THE CITIES OF ROMAGNA
AND THE MARCHES

PORTA DEL DUOMO MACERATA

THE
CITIES OF ROMAGNA
AND THE MARCHES

BY

EDWARD HUTTON 1875-

WITH TWELVE ILLUSTRATIONS IN COLOUR BY
FRANK CRISP
AND TWENTY OTHER ILLUSTRATIONS

NEW YORK
THE MACMILLAN COMPANY
1913

TO

MY FRIEND

DR. GIGLIOLI

CONTENTS

LIST OF ILLUSTRATIONS

IN COLOUR

IN MONOTONE

INTRODUCTION

IT was one evening in that cavern of Lapi's. I had just returned, as it happened, from the Marches, and after dinner we had all been talking of Italy and its by-ways— those by-ways that I love best. Little by little our party of six or seven had been increased, till about the spoiled tables and the great half-empty wine-flasks were gathered an eager and excited throng, among whom were many I did not know.

That the discussion had grown too controversial for so large a company became evident when one of the new-comers leaned across the table, and, flaming with anger, told me in a cold voice : " Believe me, Signore, you know nothing of us Italians or of our Italy."

There was nothing to be said, and if there had been he gave me no time to say it.

" You are English," said he, " therefore of the North. You dream in your fog of us in the sun here, and would deny us altogether the modern world. That you profess to dislike the modern world is nothing to us. You enjoy it. Why should not we ? We have made a new Italy in order that we may possess all that you possess. The old Italy, your dream, we have broken in pieces—utterly, utterly. There is left of it not so much as, without invention, will fill a single book. The superstition and the religion that you love is of the past : it is gone ; we have destroyed it.

The very roots of your dream we have drawn out of the ground, yes, even in the farthest and loneliest places, and there remains, Signore, modern Italy, a reality, what you see."

There was a little silence, and then Sandro Buonfigli, my friend, who for some minutes had been pulling his golden beard, said quietly : " I should not go so far as that, Caffarelli . . ."

" Oh, you," said Caffarelli, " you, what should you know ? Why, you live in the mountains and are a painter ! "

" I live," said Sandro, " in the Marches, as my fathers did, and I am a painter, as you say. I can therefore see with my eyes, and I say that you are wrong, more hopelessly wrong than my dear friend here, and, if I may so express it, without grace. Listen, and I will tell you a story, which is a double-edged sword.

" One sunny evening last February I came westward from the coast with my donkey, Grisa, laden with pretty things from Ancona for the children at home. We had walked all day, Grisa and I, at first through the steep olive gardens, by old stony ways and up steps, crossing every now and then little watercourses, happy and singing after the rain. Ah, you do not know the Marches ! Then we had come through the chestnut forests, and the oaks and the violets grew fewer and fewer, and the mountains greyer, till at last we were alone on the bare hillside. It was towards evening. The country is wild there and very lonely ; every now and then I could see the snow on a far-away peak of the Apennines—they seemed to shut out the world. . . .

" It was almost dark, and Grisa and I went forward,

hoping to reach the village, just visible, almost above us, before night. We had trudged on for another half-hour when, out of the twilight that hung like a grey curtain on either side of the way, a child leapt suddenly, and without a moment's hesitation dropped on his knees in front of me, so that I had to halt Grisa very abruptly to prevent her trampling on him. A mass of dark hair, rough and unkempt, tumbled over a round and rosy face ; his eyes were large and were looking at me in my long cloak, half in surprise, half in awe, while his hands, held in front of his nose, clasped and unclasped themselves in evident excitement or curiosity.

" ' Well,' said I, ' and when are you going to let me by ? ' But the child looked at me for a full minute in silence and then said : ' So you have come, O Signore. . . . You have come to-night ; but it was to-morrow you should have come.'

" ' I see you were expecting me,' said I, smiling at him ; ' but it is getting late, and I wish to reach the village before it is quite dark, so you will show me the way, will you not ?   Come, let us go on.'

" ' You will go to San Nicola ? ' said he in great surprise ; ' you will go to our village, and you will stay there against to-morrow ?   Eh, but yes, O Signore, I will show you the way very gladly indeed.'

" The way was more level there, and though Grisa was tired she could not have felt his little weight among so many other things ; and occasionally he would chirrup to her some little song, that seemed to help her somewhat, for she picked up her feet and we covered another chilometro.   And then we came to the village, quite suddenly, you know the sort of place—a long, straggling cobbled way, steep and rough and built in long steps. . . .

"Under the arches of houses built over the street, past long, straggling stone staircases that seemed to lead, one had to guess where—perhaps to some witches' nook out among the rocks and the tiles—up the street we went till we came to the piazza.

"I walked to the parapet to see the view. It was as always in the Marches—something beyond speech. At least I think so. A thousand feet or more below lay the sea, with the moon just rising out of the east and painting the world in silver and gold. . . . Everything was absolutely silent save for a kind of music in the air which seemed not indeed to be separate from that stealthy movement of night creeping up so ceaselessly over the woods out of the sea. . . .

"'Little boy,' I said, 'little boy, I have brought you so far for love ; and now for love you must take me to the inn.' But he had gone, stolen away as I watched the sea and the night, for I love to watch them.

"I turned to lead Grisa back to the street that I might inquire my way of someone, when I became aware that I was not alone, as I had thought, that, indeed, the piazza was full of people, full of men and women intent on something, intent as, I instantly saw, on praying. In long lines they knelt there under the stars, chanting hoarsely, monotonously, led by an old white-haired priest—a village at prayer, swaying slightly as one man to the music of the words and the rise and fall of the hoarse chanting. . . .

"Presently I saw my little friend peep out from somewhere behind the kneeling crowd and come towards me.

"'You will come this way, O Signore, will you not ?' said he.

" I followed silently, and it was only when we had once more turned into the street and were climbing again that I ventured to say : ' Tell me, then, what are they praying for ?   S. Nicola's Day is gone by, is it not ? '

" He looked at me shyly and smiled as he answered : ' They are praying against to-morrow, of course, O Signore.'

" He was ahead of me, leading Grisa, and I could not see his face, save now and again when he turned to look at me so earnestly. ' To-morrow ? ' said I ; ' and, pray, what may to-morrow be ? '

" ' To-morrow,' said he, ' as all the world knows ' (he laid such stress on the *world*), ' is the Last Day, and the Gran' Signore will once more come back to us.'

" So to-morrow was the Last Day, alas and alas ! and all the world knew it ! . . .

" ' And so the Christ comes to-morrow ? ' said I.   What could I say ?

" ' Yes,' he answered quickly.   ' Why have you come to-night, O Signore ? '

" ' I am returning from Ancona,' said I, ' where I have been busy ; and I am going home to my little children as fast as may be.'

" ' And have you brought them anything ? ' said he.

" ' Of course,' I answered.

" He said no more, but led me on till we came to a narrow alley that turned downhill out of the street.

" ' Is the inn here ? ' said I.

" ' No,' answered the boy from the donkey's head ; ' but it is not good that you go to the inn.   I will take you to my house.'

" ' But no,' said I ; ' you must let me go to the inn.'

" ' Inns are no place for you,' said my guide in his manly little way; and so I meekly followed. . . .

" We came to the house at last, dingy and desolate. His parents, he informed me, were praying on the piazza, and had been doing so for the last week. He took me to his own little bed, brought me bread and milk and some eggs, then modestly made me lie down and sleep, ' for,' said he, ' the Christ comes to-morrow.'

" I was awakened very early in the morning by the sound of groaning and chanting. I rose, pulled on my clothes, and walked out into the street. The whole village and mountain-side were covered with mist, drifting and white and damp. I wrapped my cloak about me, for it was very cold, and there was no sign of the sun ; the daylight was only sufficient to show where one was going. I found my way back to the piazza ; there were still some people praying, but the sound of chanting and groaning came from below, and I turned to the parapet and looked down upon a sea of white mist, drifting almost like smoke, hither and thither. The path wound down the mountain here, I knew, though I could see nothing for the mist ; but the groaning and the chanting kept reaching me from the depths.

" Presently I saw something moving, something black, that straggled its arms wide and moved clumsily. Next moment I knew it was a crucifix, and yet no, it was not a crucifix—and yet, again, it was a living crucifix, a huge black cross borne on the shoulders of a man in a black robe and cowl, with slits for the eyes ; and as I looked, though he was a hundred feet below me, I saw his eyes blaze with enthusiasm and passion and his body crouch to the labour of the way ; and then he was lost in the mist. And there came another and another, till I had counted forty-four men and women bearing the cross.

"I shivered; the morning was cold, and I had had not even a mouthful of wine. I felt a touch on my arm.

"'So you have come?' It was my little companion and host of last night. 'I knew you did not wish to be seen last night, O Signore,' said he, with a wise nod of his head, 'so I gave you my bed while I watched. But now you are come, what do you mean to do?'

"'I?' said I. 'I am going on when I have had something to eat.'

"He seemed surprised. 'But I thought when you came it was the end of all?'

"I looked at him for a moment ; evidently, I thought, his long night watching had made him light-headed, as though he were drunk; I had seen such things before among the mountains.

"'I am going home,' said I, 'to my little children.'

"'I think I hate you,' said he.

"'Hate me?' said I. 'What for, my little fellow?'

"'Oh, they have told me about you,' he went on; 'they have told me how you will spoil it all and burn it all—all this, and this, that I love so much. Already they have taken my mandolin and sold it to buy candles for you ; and you are come now at last to spoil the sun, and to take away the sea, that shines, as precious things shine, in the morning. And the flowers were beginning to come again, and the streams to grow young again, and not to speak with such gruff voices ; and you will spoil it all. . . .'

"'But,' said I, 'I shall do nothing of the sort.'

"He looked at me half doubtfully. 'You won't?' he

said. ' Ah, but they told me you would ; they know ; they are very much afraid ; people do not tell lies who are very much afraid ? '

" ' They told you ?—who told you ? ' said I.

" ' Father Agnolo,' said he ; ' and all the people say so.'

" ' But Father Agnolo doesn't even know me.'

" ' Father Agnolo not know you ? ' said he. ' Why, he has been to Rome and seen the Pope, and so, of course, he knows the Gran' Signore, who always comes on an ass and a colt, the foal of an ass. Eh, but yes, O Signore, he knows you very well. Why, even I knew you ! '

" So that was it, and I was—— Surely the mist must have got into my head ; and the groaning, and the mourning, and the chanting, and the crucified men and women, were they for——

" ' Come with me, little boy,' said I, ' and we will get Grisa, my donkey, and harness her, for I must be getting home to my little children.'

" He came with me reluctantly, and seemed as though he would have asked my pardon for offending me and making me sad. He certainly was not in the least afraid of me, and I wondered, till I remembered how he hated me, and then I wondered no more.

" We harnessed Grisa, and at our breakfast I explained, as well as I could, that I was not that One whom he believed me to be. But it was not until we had reached the top of the hill, whither he had accompanied me on my way, and the path once more sloped downwards into the woods that he was convinced ; for then the sun was up and the mists were scurrying away like guilty ghosts, and the groaning and the chanting were far away, and, indeed, somewhere overhead a bird was singing.

" As I wished him good-bye he smiled at me and said :
' And so, of course, I am not to hate you any more, and I
am going to buy a new mandolin with your gift, Signore,
and I will make a little song for you such as the streams
sing.'

" ' And,' said I, ' maybe when the Gran' Signore comes
one day He will be better than they say.'

" ' Per Bacco ! I believe you ! ' said my little friend."

THE CITIES OF ROMAGNA AND THE MARCHES

CHAPTER I

RAVENNA

TO the north and to the east of the Apennines, from the west of those mountains to the sea, between Venetia and the old Duchy of Modena on the north, and the Abruzzi on the south, lie the two provinces of Romagna and the Marches with which I propose to deal in this book. For the most part they lie upon either side of the great Roman roads which run northward from Rome and from Rimini, the Via Flaminia and the Via Emilia, upon which they depend and to which they have always owed their existence.

For these provinces, though precisely as we know them they have certainly less than a thousand years of history, date, if we consider them more loosely, from long before our era. In the time of the Empire they formed for the most part the provinces of Flaminia and Picenum; with the final dissolution of the Roman provincial system in the sixth century, under the pressure of the Lombard invasion, they were reformed into the Exarchate, the Pentapolis and Picenum; and at last by the acts of Pepin and of Charlemagne they came to make a great part of what our fathers knew as the States of the Church.

But, indeed, ever since the fall of the Empire they have

been formed and dominated by the action of a single city whose extraordinary situation and fate have so profoundly modified their fortunes, controlled their energies and determined their destiny, that without her they would long since have ceased to exist as we know them. That city is Ravenna ; and it is only in a right understanding of her history that we shall find the key to the story of these two little known provinces of Romagna and the Marches.

Ravenna stands in a world so desolate that only the sun, the mist and the wind seem really at home there, amid marshes so wide that everything definite is lost in their distance, where the Emilian plain in an overwhelming humility fades away almost imperceptibly into the Adrian sea.

As famous as Rome, as mysterious as Byzantium, she stands in all her hieratic beauty and incredible decay, solitary and imperial between her immense horizons ; a sepulchre rather than a city. One wanders through her silent grass-grown streets, where the melancholy campanili seem to tremble in the wind, in and out of her half-deserted churches, chill and oozing with damp, where the beautiful columns of precious marble are sinking into the marsh, and the imperishable mosaics shine through a veil of mist, from mausoleum to mausoleum empty and desecrated, from silence to silence ; and continually one asks how a city so isolated and so remote can have played any great part in history at all. That she did play such a part, that for many hundreds of years the destiny of Italy and, through Italy, of all the West lay in her hands, we know, and her monuments bear witness.

She appears to us first in a great rôle when she acted as the base from which Cæsar set out to conquer Italy, and all unknowing to found the Empire. In the first years of that great government and during the whole of its un-hampered life she proved to be one of its greatest bulwarks, the chief naval port upon the East, the gate of the eastern sea. But it was with the decline and fall of the Empire that she suddenly assumed a position, unique, not only in Italy, but in Europe. It was to her that the Emperor Honorius retreated from Milan upon the approach of Alaric in the first years of the fifth century ; and she thus became the capital of the West, and such she remained till the great Imperial tragedy was consummated and within her walls Odoacer dethroned the last of the Emperors, founded a kingdom and was in his turn supplanted, and again in Ravenna, by Theodoric the Ostrogoth. Then, indeed, her extraordinary destiny was made manifest. Upon her is directed the whole force of the Byzantine reconquest under Belisarius. It succeeds, and it is from her almost impregnable isolation that Narses issues forth on the same great business, to meet Totila and to be victorious. Again, in the midst of the Lombard flood it is she who saves what can be saved, and it is about her is formed the Exarchate and the Pentapolis, the remnants of Imperial Italy; while her fall at last in 754 brings Pepin into Italy to proclaim the new Christendom, to establish the temporal power of the Papacy and to prophesy of the resurrection of the Empire and of Europe.

When we look upon Ravenna to-day in all her loneliness and decay we may well ask, what can have given her the opportunity for such a destiny as this ?

The answer to that question, though it has escaped Gibbon and the strangely few local historians, is obvious. The secret of the greatness of Ravenna lies wholly in her geographical position with regard to Italy, the Cisalpine plain and the sea.

The Cisalpine plain, as I have tried to show in another book,[1] has always stood to Italy as a great defence. Divided from Italy proper by a difficult and barren range of

---

[1] See my *Cities of Lombardy* (Methuen, 1912). For a full examination of the geographical and political situation of Ravenna, as for a study of her history and her antiquities in detail, the reader is referred to my *Ravenna : A Study* (Dent, 1913).

mountains, the Apennines, that vast continental lowland detained and broke up the Gauls, who but for it might have overwhelmed the immature civilization of Rome; it only just failed to confound Hannibal in his great adventure; it wasted the Gothic invasions; Attila never succeeded in crossing it; it absorbed the worst of the appalling Lombard flood. We might, indeed, assert that Italy remains to us because of it.

Now, since the Cisalpine plain thus secures Italy, it is obvious that the gate between them must always have been of vital importance. That gate was held by Ravenna, and to this fact the greater part of her importance is due.

If we turn to the map we shall see that the Apennines which divide Italy from the Cisalpine plain, along a line roughly from Genoa to Rimini, actually just fail to reach the eastern sea before they turn southward to divide Italy in its whole length into two parts. This failure of the mountains quite to reach the sea leaves at this corner a narrow strip of lowland between them, and in consequence when the Romans crossed the Apennines, as they were compelled to do, for Rome lay upon their southern and western side, they were not forced to make the difficult passage at a crucial point. The road they planned, the Via Flaminia, the great north road of Rome, crossed the Apennines far to the south near the modern Scheggia and by the pass of the Furlo. It had its terminus in the midst of that narrow gate between Italy and the Cisalpine plain, between the mountains and the sea, at Rimini. Thence another road, the Via Emilia, set out for Placentia upon the Po to the north of the Apennines. Both roads thus met in Rimini, and it is obvious that the command of the gate from Italy into the Cisalpine plain lay in the hands of this city; but the command passed from Rimini whenever that narrow gate was threatened, and for this reason, that Rimini could not easily be defended while Ravenna was impregnable.

Ravenna was impregnable to any arms save those of the modern world, just as Venice was later and for the same reason. She was built literally upon the waters, on piles, traversed by canals crossed by bridges and ferry-boats. At the full tide, Strabo tells us, the sea washed quite through her, and for this reason, he asserts, though in the midst of a marsh, the air there was perfectly innocuous. So long as she could hold the road in and out over the impassable marsh or shallow lagoon, and was not taken from the sea, Ravenna was safe.

This impregnable city, the most southern of Cisalpine Gaul, for the Rubicon, the frontier between Italy and that great province, flowed between her and Rimini, directly commanded the narrow pass between the mountains and the sea, the entry to Italy, whenever that entry was threatened, and in this, I say, lay the greater part of her importance. The rest must be attributed to her situation upon the sea.

She was, as Strabo tells us and as the work of Augustus proves, as much a city of the sea as Venice is ; but of what a sea ? The Adriatic, upon whose western shore she stood holding the gate between Italy and the Cisalpine plain, was, rightly understood, the fault between Greek and Latin, East and West. To this fact she owes much of her later splendour, much of her unique importance in the Dark Age.

We may then sum up the results of her extra-ordinary geographical and political situation somewhat as follows.

Because she held the gateway between Italy and the Cisalpine plain Cæsar repaired to her when he was treating with the Senate for the Consulship, and from her he set out to conquer Italy and to make himself Dictator. For the same reason Honorius retreated upon her from Milan when Alaric crossed the Alps.

Because she was set upon the sea, and that sea was the fault between East and West, and again because she held the gate of Italy and the Cisalpine plain, Justinian there established his government when the great attempt was made to secure Italy for the Empire.

And lastly, because she was thus the seat and the fortress of the Imperial power in Italy, and commanded the southern terminus of the Via Emilia and the northern terminus of the Via Flaminia, at the other end of which was Rome ; that state which, in the last disaster, grouped itself about these great roads, on either side of them, was her creation, and remained an imperial thing when all the rest of Italy was at the mercy of the barbarian.

How all this came to pass, and how that state which we know as the provinces of Romagna and the Marches was formed, and came to be the foundation of the temporal power of the Papacy, of what our fathers knew as the States of the Church, I shall hope to show in the course of my narrative.

I

Ravenna, though situated to the north of the Rubicon, and therefore within the limits of Cisalpine Gaul, does not appear to have been a Gaulish city. Strabo tells us that it was a Thessalian colony, which later received a body of Umbrian colonists in order to maintain itself against the Etruscans. We are ignorant as to when exactly it passed into Roman hands, but this could not well have happened before 268 B.C., when Ariminum (Rimini) was occupied. The name of Ravenna does not, however, occur till a late period of the Roman Republic, and, though the city played a certain part in the civil wars of Marius and Sulla, the first really important event in its history is the great adventure of Julius Cæsar, who set out from Ravenna to make himself Dictator in 49 B.C.

In his choice of Ravenna, the most southern city of his triple command, as his headquarters during his negotiations with the Senate, the geographical and strategical importance of the place in relation to Italy and the Cisalpine plain for the first time becomes evident. He perhaps alone appreciated it. He established himself, in Ravenna, without troops in 50 B.C. ; but in the first days of January 49 B.C. the Thirteenth Legion marched into Ravenna from Tergeste (Trieste), and with that (some 300 horse and 5000 foot) he proposed to make himself master of Italy. Upon January 12, while he attended a public spectacle and dined with a numerous party of his friends, the first companies of that Legion left Ravenna by the Rimini gate and were followed after sunset by their great commander. Cæsar, according to Plutarch, went alone in a hired carriage which awaited him at a mill outside the city. He did not follow the high road, but a byway across the marshes. There, during the night, he lost his way, was compelled to abandon his carriage and to go on afoot, only finding the road again at last with the help of a peasant about daybreak. He came up with his troops on the Cisalpine bank of the Rubicon. There, Suetonius tells us, " he halted for a while revolving in his mind the importance of the step he was about to take. While he hesitated suddenly there appeared a person of noble aspect playing upon a pipe, who presently, snatching a trumpet from one of Cæsar's trumpeters, sounded the advance and himself crossed the stream. This strange act is said to have decided Cæsar : ' Let us go,' he said, ' whither the omens of the gods and the iniquity of our enemies call us. The die is cast.' And immediately at the head of his troops he crossed the Rubicon."

It is with that most famous act that Ravenna really comes for the first time into the history of Europe, to play a great and soon a chief part in it for nearly eight hundred years, before falling back into an obscurity almost as great as that out of which she had come.

If it was Julius Cæsar who first appreciated the strategical importance of Ravenna in regard to Italy and Cisalpine Gaul, the command of the great roads, the Via Emilia and the Via Flaminia which traversed them, it was Augustus who first understood the value of her position upon the sea, and much that it meant in the strategy not of Italy only but of the Empire.   Among his first acts as Emperor was the establishment of two fleets " in being "—one based upon Misenum and the other upon Ravenna.   In order to make Ravenna fit for this great office Augustus constructed, some two and a half miles from Ravenna to the south-east, a great port and harbour which were named, after the fleet they served and accommodated, Classis ; and which presently he joined to the city of Ravenna by the Via Cæsarea, upon which grew up a town of that name. " This city," says Jornandes, " has three names with which she glorifies herself, and she is divided into three parts to which they correspond : the first is Ravenna, the last Classis, that in the midst is Cæsarea between Ravenna and the sea."   It is difficult in looking upon Ravenna to-day even in the imagination to realize the city of Augustus, for not only has the sea retreated so that it is now no longer in sight from Ravenna, but the port of Classis and the town of Cæsarea have utterly perished, only the former being represented by a single deserted church dating from the sixth century.   But we may perhaps have some idea of what Ravenna was in the time of the Empire if we remember Venice and the Porto di Lido with the long Riva between them.

The city thus so splendidly founded by Augustus became one of the most important in the West.   Its strategical importance, however, was obscured by the Great Peace, but was to reappear with the first invasion of the barbarians, the Gothic raid under Alaric in 401.

And here, I think, we touch one of the vital errors of accepted history.   It has been asserted by Gibbon, to go no further, and repeated by every one of his successors, that when Honorius retreated upon Ravenna in the first years of the fifth century he did so as a mere fugitive and coward seeking an impregnable place in his desire for

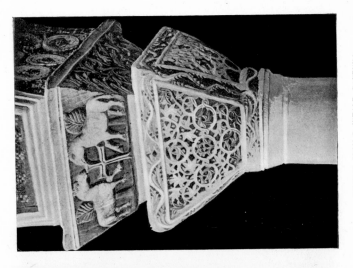

CAPITAL FROM S. VITALE, RAVENNA

CAPITAL FROM THE PIAZZA, RAVENNA

personal safety. It is impossible to defend the character of Honorius, but in thus explaining his " flight " to Ravenna it is not only his character that is at stake, but that of his advisers—indeed, the whole administration of Italy and the West. I have maintained at length and in detail elsewhere, and I shall venture to repeat here, that the " flight " of Honorius was not a flight but a well-considered retreat ; and that what has led men to consider it a flight is a misconception of the whole strategical position of Italy in regard to Europe, and especially of the peninsula in regard to the Cisalpine plain.

We do not know when that great decision to retreat upon Ravenna was come to, nor the year in which Honorius there established his court ; but we know that Alaric entered Italy in November 401, and that at the same time Radagaisus invaded Raetia. In the following year, upon Easter Day, Alaric was beaten by the great soldier of the defence, Stilicho, at Pollentia in the Cisalpine plain and again later at Asta, but he was allowed to retreat into Istria. In the summer of 403 he moved once more westward and was beaten at Verona, but again allowed to retreat. It might seem that it was now, when it was seen that these raids could only be defeated, not prevented, it was decided to secure Italy by establishing the great fortress of Ravenna as the key of the defence. It is possible, then, that in 404 Honorius there took up his residence.

It was thought, and as we shall see rightly thought, that Ravenna could hold the gates of Italy. One man, however, questioned it ; he was a barbarian and his name was Radagaisus. He did not dare to pass through the narrow way where the great road led to Rome, lest the hammer of Ravenna should fall upon him. He determined to attempt the Apennines by the old way to Fiesole. He achieved it, but when his starved and broken army issued out of those barren defiles Stilicho caught him as he saw the south, and Radagaisus and his barbarians found a grave on the confines of Tuscany. Stilicho had been right : to hold Ravenna was to hold Italy.

To hold Ravenna : but when three years later Stilicho lay dead, murdered in Ravenna, Alaric saw his chance. He entered Italy and, coming into the Emilian Way at Bologna, found the gate open, passed Ravenna without attacking it or being himself attacked, and went on southward down the Flaminian Way to make Rome desolate. Three times he besieged the City and pillaged it, taking with him when he left it hostages, among them the sister of the two Emperors, the daughter of the great Theodosius, Galla Placidia, who was to be the bride of the barbarian, his successor, Ataulfus, when the great Gothic king lay dead in that marvellous tomb in the bed of the Buxentius. The hand of Galla Placidia was the price the Empire paid for the exodus of the Goth from Italy. But Ataulfus did not long survive his wedding, and Placidia returned to Ravenna to her brother in 416, where she was given to Constantius, Honorius' colleague in the Consular office, to whom she bore a daughter and a son—Honoria who was to offer herself to Attila, and Valentinian one day to be Emperor.

The life of Galla Placidia in Ravenna during the lifetime of her brother Honorius seems to have been unhappy. Always a sincere Catholic, she must have felt like a stranger in that corrupt court, and at last she fled with her children to Constantinople. In the year of her flight Honorius died, and the western throne was filled by the obscure civil servant Joannes. This was not to be tolerated in Constantinople, and Theodosius the Emperor immediately confirmed Placidia in her title of Augusta, recognized the young Valentinian as the heir to the western throne and dispatched an army to establish them in Ravenna. This was accomplished ; and, some eighteen months after the death of Honorius, Galla Placidia reigned in Ravenna. She ruled for some twenty-five years, first as regent and then as the no less powerful adviser of her son.

Of her great buildings in the city I shall speak later.
Here it must be enough to say that her rule was rather
fortunate than unfortunate, and the last stable government
the West was to know. When she died in 450, and was
buried in the mausoleum she had prepared for herself in
Ravenna, she left Italy in a profound peace. It might
seem that the barbarian had but awaited her departure
to descend again into her unhappy country.

It is, indeed, with the advent of Attila that we come face
to face with the reality of things in Italy. Valentinian
was as corrupt and incapable as his uncle Honorius had
been, and he lacked perhaps advisers as full of resource
as those who had planned the great retreat ; but he had
in Aetius a soldier of the calibre of Stilicho. At the right
moment that soldier was not available. Aetius had broken
Attila at Châlons, but when the same barbarian descended
into Cisalpine Gaul he was not there to meet him and the
gate of Ravenna was open wide.

It was the Pope, Leo the Great, an old and unarmed
man, who, on the banks of the Mincio, turned back Attila
from Italy. In that act we may see certainly prophesied
the fall of the Empire and the rise, as its last heir, of the
Catholic Church.

That was in 453. Twenty-three years later Odoacer the
barbarian deposed Romulus Augustus in Ravenna and
there made himself king of Italy. The imperial rule in
Italy was at an end, though in theory, but certainly in
little else, the Emperor at Constantinople, upon the death
of Julius Nepos, one of the deposed Emperors in exile at
Salona, reunited in himself the government of East and
West.

Odoacer, the Patrician, for he was granted that title
by the Emperor Zeno, ruled in Ravenna from 476 to 493.
So long as he showed no sign of further ambition he was
tolerated by Constantinople, but when in 481 he led an
expedition into Dalmatia his doom was sealed. The
Emperor launched against him the barbaric legions of

Theodoric the Ostrogoth, and Odoacer perished by the treacherous hand of that barbarian in Ravenna, which had been taken by stratagem after enduring a siege of three years.

Theodoric, and far more regularly than Odoacer had ever done, ruled in Ravenna for thirty-two and a half years, doing "nothing evil." "He governed," says the Anonymous Valesii, "the two nations of the Goths and the Romans as though they had been one people. Belonging himself to the Arian sect, he yet ordained that the civil administration should remain as it had been under the Emperors. He found the treasury ruined ; he brought it by hard work into a flourishing state. He attempted nothing against the Catholic Faith. . . . He was a lover of manufactures and a great restorer of cities. He restored the Aqueduct of Ravenna which Trajan had built, and again after a long interval brought water into the city. He completed but did not dedicate the Palace, and he finished the Porticoes about it. . . . Merchants too from many provinces flocked to his dominions, for so great was the order which he maintained that if anyone wished to keep gold and silver in the country it was as safe as in a walled city. . . . Anyone who had business to do might go about it as safely by night as by day."

Theodoric succeeded because, while he was able to maintain order and to defend Italy, he ruled by Roman law and he governed by means of Roman officials. He failed to establish a new nation of Goths and Romans because he was an Arian. The chief result of that generation of peace which he gave to Italy was to prepare it to receive and even to make possible the Imperial reconquest, the final success of which was assured by the Arianism of the Gothic nation. This perhaps only became obvious when the great king was dead. Certainly he himself brought much material good to Italy, and first of all to Ravenna, where his great churches remain to this day, as does his vast mausoleum, perhaps the last work of Roman genius. But in his later

years the murder of Boethius and Symmachus, the imprison-
ment of Pope John, if not his murder, above all the quarrel
with the Pope and with Catholicism, showed the inherent
weakness of his government, which even after thirty years,
and in that society, remained utterly alien from the
Italian people. All this was visible to all men when his
daughter succeeded to his power as guardian for her son
Athalaric. The quarrel, in spite of all her efforts, grew
between Arian and Catholic—that is, between the Goth
and the Italian—and when at last, Athalaric being dead,
she was murdered by Theodahad, her cousin Justinian,
the great Emperor, who now sat on the throne in
Constantinople, was ready, the hour had struck, and the
attempt was to be made to reconquer the West for
civilization.

That reconquest began with the subjugation of the
province of Africa by the great soldier Belisarius, the
instrument of Justinian in all his heroic design. The long
campaign in Italy was begun in 535, occupied five years,
and proceeding from Sicily and Naples northward had
Ravenna for its last goal. It was fought with an army
of very small numbers, certainly at first with not more
than 8000 men, to which Vitiges the Gothic king, who had
succeeded Amalasuntha, could oppose more than 150,000 ;
and Ravenna was taken at last and again by stratagem
after a long siege.

The fate of Ravenna should rightly have ended the war
and forced the Goths to retreat from Italy. That it did
not, that the war of the reconquest had to be fought for
another thirteen years, was due in part to the recall of
Belisarius, perhaps necessary, but certainly unfortunate,
and to the poverty of Italy.

In 540, when Belisarius was recalled and Vitiges taken
as a captive to Constantinople, the Imperialists held all
Italy except the city of Pavia. In 544, when Belisarius
returned, they held only Ravenna, Rome, Spoleto and a
few other strongholds such as Perugia and Piacenza. Nor

is that all. In this second war all Italy was laid waste and ruined, Rome was twice besieged and occupied by the Goths, and in 546 when Totila had done with her during a space of forty days the City remained utterly desolate, without a single inhabitant.

The cause of this frightful collapse was, as I have said, partly military and partly financial. The incompetence of the generals who succeeded Belisarius was soon obvious. Italy was bankrupt, and in attempting to tax the ruined landowners the Imperial power invited them to turn to the Goths for deliverance. The Gothic champion, who well knew how to use every advantage the Empire gave him, was Totila. Against him and against the circumstances of the time Belisarius on his return made little headway. Nevertheless from Ravenna the reconquest was planned, and thence after a difficult and dangerous march from Illyricum Narses the eunuch issued forth to break Totila finally upon the Apennines near the modern town of Gualdo Tadino and to expel the Goths once and for all from Italy.

Thus was the reconquest achieved after not less than seventeen years of fighting (536-554).

Narses established himself in Ravenna as the representative of the Emperor at Constantinople, together with the Prefect of Italy. There he planned and contrived the resurrection of the country, applied the Pragmatic Sanction of Justinian and attempted thus to avert complete ruin. He had not been at work for more than eleven years when Justinian died, and upon the death of the great Emperor, perhaps the greatest save Augustus and Constantine which the Empire had known, he received an insulting recall from Sophia, the wife of the new Emperor, Justin ii. He retired to Rome, and as though to avenge him the Lombard hordes swept down upon Italy. In this last, and in many ways worst, invasion of barbarians, Ravenna appeared as a citadel, the citadel of what was left of the imperial administration.

For though the Lombard invasion was not so spiritually

dangerous to Italy and our civilization as those of the Goths, for the Lombards were not bitter Arians, materially it was much more disastrous, partly because after the long Gothic wars ruined Italy was incapable of any sort of defence. The very administrative system, the system of provinces, fell to pieces, and when Alboin, who crossed the Alps in 568, had been eighteen months in Italy, all the Cisalpine plain and Liguria, except the coast, Milan, Cremona, Piacenza, Ravenna and a few smaller places were in his hands ; and it is out of the fragments of Emilia, Flaminia and Picenum that we now see arise around Ravenna the impregnable citadel, the provinces we know as the Romagna and the Marches, then called the Exarchate of Ravenna and the Pentapolis. In these new groupings the only thought was for the defence, the defence of civilization against the barbarian. The Exarchate was, as it were, the official acknowledgment of this disastrous state of affairs, and it is probable that the first man to bear the title of Exarch was Baduarius, the son-in-law of the Emperor, who had appeared in Italy with an army, to be beaten by the Lombards in 575.

The Exarchate, properly so called, formed a separate province under the direct authority of the Exarch, the Governor-General of Italy. It was bounded on the north by the Adige, the Tartaro and the principal branch of the Po as far as its confluence with the Panaro. Hadria and Gabellum were its most northern towns. The western frontier is more difficult to determine with exactitude ; but it may be said to have been between Modena and Bologna. On the south the Marecchia divided the Exarchate from the Duchy of Pentapolis, whose capital was Rimini. The Pentapolis, in which a part of Picenum was involved, consisted of Rimini, Pesaro, Fano, Sinigaglia and Ancona upon the sea, and of the five inland places Urbino, Fossombrone, Jesi, Cagli and Gubbio. Largely these were set on either side of the Via Flaminia upon the eastern side of the Apennines, while the great towns

of the Exarchate were set along the Via Emilia and
were Bologna, Imola, Faenza, Forlì, Forlimpopoli and
Cesena.

Ravenna which held, as we have seen, the narrow pass
in which the two roads met, was of capital importance to
these provinces. But there was another city which was
not less vital to them. The Via Emilia lost itself in
barbarian darkness, but at the other end of the Via Flaminia
was Rome. The strength of the Latin position in Italy
lay, and continued to lie, in these two great imperial
cities, Ravenna and Rome. Little by little the position
crystallized till a new state appeared, a state which in one
way or another was to endure till our own day and which
our fathers knew as the States of the Church. With the
two cities of Ravenna and Rome as *nuclei* this state formed
itself in the very heart of Italy. It cut, and effectually,
the Lombard kingdom in two, and isolated the Duchies of
Spoleto and Benevento from the real Lombard power in
the Cisalpine plain with its great capital at Pavia ; and
indestructible as it was, it absolutely ensured the final
success of the Catholic Faith, the Latin nationality and the
Imperial power—the three necessities for the resurrection
of Europe.

We have seen the invasions of the Visigoths and the
Huns fade away into nothing ; we have seen the greater
attempt of the Ostrogoths to found a kingdom in Italy
brought to nought. One and all they failed because they
were not Catholic. The Lombards were not to fail; they
were permanently to remain and to hold a great part of
Italy. For the Lombards, never very eagerly Arian, were
open to conversion ; slowly they became Catholic, and
from the day they became Catholic there was no longer
any hope of turning them out of Italy. It was not the
Lombards but the Byzantines who were to give the *coup
de grâce* to Justinian's noble plan to gather Italy especially
once more into a universal government embracing East
and West ; and by a failure in Catholicism, by the Icono-

clastic heresy. It was this failure that raised up even in the Imperial citadel, even in Ravenna, men and armies passionately antagonistic to the Emperor, passionately Papal too. During a hundred years this movement grew, and in the eighth century it was obvious that the Byzantine cause, no longer Italian, was dying. What was to be its heir ?

That was the great question which the Pope presently called upon Pepin and his Franks to decide. Who was the heir of the Empire in Italy, to whom did these provinces of the Exarchate and the Pentapolis devolve if or when Constantinople failed ?—to the Lombard or to the Holy See ? The Lombards doubtless thought they had decided that question once and for all in their own favour when Ravenna fell in 751 before Aistulf and the Byzantine Empire in Italy thereby came to an end. They were wrong. At the Pope's bidding, as we know, Pepin crossed the Alps, invested Pavia and brought Aistulf to his knees ; and Pepin declared the Holy See the heir of the Empire and secured to it the Imperial territories. The Frank returned to the north, and for twenty-two years the Lombard sought to maintain his claim ; but in 773 a greater than Pepin crossed the Alps on the same mission, and Charlemagne confirmed, renewed and enlarged the donation of Pepin, to be in return crowned Emperor and acclaimed and acknowledged by the Roman people.

From that time, as it happened, Ravenna ceased to be of any pre-eminence in the history of Europe. The pass it held was no longer of importance, for the barbarian invasions were at an end, and a new road into Italy over the Apennines was coming into use, the Via Francigena, the way of the Franks. As the port of the sea which was the fault between East and West it too ceased to exist, for East and West were no longer of any real importance the one to the other, and already the alteration of the coastline, which was one day to leave the old sea-port some miles from the coast, had begun. The city which had played

2

so great a part in the fortunes of the Empire herself passed into oblivion when the Empire, Holy now and Roman still, rose again in the West with the crowning of Charlemagne in St. Peter's Church in the year of Our Lord 800.

II

The traveller who would see to the best advantage what remains to Ravenna from the dark age of her glory will do well to visit the monuments she possesses in such abundance in order, according to the periods in which they were produced, and which may be named as follows : the Roman time of Honorius and Galla Placidia, the Arian and Gothic interval of Theodoric, and the Byzantine period of Belisarius, Narses and the Exarchate. To these periods must be added those of the Middle Age and the Renaissance, in which, however, Ravenna appears as little more than a remote provincial city, interesting to us for the most part on account of two episodes which interrupt for a moment her curiously uninteresting story—the apparition of Dante and the battle of 1512.

The oldest buildings remaining to us in Ravenna are to be found in the Baptistery, the Cathedral, the Chapel in the Arcivescovado and the Mausoleum of Galla Placidia, the oldest complete building being the last.

The first Bishop of Ravenna, S. Apollinaris, who may perhaps be considered as the " Apostle " of Emilia, was a Syrian of Antioch, the friend and disciple of S. Peter, who appointed him Bishop of Ravenna. It was not, however, till the fourth century that a great church was built in the city. This was the work of the Bishop S. Ursus (370–396), who, according to the ninth-century chronicler Agnellus, " first began to build there a temple to God, so that the Christians previously scattered about in huts should be collected into one sheepfold." This church, which was on a grand scale and of great beauty, adorned with marbles and mosaics, and possessing a wonderful altar and ciborium of silver, was sacked by the French in 1512, and was utterly destroyed by the *accademici* of Ravenna in the eighteenth century. In 1734 the church we see was begun on the same site by Gian Francesco Buonamici da Rimini and, fine and spacious though it be, its only interest for us lies in the fragments which it possesses of its glorious predecessor. These unhappily are few in number and of little account, consisting for the most part of marble columns and tombs. In the second chapel on the right, for instance, is an ancient marble sarcophagus said to be that of S. Exuperantius, Bishop of Ravenna about 470. In the chapel of the Madonna del Sudore in the south transept are two more sarcophagi of marble : that on the right is said to be the tomb of S. Barbatianus, the confessor of Galla Placidia, and comes from the destroyed church of S. Lorenzo in Cæsarea ; that on the left serves as the tomb of a fourteenth-century Archbishop, Bonifazio dei Fieschi. Within the high altar, too, is another sarcophagus which holds, it is said, the dust of nine bishops of the sixth century. But the noblest thing left to us from of old in the church is the beautiful processional cross of silver which stands before the high altar. This, however, is a work of the eleventh century.

In the left aisle are some fragments of a sixth-century ambo with the inscription " SERVUS CHRISTI AGNELLUS EPISCOPUS HUNC PYRGUM FECIT." And a few pictures from the time of the Renaissance—some frescoes by Guido Reni—still remain in the church.

As it is with the Cathedral so it is with the Arcivescovado, only here most fortunately a wonderful little chapel remains to us from the fifth century, though sadly restored, the chapel of S. Peter Chrysologus. It is a square and vaulted chamber of small size adorned with mosaics originally of that time. On the angles of the vaulting on a gold ground are four angels in white raiment holding aloft the symbol of Our Lord. Between them are the symbols of the Four Evangelists. In the key of the arches east and west is a medallion of Christ, and under the arch on either side the eleven Apostles and S. Paul. In the key of the arches north and south is a medallion of the symbol of Our Lord, and three by three under the arch on either side six saints, the men to the right : SS. Damian, Fabian, Sebastian, Chrysanthus, Chrysologus and Cassianus ; and the women to the left, SS. Cecilia, Eugenia, Euphemia, Felicitas, Perpetua and Daria. These mosaics, lovely as they are and still Roman in feeling, have suffered very much from restoration. The pavement is old and fine, but the frescoes, once by Luca Longhi, are unworthy of the place. The recess which now contains the altar is an addition of the eighteenth century, the mosaics there of the Blessed Virgin, S. Apollinaris and S. Vitalis having come from the old cathedral.

One other thing at least, of the greatest interest, the Arcivescovado possesses. This is the ivory throne of S. Maximianus, a magnificent work of the early part of the sixth century, entirely covered with carvings, some of which are unhappily now missing ; in front there remain S. John Baptist and the Four Evangelists, at the sides the story of Joseph and at the back the life of Christ.

From the Arcivescovado we pass to the only building of the Cathedral group which is still intact, the Baptistery. This is an octagonal building with a cupola constructed of *amphoræ* covered with tiles. It was originally, perhaps, one of the halls of the Roman baths that stood near the Cathedral, and was converted into a Baptistery and covered with mosaics by Archbishop Neon of Ravenna (449 *c.*-459). It is certain, however, that there has been more than one rebuilding here. Within, the present pavement is raised nearly ten feet.

What we see is a building of two arcades, one over the other, covered by a cupola, the whole most lavishly decorated with mosaics and marbles. The mosaic of the cupola, originally of the fifth century, is perhaps the finest left to us in Ravenna. In the midst we see the Baptism of Our Lord on a gold ground. About this circle is set a greater in which on a blue ground are the twelve Apostles in procession, each bearing a crown. Beneath this is another circle in which are eight open temples, four with thrones and four with altars and the Book of the Gospel. Nothing more masterly in its way remains to us in Europe.

The upper arcade beneath the cupola is decorated with sixteen figures of Prophets in stucco, while the lower is encrusted with mosaics, restorations of our own time; the walls are panelled with rare marbles. In the midst is set the huge octagonal font with its ambo.

A few other churches retain notable fragments of the time of the Empire in Ravenna, but not one of them is in any sense a complete monument. Among these is S. Agata, with its beautiful columns of bigio antico, cipollino, porphyry, granite and other marbles, with Roman and Byzantine capitals. The altar here, too, is formed of an ancient sarcophagus which holds the dust of the two Archbishops, Sergius and Agnellus, and there is a curious ambone formed from a fragment of a gigantic column. It was in this church that S. John, surnamed Angeloptes, Archbishop of Ravenna, 477–494, was singing Mass when suddenly an angel from heaven appeared to serve him.

The churches of S. Francesco, S. Giovanni Evangelista and S. Giovanni Battista too are still upheld by their ancient columns and contain several old sarcophagi. With S. Giovanni Evangelista, indeed, Galla Placidia is more especially connected, for she founded the church in fulfilment of a vow made when she was in danger of ship-wreck on her way as Augusta from Constantinople to Ravenna. She was to build a church to S. John Evangelist if she came safe to land, but it seems when the church was to be consecrated no relic of S. John was to be had. But when the Bishop came to the altar to consecrate it suddenly S. John himself appeared, vested as a Bishop with a thurible in his hand with which he censed the church. And when the Augusta would have venerated him he vanished away, leaving in her hand, however, one of his shoes.   This legend is represented in relief over the fourteenth-century doorway of the church and is also the subject of a picture by Rondinelli now in the Brera in Milan.

But certainly the oldest and, I think, the loveliest complete monument of the time of Galla Placidia left to us in Ravenna is her Mausoleum.   This, Agnellus tells us, she built close to her palace, and really as a part of the church she dedicated in honour of the Holy Cross, which has long since disappeared.   It is a simple cruciform build-ing of plain brick, but within it is so splendidly adorned with mosaic and marble that not an inch anywhere remains uncovered.   The roofs and dome are encrusted with mosaics of a wonderful night-blue powdered with stars. In the cupola is a cross and at the four angles are set the symbols of the Four Evangelists.   Over the door we see Christ the Good Shepherd, a beautiful classical figure seated on a rock in a hilly landscape, a cross in His left hand, caressing His sheep with His right.   Opposite we see a different figure, a majestic and angry Christ moving swiftly, the Cross on His shoulders, in His left hand an Arian book which He is about to cast into the furnace in the midst.   In the lunettes are some beautiful arabesques— stags at a fountain and doves drinking from a vase. Above in the spandrils are figures of saints.   The pave-ment is composed of fragments of the same precious marbles as line the lower parts of the walls.   Nothing can be finer than this interior, which has, however, not escaped restoration.

Under the mosaic of the burning of the heretical books we see the great sarcophagus of Greek marble which once held the body of the Augusta.   This was once richly adorned with carvings and perhaps with silver and mosaic, and we know that in the fourteenth century it was possible to see, within, the figure of a woman, richly dressed, seated in a chair of cedar.   This was believed to be the mummy of Galla Placidia. But it seems that in 1577 some children, curious about it and anxious to see a thing so wonderful, thrust a lighted taper into the tomb through one of the holes in the marble, when mummy, vestments, chair and all were consumed in a moment.

The sarcophagi under the arches on either side are thought to hold the dust of the Emperor Honorius, of the Emperor Valentinian III, the brother and the son of the Augusta.

It was in 493 that Theodoric, king of the Ostrogoths, entered Ravenna as the representative of the Emperor at Constantinople. Among his first acts was the erection of a palace for himself and his successors. Perhaps the Palace of Honorius and Galla Placidia had been destroyed in the wars, at any rate Theodoric built a new one. Nothing of all his work in it remains to us. The ruin which passes under its name is a work of a much later time, the time of the Exarchs, and seems to have been merely a guard-house.

Very different is it with the great church, the noblest left to us in Ravenna, which he erected close to his palace, and which we know as S. Apollinare Nuovo. It was the chief temple of Arianism in Ravenna, and has come down to us almost intact as a work of the earlier part of the sixth century. It consists, as we see it, of a basilica divided by twenty-four pillars of Greek marble with romano-byzantine capitals into three naves. Of old, however, it had an atrium, but this was removed in the sixteenth century, as was the apse in the eighteenth. The portico we now see before the church is a work of the sixteenth century, as is the façade of the church, though it contains some ancient marbles. The campanile, a noble round tower, dates from the ninth century.

Dedicated by Theodoric to Jesus Christ, and by the Catholic Archbishop S. Agnellus, when it came into his hands, to S. Martin, it got the name of S. Apollinare from Archbishop John, who asserted that he had translated thither the relics of S. Apollinare when the church of S.

Apollinare in Classe was threatened by the Saracens. In early times it was generally called, however, *Cœlum Aureum*, from its roof of gold destroyed in 1611.

The great splendour of S. Apollinare, though indeed the whole interior of the church is lovely and still largely of the sixth century, is the great series of mosaics in the nave which cover the walls over the arcade under the windows and represent two vast processions of saints. Upon the right we see a procession of twenty-five martyrs out of the city of Ravenna (which is magnificently represented with the palace of Theodoric in the foreground), led by S. Martin Confessor, who alone bears no palm, along a way strewn with flowers, to the throne where Christ sits guarded by four angels. Upon the left we see a similar procession of twenty-one virgins out of the Castello of Classis, through whose gate we see the sea, led by S. Eufemia and the three Magi to the throne where Madonna sits, her little Son in her arms between four angels. Above on both sides between the windows are figures in mosaic of the Prophets and Fathers, and above again scenes from the life of Our Lord.

What can be said of these marvellous things ? This, at least, that they are only in part the work of the time of Theodoric. It would seem that the city of Classis, and, in the general opinion, the city of Ravenna, the Christ enthroned with the angels, the Virgin enthroned with angels, the Prophets and Fathers and the scenes from the life of Our Lord, are of Theodoric's time ; the rest is the work of the Byzantine and Catholic mosaicists after Ravenna had been taken by Belisarius. It is certain that mosaics similar to these were here from the first, but it is probable that they represented certain Arian doctrines and were taken down, and those we see substituted when Ravenna again came into Catholic hands. Such as they are they are beyond our praise—beautiful everlasting things.

Little else remains in the church worth notice, except the ancient ambo in the nave and the chapel of the relics

at the top of the left aisle, which is a sort of museum of
fragments put together in the sixteenth century. Here is
a curious mosaic portrait of Justinian as an old man,
unfortunately hopelessly restored.

Two other churches, originally Arian buildings of Theodoric's time, remain in Ravenna. These are S. Spirito
and the Arian Baptistery now called S. Maria in Cosmedin.

S. Spirito, originally S. Theodore, was almost entirely
rebuilt in the sixteenth century, and all that really remains
of the earlier time is the fourteen columns of rare marble
with their capitals in the nave and the eight columns that
uphold the portico. In S. Maria in Cosmedin we have
something more. Like the Catholic Baptistery, originally
a bath, it is an octagonal building covered with a cupola
which, within, is encrusted with mosaics in circles. In
the midst we see Christ baptized in Jordan ; about this is
a band of palm leaves, and in the outer circle the twelve
Apostles ; between S. Peter and S. John (?) a throne is set
on which stands a jewelled cross. It is difficult to say to
whom we owe these mosaics, for they have been very much
tampered with. The Apostles certainly look like work
of the Byzantine time.

Theodoric was, as these works serve to show, a great
builder ; that his masons were Romans is, I think, evident
in the greatest of his works, the mighty Mausoleum where
his body was destined to lie for so short a time. This vast
monument is situated outside the city on the north-east
in a curiously-tangled garden at the end of a long green
alley way which leads up to it. It is built in two stories
of huge blocks of hewn stone, the lower story decagonal,
the upper circular, having about it eighteen blind arches
and over it a vast circulr aroof formed of a single block of
Istrian marble. Here in a tomb, modelled perhaps on
Hadrian's, the Gothic king lay, but not for long. Before
the ninth century certainly, and probably long before, his
body was thrown out, and it is thought that in 1854 his
skeleton, " armed with a golden cuirass, a sword by his

side and on the helmet large jewels," was discovered near the Corsini Canal by some navvies, who made off with most of the spoil.   What was recovered is now in the museum.

Theodoric died in 526, and thirteen years later Belisarius entered Ravenna and established it once more as the imperial capital in Italy.   From the hands of the Byzantines beside the redecoration of the reconciled Arian churches, the city received two great monuments which have come down to us more or less intact, I mean the churches of S. Vitale and S. Apollinare in Classe.

S. Vitale had been begun by the Archbishop S. Ecclesius some years before, but it was not finished when Belisarius entered Ravenna, and it remained for the Archbishop S. Maximianus to complete, decorate and consecrate it. It is an octagonal church, 114 feet in diameter, covered with a cupola, with a rectangular choir and a narthex set obliquely across one of the angles of the octagon.   Within, the octagon is divided by eight vast piers, which with the pillars between them uphold a great loggia, into a central space and an ambulatory.   The piers are in their lower parts lined with slabs of African marble, and the capitals, both below and above in the loggia, are capped with most exquisite Byzantine capitals.

In the presbytery stands the altar consisting of slabs of semi-transparent alabaster, the altar stone itself supported by four columns, the frontal carved with a cross between two sheep.   Across the apse behind the altar are set beautiful low fretted screens.   The vault of the apse, the lunettes and the walls are entirely encrusted with gorgeous mosaics.   In the curve of the triumphal arch through which the presbytery is approached we see, amid much decorative ornament, fifteen circular discs containing the busts of Our Lord, the twelve Apostles, S. Gervasius and S. Protasius.   Beneath are two monuments made up from antique fragments in the sixteenth century ;   the columns coming from the old baldacchino here and the reliefs from a frieze in the Temple of Neptune.

MOSAIC OF THE EMPRESS THEODORA

S. *Vitale, Ravenna*

Within the triumphal arch on either side are the beautiful tribunes supported by columns with marvellous Byzantine capitals. The arches and the lunettes are encrusted with mosaics. Upon the right we see the Sacrifice of Abel and Melchizedek, and on the face of the arch Moses tending the sheep of Jethro, and Moses and the burning bush. On the left we see the Sacrifice of Abraham and the visit of the Three Angels and on the face of the arch Moses upon Sinai. Above, the vault is filled with ornament, amid which three angels uphold the Agnus Dei.

In the apse itself, which we enter under a second triumphal arch upon the face of which we see the two cities, Jerusalem and Bethlehem, and above some wonderful ornament, is Our Lord enthroned, an angel on either hand with S. Vitalis and S. Ecclesius. Beneath upon either side are the two great mosaic pictures, the most wonderful works of the sixth century that have come down to us. Upon the left we see the great Emperor Justinian bearing a gold dish in his hands, the Archbishop S. Maximianus beside him with attendant priests and soldiers. Upon the right we see the Empress Theodora, straight-browed and gorgeously arrayed, with two priests and her attendant ladies. Here, indeed, we have work at once more gorgeous, more mysterious and more artistic than any Roman thing, a symbolic and hieratic art, the gift of Byzantium.

As a whole the church of S. Vitale should be compared not with anything in the West, but with S. Sophia and SS. Sergius and Bacchus of Constantinople. It is worth any trouble to see, and many a morning's study will not exhaust it.

Nothing can be more desolate and sad than the other Byzantine church of Ravenna, S. Apollinare in Classe, which is not in Ravenna at all, but in the wide marsh some two miles and a half from the city to the southeast, where once stood the port of Classis. It looks like a ruin with its tottering round campanile and melancholy dilapidation, deserted in the silence of the marsh ; and, indeed, it is not much more than a ruin we see. For this great basilica, which S. Maximianus consecrated in 549, was stripped of its marbles in 1449 by Sigismondo Mala-testa of Rimini, who was eagerly transforming the old church of S. Francesco in that city by the hand of Leon Alberti.

In spite of this vandalism S. Apollinare remains one of the most interesting churches in Italy. In the midst of the nave, which is upheld by twenty-four columns of great size and beauty, there still stands the altar which S. Maximianus erected. Beneath it of old was the tomb of S. Apollinare, the first Bishop of Ravenna, who now, after more than one translation, lies under the high altar, which is reached by a flight of steps built in the eighteenth century. In the apse is part of the marble throne of Arch-bishop Damianus (688–708), and in the tribune the latest of the Ravenna mosaics, a work of the late sixth century. In the midst is a large Cross bearing the head of Our Saviour. Above we see the hand of God the Father, and on either side Moses and Elias. Beneath, his hands uplifted, stands S. Apollinare, while on either side six sheep move among flowers and trees ; in the background are three other sheep, representing perhaps SS. Peter, James and John. Be-neath between the windows are four Bishops of Ravenna, and to the right Abel, Melchizedek and Abraham, to the left the gift of privileges to the church of Ravenna, by the Emperor Contantius IV. This mosaic dates from 668. Over the arch of the tribune is a bust of Our Lord, and upon either side symbols of the Four Evangelists. Be-neath we see the cities of Jerusalem and Bethlehem, from each of which issue six sheep. All these mosaics have suffered very much from restoration.

There is much else of interest in the church : the crypt should be seen, with its ancient sarcophagus of S. Apolli-naris and its columns ; the ten sarcophagi which stand about the church should be noted and the curious tabernacle at the end of the north aisle. Indeed, a whole morning is not too much to spend in this deserted sanctuary.

S. Apollinare in Classe was the last great work to be undertaken in Ravenna by the Byzantine Empire. With the restoration of the West by Charlemagne, as I have said, Ravenna suddenly loses its importance. Indeed, all that really concerns us in the Ravenna of the Middle Ages is the visit of Dante ; the most eager mediæval apologist of the imperial idea, most fortunately, as we may think, there finding a refuge and a tomb.

Dante would seem to have come to Ravenna in 1317, at the earnest invitation of Guido Novello da Polenta. We know little of his life there. He does not seem to have occupied any official position either at the Court of Guido or at the University, but we hear of him as lecturing and " training many scholars in poetry, especially in the vernacular." He was, however, not without good friends and eager admirers, not the least of which was his host. It is possible, too, that his daughter Beatrice, who became a nun in S. Stefano dell' Uliva, was with him, and that his two sons were not altogether separated from him. It is said to have been at his invitation, too, that Giotto was invited to Ravenna to paint, if not in S. Maria in Portofuori, certainly in S. Giovanni Evangelista. For Guido Novello da Polenta Dante seems to have had a real regard, which was enthusiastically returned, and it was in the service of this man that the great Florentine met his death. For having gone to Venice on an embassy, on his way back he caught a fever in the marshes and died in Ravenna in 1320.

Dante was buried in a temporary resting-place in the church of S. Francesco, Guido Novello intending to raise a great monument in his honour. But Dante was scarcely laid in his temporary resting-place when Guido lost his lordship, and the noble sepulchre which had been planned was not built. A strange fate awaited those neglected ashes. Boccaccio had prophesied that Florence would one day regret her treatment of her greatest son. This prophecy was many times fulfilled, and first in 1396. In that year Florence made the first of her many demands for the body of Dante. None of these had any chance of success except that which was made to the Medici Pope in 1519, when permission was given to the Florentines to carry off the bones of him she had despised and to bury them in a tomb Michelangelo was to make in S. Croce. But when the ambassadors came to Ravenna and opened the ancient sarcophagus in which the great poet had been buried by Guido, it was found to be empty, and the mystery thus disclosed remained unexplained till our own time. In 1865, however, workmen were making certain repairs to the Braccioforte Chapel, when one of them struck his pickaxe through the wall and found a wooden box in which was discovered a human skeleton. Upon the box was found this inscription—

> Dantis ossa a me
> Fra Antonio Santi
> Hic posita An. 1677
> Die 18 Octobris.

It seems that in 1520 the Franciscans entered the mausoleum which had been erected and adorned at the command of Cardinal Bembo by Pietro Lombardi when the Venetians held Ravenna, abstracted the body and hid it to save it from the Florentines. In June 1677, as another inscription found within the coffin tells us, Fra Antonio visited the bones in this hiding-place and verified them, and in October of the same year built them into the wall, where they were discovered in 1865. Upon June 26 of that year the bones of Dante were replaced in their original sarcophagus, to remain, let us hope for ever, in the city which succoured him.

All that is of any interest in mediæval Ravenna we shall find spoken of in the pages of the *Divine Comedy*. It is there we hear of the Polentani, of the Mainardi, and the

Traversari, and of that Francesca who loved Paolo Malatesta, whose pitiful story as told by Dante is one of the great tragedies of the world. It is there too we hear of S. Romualdo, S. Peter Damiano and that Blessed Peter called Il Peccatore. All were famous and all were of Ravenna, but it is the last and, I suppose, the least of them who is most closely connected with the city. The others went away and won an everlasting fame, but Blessed Pietro Il Peccatore stayed in Ravenna and built there outside the walls in the marsh the great home of Our Lady S. Maria in Portofuori.

This lonely and melancholy church, as we see it to-day, is a basilica consisting of three naves which formed a part of the original church of the Blessed Pietro, and a presbytery, apse and chapels which are of the thirteenth century. There we see some frescoes of a very fine and early character erroneously attributed to Giotto, but really the work of Maso da Faenza, Rastello da Forlì and Giovanni da Ravenna in the fourteenth century. The best preserved and the noblest in design are those which represent the Death of the Blessed Virgin, the Last Supper and the Incredulity of S. Thomas. The old church has sunk deeply into the marsh, and its pillars are half immersed. The mighty tower beside it has been thought to be the famous Pharos of the port, and it is probably founded upon it, but what we see is a work of the end of the twelfth century.

The earliest of the Friars churches in Ravenna is that of S. Chiara, which is now suppressed. It dates from 1255, when it was founded by Chiara da Polenta, and it still possesses frescoes by the masters whose work is seen at S. Maria in Portofuori.

Not much later, the church of S. Pietro Maggiore, which we know as S. Francesco, came into Franciscan hands, but it is, as I have said, of very much earlier foundation, dating indeed from the time of Galla Placidia, to which its pillars bear witness. Its chief mediæval interest lies in the fact that it was within its precincts Dante was buried. It possesses, too, a few monuments of some interest, such as the tomb of Ostasio da Polenta (1396) and that of Enrico Alfieri, General of the Franciscan Order, who died in 1405. The fine Renaissance pilasters in the Cappella del Crocifiso should be noted also and the beautiful sixteenth-century monument of Luffo Numai by Tommaso Flamberti at the end of the left aisle.

Somewhat to the north of the Piazza stands the Dominican church of S. Domenico dating from 1269, enlarged in 1374 and rebuilt in the eighteenth century. The façade and side porch are the only parts left to us of the original church, but within are four paintings in tempera, possibly organ shutters representing the Annunciation of S. Peter Martyr and S. Dominic, the work of Niccolò Rondinelli.

From S. Domenico we pass to S. Giovanni Evangelista with its beautiful Gothic portal of the fourteenth century and the utterly spoilt frescoes of Giotto in the vaulting of the fourth chapel on the left. They represent the Four Evangelists and the Four Doctors of the Church ; in the centre is the Lamb with the Cross. These works have suffered so much from repainting that they can no longer be considered as Giotto's in anything but their design. In the chapel to the left of the choir is a mosaic pavement dating from 1213 representing scenes from the Third Crusade.

We must not leave S. Giovanni Evangelista without noting the great tower of the eleventh century which overshadows it. It is contemporary with the greater Torre Communale in the Via Tredici Giugno. Nor should we omit to visit the old house, the Casa Polentena, near Porta Ursicina and the Casa Traversari in Via S. Vitale, grand old thirteenth-century houses of Dante's day, before we pass to examine what is left of the time of the Renaissance in Ravenna.

The Middle Age may be said to have come to an end in this lonely city with the advent of the Venetians in 1441. Their first work was the fortification of the city

PIAZZA MAGGIORE RAVENNA

when in 1457 they built the tremendous Rocca whose ruins we still see. To them is also due the Piazza Maggiore in which they raised the two columns we know before the Palazza Comunale, bearing now, though not from of old, the statues of S. Apollinaris and S. Vitalis. But the Palazzo del Comune was entirely rebuilt by the Papal government in 1681 and the Palazzo Governativo in 1696. The Orologio Pubblico, dating from 1483, was transformed as we see it in 1785. The Portico Antico here would seem to have been built from the débris of the Arian church of S. Andrea when the Venetians destroyed that church to make room for their Rocca.

But undoubtedly the greatest monument which the Renaissance has given us in Ravenna is the church of S. Maria in Porto, built in 1553, when for nearly fifty years the Canons Regular had been compelled to abandon S. Maria in Portofuori. Even this church has, however, suffered from restoration, and the façade is a work of the eighteenth century. The church as a whole, however, remains a noble sixteenth-century building with a fine choir and a beautiful ciborio. The marble relief of the Madonna in prayer in the transept should also be noted ; it is a Byzantine work, brought to Ravenna in the time of the Crusades. Here, too, is a fine Renaissance Cloister, as there is at S. Giovanni Evangelista and at S. Vitale.

Ravenna is the last place in which to look for pictures, for, as I have said, her life in the Middle Age and the Renaissance was languid and isolated. What is to be had in the way of painting has been gathered in the Accademia in the Via Alfredo Baccarini. Among much that is negligible there remain a few delightful pieces. The best of these are the work of Niccolò Rondinelli, a native of Ravenna and the pupil and assistant of Giovanni Bellini. Three works by this master hang in the Accademia, a Madonna and Child with S. Catherine and S. Jerome (6) which comes from S. Spirito ; a Madonna with SS. Catherine, Mary Magdalen, John Baptist and Thomas Aquinas

3

which comes from S. Domenico ; and a Madonna and Child
with S. Alberto and S. Sebastian which comes from the
Carmelite church of S. Giovanni Battista.

Beside these fine works hang a number of pictures by
Francesco Zaganelli da Cotignola, a follower of Rondinelli's,
of which the better are the Presepio (10) and the Crucifixion
(13) from S. Agata. Three of his works remain in various
churches in the city, one in the ex-church of S. Romuald
in Classe, now part of the Museo, another in S. Girolamo,
and another at S. Croce. His brother Bernardino has a
picture here in the Accademia, the Agony in the Garden
(194).

Here are two works by Marco Palmezzano, a master of
the Romagunol school, a Nativity and a Presentation of
the Blessed Virgin (189, 190) ; another work by this master,
a Madonna and Child with four Saints, hangs in the
Vescovado.

Not one of these men had really much to do with
Ravenna, but a lesser painter, Luca Longhi (1507–80),
belongs to her altogether. Eight of his works, of which
three are portraits, hang in the Accademia ; by his son
Francesco there is one, and by his daughter Barbara, three.
It was with Luca Longhi that Vasari stayed when he came
to Ravenna ; he speaks kindly of his work and praised
that of " a daughter of his called Barbara, still but a child,
who draws very well and has begun to paint too in a very
good manner and with much grace."

These pictures with others fill the first two rooms of
the Accademia ; the third is full of various late pictures
which may be neglected ; the fourth, however, is devoted
to the tomb of Guidarello Guidarelli who fell at the battle
of Imola in 1501, the glorious work of Tullio Lombardo
which no one should miss. The young knight is represented life-size in complete armour lying on his back ; he
seems, weary of fighting at last, to be sleeping. Truly a
knight of the olden time.

The fifth room of the Accademia, again, is hung with

late and uninteresting works, but in the sixth there are some delightful early Italian pictures ; a Madonna and Child with SS. Peter and Barbara (191) by Matteo di Giovanni of Siena among them, together with a Christ with the Cross between two angels (202) by Niccolò da Foligno. The room is, however, overcrowded with an immense number of pictures in the Byzantine manner of considerable interest.

We leave the Accademia for the Museo close by. The building in which the collections are housed is the old Camaldulensian monastery of Classe, built in 1515 ; it has beautiful seventeenth-century cloisters, and altogether is far more interesting than anything it contains. Here, however, we may find all that remains of the Ravenna of the old Empire, and certain fragments of the suit of gold armour thought to be Theodoric's, which was discovered near the Corsini Canal not far from the great Mausoleum.

No one should leave Ravenna without visiting the Pineta beyond S. Apollinare in Classe, yet few there be who get so far, for the country is too desolate and uninviting for so long a drive to prove very attractive. Yet the Pineta should be seen for its own sake, and certainly in memory of Dante, Boccaccio and Byron, who have each loved it in his own way. It is perhaps, even yet, the loveliest thing to be had in Ravenna.

CHAPTER II

ARGENTA, PORTOMAGGIORE, POMPOSA COMACCHIO

IT was very early one April morning that I set out from Ravenna to explore those two provinces which she had created and conserved, as I have tried to show, when the appalling Lombard flood threatened to overwhelm everything, and the old provincial system of the Empire was broken in pieces at last. I went northward, intent on Ferrara, but hoping by the way to see something of that strange country of which Comacchio is a sort of capital, a country of vast lagoons and low marshes in which Argenta lies like a jewel and Portomaggiore like a discarded buckler.

This country which, under a grey sky, is perhaps the dreariest in Italy, and the emptiest in the world, in the spring sunshine laughs and dances for joy as the silver footsteps of the wind come softly over the great lagoons, and the marvellous white clouds of those vast skies lend the enormous loneliness something of their own loveliness, fleeting and indescribable. One feels indeed often upon these endless lost roads, in a world that seems to have fallen away from one, rather of the sky than of the earth, as though those great white clouds, which, in their beautiful shapes, lift one's eyes from the way, were indeed those blessed islands which the ancients sought, or those delectable mountains the Pilgrim found far away, or again, some sunny argosy sailing up from the Ionian sea with Andromeda and all her wronged maidenhood, in pursuit of Theseus. It is a world in which heaven constraineth us.

In the midst of this towering unearthly world of cloud, of water and fen, and mist and sun and wind, Argenta lies, its wonderful church, its pictures, its simple delight for the most part unknown. Yet what is there more strange than the church of S. Giorgio with its round-arched, Lombard doorway carved with curious beasts, and its beautiful immemorial altar ? What is there more light, more delicious in all Romagna than the Duomo in its Renaissance graciousness and airy space ? What is more beautiful than the lofty apse of S. Francesco, or more splendid than the round church, with its lofty buttresses, of Calletta ? And there are pictures too : in the Chiesa della Saliciata, for instance, a spoilt but charming Pietà of the Ferrarese school, and a noble great ancona by Aleotti, who was born here ; in S. Domenico, a fresco of S. Gregorio Magno by no less a master than Rondinelli. There is, too, a Pinocoteca which, among other works, boasts a polyptych by Aleotti in which we see the Madonna and Child enthroned with two angels playing music at their feet, and about their heads six Cherubim, while four saints stand on guard, two on either side. Here, too, is a Madonna and Child enthroned between SS. Lazarus and Job by Garofalo, and a curious picture representing the earthquake of 1570 in Argenta.

Nor is this all. I know not rightly how to speak of this little place which has won my heart. I have said nothing of the Piazza so dear in its littleness between its fine arcades ; I have said nothing of the Terraglio della Mura or the great Torre dell' Orologio over the gate. I have not told you yet of the palaces, Palazzo Aleotti, Palazzo Dorini, or spoken of S. Domenico, that great church of brick with its tower and steeple, or of the unforgettable apse of S. Francesco over the green of the orchard, or said anything at all of the gardens. Go and see, and if you are wise and bold enough to find this dear forgotten place, only leave it to go to Portomaggiore, that gay little town with its great Estensi villa and tower, glorious Palazzo Aventi and noble garden, its curious church, Chiesa di Maiero, and fine picture by Dosso Dossi in the Palazzo Comunale, Madonna and her little Son enthroned under great trees while S. John Baptist and another worship them.

From Portomaggiore it is a drive of a whole long spring morning to Comacchio by way of Ostellato. This strange and delightful place is as it were the capital of all this country of waters, and so wonderful is it that nothing can really excuse one for failing to find it. It is a town of fishermen built really upon the waters of vast lagoons, and everywhere traversed by picturesque canals and lofty bridges many of them of great beauty, as the Ponte del Carmine, the high Ponte del Borgo and the charming Tre Ponti. Here and there are some fine churches, as the Chiesa dei Cappuccini and the Chiesetta del Carmine, and everywhere there are gardens full of shade; but Comacchio is yet in a waste of waters, and what strikes one there first and last is the beauty of those infinite lagoons across which the sky leans so nobly, with the great white clouds of spring and autumn, most wonderful in their lovely majesty, towering up into the blue.

One could spend half a year in Comacchio without being weary, it is so exquisite in its strangeness and its fisher folk are so hospitable and kind, as human a people as abide in Italy ; but before turning to Ferrara, the true refuge and fortress of all this country of great waters, there is another wonder that will not be denied, I mean the great abbey of Pomposa.

The way lies across the northern *Valli* to Codigoro, where the Germans are now continuing the work of re-claiming this country, first undertaken by the monks and then in the modern manner by the English. Codigoro is without charm, but there is nothing more strangely beautiful in all this world of marsh and water than the Badia di Pomposa, some three miles beyond it.

This most ancient Benedictine Abbey would seem to

date from the appalling years of the Lombard invasion.
It is deserted now, but still its great tower, the loftiest and
the noblest in all this country, salutes the dawn, and still
the little church beside it offers a shrine to all who pass by
in this enormous silence.

It is possible, though by no means certain, that even in
the earliest days of Christianity there was a hermitage and
an altar here which passed, though we know not when, at
last to the Benedictines, who at once set about repairing
the banks of the streams and reclaiming what they could
of all that had fallen into decay in the decline of the
western Empire, and the invasions which followed the
failure of that great administration. The success of the
monks cannot be denied, for Pomposa became very famous,
the shrine and the sanctuary of the Bocca di Po as long as
the main stream emptied itself through the Po di Volano.
Indeed such was the glory of the place that it was known
throughout Europe for its learning, and was not only
patronized but visited by many of the greatest figures of
the Middle Age. In the time of the famous and holy
Abbot Guido, the Marquis Bonifazio of Tuscany frequently
sojourned there, as in disguise one day did the Archbishop
of Ravenna, sent by the Pope to inquire into the state of
the community, which, according to common report, was
puffed up with pride on account of its learning and extremely lax in discipline. The Archbishop, however,
found all to be very well, and from that time on the Badia
di Pomposa increased in fame. Guido Aretino the musician,
Otho III, the Emperor Frederick Barbarossa too, and a
host of Crusaders came to sojourn there from time to
time, and it is possible that Dante did not leave it unvisited
on his last journey between Venice and Ravenna in the
year of his death.

By then the place had already lost much of its unique
pre-eminence. In 1270 it had come under the protection
of the Estensi, but the real cause of its decline was the
opening of the present main bed of the great river in the

previous century. Little by little Pomposa lost touch with life till in 1550 the Benedictines abandoned it for their monastery of S. Benedetto in Ferrara.

What we see to-day at Pomposa is a vast and lofty Romanesque campanile towering out of the marsh over the little Romanesque church beside it. This church, dedicated in honour of the Blessed Virgin, is a rebuilding of 1150. Before it there stands a long, low vestibule, into which we pass through an arcade of three arches. The walls of the façade are decorated with beautiful sculptured friezes of Romanesque work, and with two vast roses of sculptured ornament. The church is a basilica divided within into three aisles by two arcades borne by fine marble columns with very lovely capitals, at the end of the central nave being a raised semicircular choir or apse. The aisle has been divided into chapels, and thus the beautiful design of the church, its effect of space and beauty, has been spoilt. But the glorious pavement of mosaics still remains, and the whole church is covered with fading frescoes. On either side of the nave there are three series of these frescoes one above another. The highest series consists of scenes from the Old Testament; the middle, of scenes from the life of Christ; the lowest, of scenes from the Apocalypse. In the aisles and apse are others almost indecipherable. All are Giottesque works of the Romagna, without much distinction, but full of tender and beautiful colour that even now gives light and sweetness to the old church. In the refectory are other works of the same kind.

The mighty tower is a work of the eleventh century. From its summit a marvellous view of earth and sky and sea and sealake lies before the traveller, which he should on no account miss. Close by is the beautiful Palazzo della Ragione. A whole day of delight may easily be spent about this lovely old abbey, before the mists of evening drive one back to Codigoro and the steam tramway to Ferrara at last.

CHAPTER III

FERRARA

I

ANYONE who will take the trouble to make the journey from Ravenna to Ferrara by road will understand Ferrara at once. It is a place dyked and very strong, a refuge from the great waters that lie about it, and that, when Po is angry, inundate all these vast marshes in which it alone stands impregnable.

Ferrara is a lonely and silent city, half empty now, a city of stone, cold and despondent, in which the misery of Tasso seems still to haunt the ways, an expression of the melancholy of the place. All the splendour in which the great house of Este involved it has utterly fallen away. The Cathedral, half forbidding in its dark façade and the curious twilight of its interior, the mighty Castello, rather a prison than a palace, where, of all that famous family, only the guilty Parisina and her unhappy lover seem at home, strike a forbidding and unhappy note with so much intensity that the whole city is caught as in some sinister misfortune. Ferrara is the stronghold against the marshes, but often it might seem as though something of their emptiness and grim desolation had overwhelmed this citadel in their heart.

As a refuge, indeed, she is without confidence, a city of burning sunshine and of many days of rain. There is always fear in her heart, fear of fever or of flood ; it is as though she would not be taken unaware. Her mood, which one feels at once on entering her gates, is curiously emphasized by her history. She has not the confidence of antiquity ; she is of the Dark Age, but unlike Venice, her contemporary, she has not been given the strength, the beauty, and the joy of the sea. She was probably founded by the provincial refugees who were in flight before the barbarian Lombard. Those fugitives, like others who established themselves finally in the Venetian lagoons, sought the safety of the marshes and shallow waters and there, upon such islands of dry and good ground as they could find, built their hovels, and were really impregnable because they could not be reached. Even to-day when all this marshy land is in slow process of redemption it is easy to understand how secure Ferrara essentially was. The great and, alas, half-empty town lies right in the delta of the Po to the north of the southern arm which there, where Ferrara stands, divides itself into two branches, the Po di Volano and the Po Morto di Primaro. This southern branch, now without importance, was of old the main stream, for the great bed on which the main waters of the river now pass to the north of the city, the Po della Maestra, was only formed in the twelfth century. Until the Lombard invasion in the sixth century all the region to the north of the Po Morto made a part of the province of Venetia. That province was, as I have tried to show, broken in pieces by the final ruin of that invasion, and the Imperial governor established himself in Grado. With this town for a centre the eastern part of the old province of Venetia re-formed itself together with part of Istria. But the western part, cut off from the capital, attached itself by force of circumstances to what remained of Emilia and Flaminia ; and these fragments all found their centre in Ravenna, the capital of Flaminia and the residence of the Prefect of Italy and later of the Exarch.

It is probable that that reconstruction in the sixth century, fundamentally a measure of defence, was as necessary on account of the physical changes in the country consequent upon the ruin of the Imperial administration and the neglect of public works as on account of the barbarian conquests. The great works of engineering, which are still necessary to save the country,from inundation, fell into decay, and the Po, instead of being confined to its old channels, spread over the fields and every year claimed a wider territory. Thus the island of good land upon which Ferrara stands offered itself in a waste of marsh and water as a refuge, and it is for this reason that we find the Exarch Smaragdus (585-9 and 602-11) constructing to the north of the old bed of the river—for all this country was now within his real jurisdiction—the stronghold of Ferrara.

This stronghold, almost as impregnable as Ravenna, became the centre as it were of a group of cities, among which were the ancient Roman towns of Hatria (Adria) and Gabellum (Gavello), the most northerly of the Exarchate.

But the Exarchate began to fail in the eighth century, and we then find the débris of the Roman province of Venetia to the south of the Adige, formed into the Duchy of Ferrara. Its limits would seem to have been, the Adige on the north, the Panaro on the west, and the Po di Volano on the south. This duchy presently came into the hands of Liutprand, king of the Lombards, but when Ravenna fell at last in 754, and Pepin crossed the Alps and gave the whole of the old Exarchate and the Pentapolis to the Pope, Stephen II received the keys of Ferrara with those of the other cities (757).

The Holy See, as we might expect, soon found that it had not the means at its disposal, in the condition of society at that time, for an armed civil government. Its dominion was in many ways a failure, and Ferrara, like other cities, acquired little by little a veritable though a limited autonomy. In the eleventh century she recognized the suzerainty of the Marquis Bonifazio of Tuscany, and after his death that of his daughter, the Countess Matilda. In the twelfth century she appears as one of the most

flourishing cities south of the Po, but uncertain in her
allegiance, and consequently already at the mercy of those
great families whose prey she was to be. We see the city
divided into two factions, whom we may call Imperialists
and Nationalists, and later Ghibellines and Guelfs. At the
head of the Imperialist party was the family of Salinguerra
Torelli ; at the head of the Nationalists the Adelardi. In
the time of Frederick Barbarossa it was the latter who
prevailed, and Ferrara entered the Lombard League.
And when, with the thirteenth century, the quarrel
developed and the factions everywhere in Italy became
either Guelf or Ghibelline, the city was involved in this
ferocious personal and political vendetta, here most
fiercely fought by the Ghibelline Ezzelino da Romano and
the Guelf house of Este.

Ferrara became involved in this unappeasable hatred,
if we may believe the chroniclers, in the following way.
It seems that a marriage had been arranged between one
of the Ghibelline house of Torelli and Mascherella the
heiress of the Guelf house of Adelardi, with the object of
reuniting the two factions in Ferrara. This was too much
for the Estensi, Guelfs too, who had doubtless expected to
possess themselves of the Adelardi power when that house
failed. The Marchese Obizzo swooped down from his
hills and carried off Mascherella and married her. Mascherella was, as I have said, the heiress of the Adelardi,
and thus their great wealth passed to the house of Este,
who now set foot in the Ferrarese. The twelfth century
came to an end in Ferrara in the midst of the struggle
of the Estensi to establish themselves there. Time and
time again they were chased out of the city by the Torelli
house which they had robbed of a bride, till the Marchese
Aldobrandino d'Este made a peace with Salinguerra
Torelli by which the two rivals agreed to divide the government of the town. But Aldobrandino was beaten by
Ezzelino and disappeared in 1215. His young brother,
Azzo VII (1205–61), was at first unable to continue the

struggle, and Salinguerra, who was married to a sister of Ezzelino, dominated Ferrara till 1240, and with considerable success. But after 1229 the struggle was renewed and assisted by the Lombard League. Azzo d'Este attacked the Ferrarese with such ferocity that they at last found it wiser to surrender to the Guelf party. The gates of the city were opened by Ugo Ramberti, Salinguerra was imprisoned, his palace demolished, and his partisans banished (1240). Ferrara passed under the dominion of Azzo, who immediately transferred the centre of his power to Ferrara, and though for a time all looked dark enough for the city, for Ezzelino still lived, in 1259 that monster perished, and the Guelf cause with the Este house at its head finally triumphed. Azzo gave peace to the Ferrarese, and when he died was borne to S. Francesco amid the lamentations of the citizens.

He was succeeded, not by his son, who had died a prisoner of Frederick II's in Sicily, but by his grandson Obizzo (1240–93), who succeeded in adding Modena and Reggio to his lordship. His son, Azzo VIII (d. 1306), inherited these three states, but his brothers, Francesco and Aldobrandino, successfully disputed them with him, and in 1306 he lost Modena and Reggio. Nor was he then done with his brethren. He had chosen as his successor Folco, son of his bastard Fresco, but Francesco and Aldobrandino appealed to the Pope, who was very ready to hear them, hoping to obtain once more the real overlordship, for Ferrara was by right a fief of the Holy See. In despair Fresco ceded Ferrara to Venice, and retired there with his son. For a time a Venetian Podestà governed the city, but it was presently retaken by the Papal troops, and Clement V gave it to Robert of Naples. Francesco and Aldobrandino opposed him, but without success, and the Estensi were reduced once more to the original marquisate of Este. They both disappear from history in 1312, but their sons, with others of the house, were able to re-enter Ferrara in 1317, for the population, bullied and butchered by the Catalan soldiery of Robert of Naples, rose, and, with the help of the Estensi and the Bolognese, took the Castel Tebaldo, where the Catalans held out, and massacred them. The three sons of Aldobrandino thus repossessed themselves of the lordship. Pope John XXII answered their success by excommunication and an interdict against Ferrara, with the result that the Estensi joined the Ghibellines and Aldobrandino III (1335–61) became Vicar Imperial for the Emperor Charles IV.

But there was an enemy more ambitious, more jealous, and more formidable than the Pope, which the Estensi had now to face. This was the Visconti. Against them and against the Gonzaga of Mantua, Aldobrandino's brother and successor, Niccolò II (d. 1388), made war ; but his brother Alberto (d. 1393), hoping for the lordship, first joined them and then in 1390 allied himself with Bologna and Florence against them.

The Estensi were divided against themselves. Niccolò III (1384–1441), the son of Alberto, during his minority was placed under the protection of Venice, and later with the assistance of Venice, Bologna, and Florence succeeded in holding Ferrara against his kinsman Azzo and the Visconti. He was a man very splendid in all his ways, a great traveller, a fine soldier, an insatiable lover. It was said of him by the Ferrarese, and with obvious double meaning, that "Di qua e di là del Po, tutti son figli di Niccolò." A great personal tragedy clouded his reign. As his second wife he had married Parisina Malatesta of Cesena. One day it was told him that Ugo, his son, was her lover. In his immense anger he refused to hear reason, but on the same night had them both put to death in Castel Vecchio in the dungeon of the tower called Marchesana. Before dawn their bodies were borne to S. Francesco and buried at the foot of the Campanile.

> No tomb, no memory had they ;
> Their's was unconsecrated clay.

The wars in which Niccolò III was involved against the Visconti, though diversified by various treaties of peace, only came to an end with his death. Nevertheless it was Niccolò, soldier though he was perforce, who first made Ferrara the brilliant centre of learning and the arts it was to remain throughout the Renaissance and the Catholic Reaction. His court rivalled that of Milan, and the city boasted, by reason of his munificence and that of his son, a school, a university, and museums, as well as wharves which served a growing commerce. Niccolò's son Leonello (1441–50) had been educated by the famous Guarino da Verona, and he came to hold quite as great a position in Italy as his father had maintained. It was he who mediated between Alfonso of Aragon and the Venetians, and it was at Ferrara that peace was signed. His son Borso, who ruled from 1451 till his death in 1471, was one of the most magnificent princes of the age. Indeed, such was the splendour of his court that it may be said to have won him the title of Duke from the Emperor Frederick III in 1452 ; this for the imperial fiefs of Reggio and Modena, while the Pope, Pius II, granted him a similar title for the papal fief of Ferrara, as reward for the entertainment he had received on his way to the Council of Mantua. When he died at last the peace of his dominion was endangered for a time by the rivalry of his brother Ercole and Niccolò son of Leonello. Ercole was supported by Venice and was eventually successful, but the horrors of this civil war, in contrast with the luxury and immorality of the Court, struck the imagination of Savonarola, who, it will be remembered, was a Ferrarese, the grandson of Niccolò III's physician, and in 1475 he entered the Dominican Order at Bologna and found, as we know, an amazing career in Florence.

Venice had supported Ercole, and it was her support which had decided the civil war in his favour, but in 1482 we find the Republic plotting with Pope Sixtus IV to divide the Este dominion. It seems Ercole had been taxing Venetian merchant shipping on the Po, and had especially levied duty upon the salt from Comacchio. A Venetian fleet appeared, and Rovigo was taken and the Polesina was occupied by the troops of the Republic.

Ercole, however, was a sufficiently clever politician to know how to convince the Pope that his action could only end in the aggrandizement of the Venetians. The Pope agreed to come to terms, but the war with Venice persisted for two years more, when Ercole agreed to give up any rights of taxation he may have had and obtained in exchange the Polesina.

During the peace thus established which endured to the end of his reign, the brilliancy of his court increased. Boiardo became his minister and Ariosto his guest. But he owes less than his successor, Alfonso I, to the men of letters he patronized and supported. Alfonso, however, was an unfortunate ruler. Inveigled into the League of Cambray for the utter destruction of Venice, he played no mean part; his artillery broke the Venetian fleet in 1509 at Polisetta on the Po, and as the ally of the King of France, when the Pope had made peace, this same great arm of his played by no means the least part in the battle and victory of Ravenna. Excommunicated by the Pope, he was forced to humble himself when the French retreat began after the death of Gaston de Foix at Ravenna. Julius II claimed Modena and Reggio and Parma, and Alfonso was compelled to relinquish them to Leo X, but recovered them in 1516. He did not forget his injuries, however, and in the appalling invasion of 1527 when Rome was sacked by the rabble of the Constable Bourbon, it was Alfonso d'Este who opened the road. All the wars he waged and those of his predecessors when Charles V came into Italy in 1529, had gained him nothing and lost him nothing; he was just able to hand on his dominion unimpaired to his successor, Ercole II, when he died in 1534.

Alfonso I had carried on the tradition of his house in his vast patronage of letters. As his second wife he had

married the famous Lucrezia Borgia ; his successor married
the almost equally famous Renée of France, and their courts
were the real centre of the literature of the sixteenth
century in Italy. He had built in Ferrara the finest theatre
in the peninsula and the city became the shrine of dramatic
art. He died in 1555, and his successor Alfonso II carried
on the tradition. It was he who employed and befriended
Tasso. His court was perhaps the most splendid that had
ever been maintained in Ferrara. He had married the
ill-favoured Lucrezia de' Medici, but both his beautiful
sisters Lucrezia and Leonora d'Este, the one the wife of the
Duke of Urbino, the other, as it is said, the lover of Tasso,
lived at Ferrara. Life in the city was one long festa
diversified by the theatre and discussions of poetry, science,
and manners. A sort of political equilibrium had been
obtained for the Duke by the fact that he remained the
faithful supporter of the Emperor, while his brother
Cardinal Ippolito had embraced the French cause, and thus
the Estensi had a representative in both camps, but his
extravagant pride finally ruined all. In order to send presents which he thought worthy of himself to the Emperor
and to maintain the splendour of his court he broke his
people with taxes, but neglected the public works, such as
the dykes and canals which were the very source of his
country's wealth ; nor did he stop at murder to obtain
money for his pleasures. Such a state of things could not
endure. His subjects were alienated, he had no legitimate
heir in spite of his three marriages, and though the Emperor was willing to recognize a son of a bastard of Alfonso I
as his successor, the Pope was not. When Alfonso II died,
in 1597, Clement III declared that all the pontifical fiefs
of the Empire must return to the Holy See. Cesare, the
feeble prince nominated by Alfonso and accepted by the
Emperor, retired to his imperial fiefs of Modena and Reggio,
and at Ferrara the dominion of the Holy See was erected.
The splendour and prosperity of Ferrara were at an end ; the
town grew poor with the country, and presently an entire

quarter, half depopulated, for the Ferrarese were emigrating in large numbers to Modena, was pulled down and a citadel erected upon its site. It is useless and melancholy to follow the story further, for, as we may believe, its misery is past and its poverty about to be cured by the energy, enterprise and new-born hope of the Italian people in their new unity.

II

Such in briefest outline is the history of Ferrara. How far may we trace it in the monuments that remain in the city to-day ? It is true that the depopulation of the city that followed upon the fall of the Este house allowed much to fall into decay and at length to be destroyed that we should be glad to possess in Ferrara, but nevertheless I think there is no city in all Italy which is materially more at one with its history than is this lonely stronghold in the marshes.

Mediæval Ferrara, the old, crooked, and crouching city of refuge, is indeed almost startlingly brought before us in those ancient byways, the Via S. Romano, the Via delle Volte, and the Via Porta Reno. In the Duomo we remember the Adelardi, for it was founded and in great part built by them. The Castello, S. Francesco, the Palazzo Schifanoia, the Palazzo de' Diamanti are the enduring work of the Estensi in the great period of the city's story ; while in the house of Ariosto and the Hospital of S. Anna we are reminded of the two great poets who made Ferrara their home. It is in these buildings and the works of art which they contain that the city of old lives for us again.

Ferrara may be said to be quite divided into two parts, a northern and a southern, by the Corso della Giovecca. It is the latter of these which is the true city, and its centre lies in the Piazza del Mercato, which was the gathering place of the people in the Mediæval and Renaissance city, where the riots and festas, the executions and bull-fights took place. All the life that remains to Ferrara will still be found there, and on a market-day one may easily deceive oneself that the city is still a great capital and very much alive. It is out of this Piazza to the south that the Via S. Romano and the Via Porta Reno, two of those old, picturesque streets of which I have spoken, pass upon either side of the Palazzo della Ragione at last to join the third, the Via delle Volte.

The Palazzo della Ragione, as we see it, is an ugly modern building, but it occupies the site of an Italian Gothic palace built in the early part of the fourteenth century in which the Courts of Justice were held. At either end of this palace stood a tower, upon one of which the bodies of those who had suffered the death penalty were exposed, while from the other the decrees of the dukes were announced.

Beside the Palazzo della Ragione stands the ex-church of S. Romano with its charming façade of the fifteenth century. It occupies the site of a much more ancient building, once the church and monastery of the Benedictines of Ferrara.

The long south wall of the Cathedral, so delightfully supported by booths and shops, closes the greater part of the Piazza upon the north. This remarkable rather than glorious church possesses a very noble western façade before which the Piazza stretches to be closed here on the north by the Arcivescovado. This façade, almost unique in Italy, is a lofty and cavernous triptych, always full of dense shadows, and especially on a misty spring or autumn morning, when if it be market-day the Cathedral will be filled with people as of old, for Mass. This noble and rather tragic structure has two principal faults—it has no relation to what lies behind it, and is not at one with itself ; but it is finely picturesque, always full of mystery, and on a market-day in the morning mist that is so common in Ferrara rises there like a cliff roaring with the sea and full of caverns.

The Duomo was founded, it is said, by Guglielmo Adelardi in 1133, and was dedicated in honour of S. Girogio on 8th May 1135, when the throne of the Bishop was transferred hither from the old cathedral across the river. It was the work of one Niccolò. All of this is rudely reported in the old verses on the façade :—

> IL MILO CENTO TREMPTA CINQUE NATO
> FO QTO TEMPLO A ZORZI CSECRATO
> FO NICOLAO SCOLPTORE
> E GLIELMO FO LO AUCTORE.

The lower part of the façade would seem to date from 1135 and is in the Lombard style, but the isolated arcades of the upper part are of a hundred years later and Gothic in feeling and intention as the Italians understand that great northern style. But to our eyes at least the effect is not Gothic ; it fails everywhere to impress us with its sincerity of construction, suggests breadth rather than height, and is overwhelmed by the great blind *oculi* under the three gables. Its one distinctive feature, if indeed a thing so composite can be called one, is the great round-headed porch, purely Lombard in feeling, with a fine relief of S. George and the Dragon surmounted by the rich Gothic loggia in which stands a great statue by Aristofero da Firenze (1427) of the Madonna and Child, beneath the reliefs of the Last Judgment of the early fourteenth century in the pediment and tympanum.

Within, the church is noble in its effect, but with a nobility very different from anything the façade has led us to expect. It consists of nave, choir, double transepts, and aisles ; its beauty is wholly due to its dim spaciousness, which has not been spoiled by the rebuilding of the eighteenth century. Its chief interest, however, lies for us to-day in the paintings it contains, which, though of a late period, are fine of their kind.

In the second transept on the south is a ruined work by Guercino of the Martyrdom of S. Laurence. Upon the altar here is a noble group of figures in bronze by Niccolò Baroncelli and Domenico di Paris, fifteenth-century works consisting of the Crucifixion with the Blessed Virgin and S. John, S. George, and S. Maurelius. Here, too, and in the other transept, are figures in terra-cotta of Our Lord and the Apostles by Alfonso Lombardi, sixteenth-century works spoiled by repainting. The best pictures in the church, noble masterpieces in their own way, are in the choir ; two panels by Cosimo Tura of the Annunciation and S. George and the Dragon. That adamantine master of Ferrara here seems to be working in bronze, so sculptural is the effect of his work, especially in the S. George.

Two other pictures remain in the church which are worthy of notice, a late work by Francia upon the sixth altar in the south aisle, a Coronation of the Virgin, and a Madonna enthroned with Saints by Garofalo over the third altar on the north. Two repainted frescoes by this master, of S. Peter and S. Paul, remain to right and left of the main door, while in the sacristy there is an Annunciation from his hand and a charming fifteenth-century statue of the Madonna by Giacomo da Siena. Here, too, is a lovely fragment of mosaic, the head of the Madonna dating from 1135.

The beautiful unfinished campanile of the fifteenth century stands a little heavily to the south-east of the great church.

Opposite the western façade of the Cathedral, a little to the north, stands the Palazzo del Municipio restored in 1739. This was the first home of the Estensi in Ferrara. Here, according to Vasari, Giotto painted some frescoes, as he did also in the church of S. Agostino now no more. Later Duke Borso employed Piero della Francesca to decorate his house, but these works too have perished, and all that remains of the numberless splendours that the Dukes lavished upon this, their first palace, is the columns of the Volto del Cavallo, a loggia which Ercole I built towards the end of his life and adorned with a statue of his father Niccolò III. All was swept away in 1796, save these ruins and, within, a beautiful staircase also of that time.

From this first palace of the Estensi we pass to the Castello which Niccolò II built in the last years of the

fourteenth century by the hand of Bartolino da Novara.
As we see it, it is a restoration of the sixteenth century,
but it is impressively strong and picturesque, a fortress,
one might think, rather than a palace surrounded by a moat
with a tower at each of its four corners and armed at
all points. In the old days, indeed, it must always have
successfully overawed and threatened the city and have
been a continual reminder of him who was master. This
was, of course, its intention.[1]

I do not think that anyone can affect to be much interested in the apartments now so unromantic with their
frescoes of the schools of Dosso Dossi and Garofalo. What
is fascinating, however, in spite of their dubious claim to
authenticity, is the dungeons at the base of the Marchesana
tower, where, the custodian assures one, Niccolò iii confined
Parisina his wife and Ugo his son, her lover, in the long
night before they were beheaded. Here, too, Alfonso i
imprisoned his brother Giulio and Ferrante d'Este after the
conspiracy of 1506. The Castello itself has seen, of course,
all the splendour that was Este. And it is curious to recall
that among those brilliant ghosts of great men and fairest
women—Ariosto, Tasso, Lucrezia Borgia, Leonora and
Lucrezia d'Este, to name no more—we may find the tragic
figure of John Calvin, who was protected by Renée of
France, wife of Ercole ii. He came to visit her in 1536,
and so corrupted her mind with hatred and error that he
destroyed her happiness and broke her marriage. The
ghost of Calvin only, I think, emphasizes the essential gloom
of this strong and cruel place so full of the memory of dead
pleasures.

The Piazza before the Castello is now named in honour

[1] It would seem that it was the murder of his tax-gatherer
Tommaso da Tortona which induced Niccolò to build this fortress.
That unhappy creature had been mobbed and had taken refuge
with his master, who, to save himself, was obliged to surrender
him to the crowd that tore him limb from limb. It was then in
1385 that Niccolò built this great stronghold.

of another reformer, Savonarola, who was born in Ferrara, as I have said, in September 1452. He left his native city to enter the Dominican Order at Bologna, however, when he was twenty-three. He only returned once, in 1482, when he preached the Lent in the Duomo here, but either his political notions or his prophecies caught the restless fancy of Duke Ercole, and in 1495 he began a long correspondence with the Frate, then famous in Florence. Even two years later, on the eve of Savonarola's exposure, the Duke was writing to him, but when Pico della Mirandola dedicated his defence of the Friar to him, and the Pope protested, Ercole excused himself. Yet there was much in common between them, as presently became obvious. For if Savonarola was in league with Charles VIII, Duke Ercole was even more eager and joined Ludovico il Moro in his invitation to the French to descend upon Italy. Ludovico was Ercole's son-in-law, for he had married Beatrice, his daughter, who was so brilliant a figure in the corrupt Milanese court, and whom the Moor seems really to have loved to the end of his life. He had a palace in Ferrara near the Porta Romana, now called Palazzo Calcagnini, but it was never finished.

Just out of the Piazza Savonarola, to the west of the palace, is the Piazza named in honour of Tasso. At the end of it is the church of S. Giuliano with a pretty Renaissance façade.

Tasso came to Ferrara in 1569, and presently is said to have conceived a hopeless passion for the Duke's sister, the Princess Leonora. This story, however, which has delighted generations of men with its pathetic romance of love unhinging a noble intelligence, is now wholly discredited. Tasso's mental affliction seems to have been a very different affair—to have had nothing whatever to do with a hopeless love at any rate. Nervous and self-centred as he always had been even in his boyhood, the victim of a precocious talent and an unwise upbringing, his whole character at Ferrara little by little went to pieces. He imagined himself to be the victim of a ridiculous persecution, and at last, really to save his life, the Duke Alfonso II had him confined to his rooms in the Castello. He escaped, however, and, how we know not, travelled on foot as far as Sorrento in southern Italy, where he had a sister. Unfortunately, he returned to Ferrara, where every one at the moment was busy with the marriage of Alfonso and Margherita Gonzaga. Wounded in his vanity, always his weakness, and still suffering from a mania of persecution, he insulted the Duchess and cursed the Duke, who had the poet carried to the Hospital of S. Anna opposite the Castello on the other side of the Corso, where he was confined as a madman from 1579 to 1585. His cell is still there, but is chiefly interesting by reason of the poets who have visited it and there scrawled their names ; among these we see Byron's.

The English poet, as he tells us himself, had been very eager to see " the cell where they caged Tasso," and it seems to have inspired the famous *Lament*, as the "Court where Parisina and Hugo were beheaded " did the finer *Parisina*. We, perhaps, are more exacting or less susceptible ; and then for us the love-story has faded out of Tasso's tragedy. Nevertheless, I for one always recall there the lovely lines which Spenser translated so exquisitely in the " Faerie Queene " ; are they better in the Italian or in the English ?

> Cosi trapassa al trapassar d'un giorno
> De la vita mortale il fiore e 'l verde . . .

So passeth in the passing of a day
Of mortall life the leafe the bud, the flowre
Ne more doth florish after first decay
That earst was sought to deck both bed and bowre
Of many a ladye, and many a paramoure.
Gather therefore the rose whilest yet is prime
For soone comes age that will her pride defloure
Gather the rose of love whilest yet is time
Whilest loving thou mayest loved be withe equal crime.

Returning through the Piazza del Mercato past the Seminario Arcivescovile, where there are some fine ceiling paintings by Garofalo, one comes to the University built by Aleotti in the end of the sixteenth century, with its manuscripts of Ariosto's *Orlando Furioso,* Tasso's *Gerusalemme Liberata* and Guarini's *Pastor Fido,* and the monument of Ariosto which was brought here from S. Benedetto in 1801.

Ariosto was born in 1474, within the Este dominion, but at Reggio, not at Ferrara. His father, however, who was governor of Reggio, had property in Ferrara—indeed his house is just opposite the University—and from his eleventh year the poet lived in the capital and all his life was essentially a Ferrarese. His father died in 1500 and he was compelled to exert himself for the support of his family. It was the Cardinal Ippolito d'Este who introduced him to the court of Ferrara, and though mean in his rewards, employed him continually. Thus patronized, Ariosto found leisure to write in the ten years between 1506 and 1516 his great poem the *Orlando Furioso,* a continuation of Boiardo's *Orlando Innamorato.* Ferrara was his home, and when he was away from it he was miserable. He died there in 1533 and was buried in S. Benedetto.

From the University we return along the Via della Scienza and come to S. Francesco. The friars founded a church here as early as 1232 and this was rebuilt in 1341. Very many of the Este house were buried in the old church, for it was under their especial protection. There lay Azzo VII, Aldobrandino, Niccolò II and Alberto in a great tomb of red marble. But the church was again rebuilt in 1494 by Biagio Rossetti, and now no trace is left of all that once noble dust. The present church is large and spacious, a brick building with a terra-cotta façade, the interior light and beautiful in the manner of the Renaissance. It contains some works by Garofalo in the first chapel on the north; frescoes of the Betrayal of Our Lord, with donors;

and others in a chapel on the other side of the church, of the Nativity.

S. Francesco has lost its memories of the Estensi, but in the neighbouring church of Corpus Domini, if you can get into it, you will find the tombs of Duke Alfonso I and Lucrezia Borgia, Isabella d'Este, Duke Ercole II, and Princesses Lucrezia and Leonora. And then we come upon them again in all their indifferent pleasures, their curious aloofness, as we may think, from reality, in that Palazzo Schifanoia in the Via Scandiana on the verge of the city. This palace, though begun by Alberto d'Este, is really the work of the Dukes Borso and Ercole I. Borso finished what Alberto had but begun, adorned it with festoons by the hands of Cossa, of the pupils of Cosimo Tura, and surrounded it with gracious gardens, and here he and his successor took their pleasure in the hot weather amid all those fairest ladies whose eyes have lingered upon the frescoes we see, but of whom we, alas, shall never have a glimpse. The place is now a museum full of all sorts of litter and fragments and precious things which are no more thought of in the world.

It is much the same with all those pictures which have now been gathered into the Palazzo de' Diamanti in the northern part of the town, the *Addizione Ercolea*, built by Ercole I in 1492. This fine palace, built for Sigismondo d'Este by Biagio Rossetti and completed in 1567, is now the Picture Gallery of Ferrara, and contains a fine collection of those late works characteristically Ferrarese, pictures by Panetti the master of Garofalo, by Garofalo himself and by Dosso Dossi for the most part—things not to linger over but certainly to admire if you can, though I think without any real enthusiasm. Dosso has been called the Giorgione of the Ferrarese, of which school, it is said, Garofalo is the Raphael ; it is with much the same feelings as this inspires, that one hears certain towns at home called the English Naples or Florence. Dosso Dossi we know was a man of the greatest talent who does not always please us so well as he does in his Circe in Rome. If Garofalo is a lesser master, he is yet able to defend himself, and is only made ridiculous when labelled with Raphael's name. These men were what we might expect from the fact that the Ferrarese had only a sixth-rate talent for art. They issue out of nothing native to the soil, but from the spirit, then almost exhausted, which had breathed over all Italy, the glory of life and the desire for art the noblest expression of life. No one will refuse his admiration before the great ancona of Dosso Dossi in which we see Madonna with her little Son and S. John Baptist enthroned on high amid saints and angels ; it has a noble gesture, but it is only ducal in its glory, not divine. Again no one can but be enchanted by such a thing as Panetti's Annunciation with its delicious landscape in which a little city towers beside a great river under far-away fair mountains ; but the figures are not so lovely, not lovely enough for enchantment. These things abide, but what is there to interest or charm us in such a thing as Garofalo's Invention of the Cross, unless it be the portraits ? The whole picture is incredible in its courtliness, and only the landscape—and even that is too fantastic—can hold us at all.

Before leaving Ferrara for good no one should forget to visit two places outside her gates. One of these is the church of S. Cristoforo, once the sanctuary of a Carthusian monastery, now the church of the Campo Santo, a very noble Renaissance building. There, too, we shall find the sepulchre of Borso d'Este, whom we seem to know better than any other of his house because of the frescoes in the Schifanoia.

The other place no one must fail to see is also a church, the church of S. Giorgio suburbano, where Pope Eugenius IV opened the great Council of 1438 for the reconciliation of the Latin and Greek Churches in the presence of the successor of Justinian, John Palaeologus. The Council was removed in 1439 to Florence on account of the marsh fever. One goes there, however, not in memory of this futile attempt at reconciliation, but for the sake of what, when all is said, is the fairest tomb in Ferrara, that of Bishop Lorenzo Roverella, who died in 1475, by Ambrogio da Milano, the pupil of the Florentine Antonio Rossellino.

CHAPTER IV

BOLOGNA

I

I HAD been in Bologna many times, and had never really liked this sombre and learned city, with its gloomy arcaded streets and grotesque leaning tcwers, its sober brown churches, its gallery full of late pictures, its general air of disillusion, when circumstances compelled me to spend a month there, and it was only then I discovered, not without astonishment, that I had never really understood Bologna at all—how essentially charming she is, how cool and delightful those arcaded streets, how glowing those numberless churches where the people worship with so simple an earnestness, how beautiful her environment, that countryside neither of the plains nor of the mountains, among the foothills of the Apennines.

And certainly my experience is not unique. Very many travellers, I think, have felt much the same disappointment in Bologna, nor is it strange perhaps that this should be so. For the most part we come to this sober university town from all the dancing light and colour of Venice, from the sheer beauty of Florence, or from the inexhaustible interest and strength of Milan, and we feel that Bologna beside these is insipid and without a character of her own, a place to which one can only be indifferent.

But, indeed, if approached in the right way, Bologna may be loved at once, and without an afterthought. Only to come to her directly, with the best of all in your heart, is too hard a test. Let the traveller who would understand her great delight come to her not from Venice or Florence, but from the cities of the plain, from Ferrara, or best of all along the great Roman road, the Via Emilia, from Piacenza, through Parma, Reggio and Modena ; only thus can he truly appreciate her dry superiority and that strange beauty of hers which is neither of the plain nor of the mountains, but of the marriage here made between them.

Neither of the plain nor of the mountains ! If you would really understand the secret of Bologna, before exploring the city itself go afoot out of Porta Castiglione by the beautiful Giardini Margherita past the fifteenth-century church of the Misericordia, which holds a fine work by Lorenzo Costa, up to S. Michele in Bosco, that old Olivetan Monastery from which the white monks have long since departed, where in the beautiful empty cloisters you will see only the fading frescoes of the Carracci and their pupils, but where, too, if you look out over the wonderful world before you, the city at your feet, you will begin to understand what manner of place this is.

Or in the morning early go up to the Madonna di S. Luca by way of the Certosa of the fourteenth century and the Campo Santo of the city. Up there you are twice as high in the blue air as you are at S. Michele, and if it be hot you may descend all the way in the shade under those strange arcades which the Bolognese have built even so far and so high as this for love of that picture of Madonna, painted by S. Luke they say, which names this sanctuary. If you look out from the dome of the church, as you may do for a few *centesimi*, you will see half the Romagna stretched out before you, and Bologna on the foothills of the Apennines, and the far-away sea, and you will understand how strange is the situation of this city, in which the plain is married with the mountains and things naturally opposite are become one.

It is, I think, in just that marriage of irreconcilable things that the charm of Bologna really lies hid. The seat of perhaps the most famous University in Italy, a sad and learned town, full of professors and all sorts of intellectual reservations and compromises, she is yet altogether confident, as may be known from that proud boast of hers, *Bononia docet*, and at all times the gloom and silence of her melancholy arcaded ways through which one may pass about the whole city, dry in the rain and cool in the summer heat, are confounded in the most astonishing way with the joyful noisiness of youth, the rather boisterous gaiety of her students, here for once really charming, and something to be thankful for, in a city inclined, but for them, to be a little dry and sombre.

It is such contrasts as these, which she always contrives to reconcile with herself so that they are really a part of her life, that must, I think, strike the traveller at once on his first coming to her. He drives perhaps from the station, through what might often appear to be a deserted town, down the long empty vista of street after street, only to find at last that the people are all afoot under the arcades which are thronged and crowded. Nor I think does any other city in Italy offer so extraordinary a contrast as at any time may be found in Bologna between the vast emptiness and silence of the Piazza Maggiore before S. Petronio, and the crowded movement and noise of the Piazza del Nettuno, between the Palazzo Pubblico and the Palazzo del Podestà. These Piazzas are so close together that they might appear in a map to form but one square, yet in reality they are divided by the whole distance which separates life from death.

Little by little the traveller learns to expect such contrasts in Bologna and to look for some astonishment. Yet she will beggar his wonder. There can have been no one coming to Bologna for the first time, but has thought to see in the vast church of S. Petronio, in the Piazza Maggiore, obviously the Cathedral of the city. But in fact S. Petronio, though it is dedicated in honour of the patron saint of Bologna, is not the Cathedral at all. That is to be found in the comparatively small church of S. Pietro before which no Piazza opens, in the Via dell' Independenza.

But it is everywhere the same in this curious town, it is ever the unexpected that one finds. From the sevenfold wonder of S. Stefano to the spacious beauty of S. Petronio, from S. Domenico which holds one of the most precious tombs in Italy, to S. Francesco which is empty of everything but light, with its tombs set about it, as it were in the street, there is not a building dull and forbidding though it may appear, but holds some delightful surprise for one, something wonderful or beautiful at which one cannot but admire. It is as though the city kept the best of herself only for her intimates and for her friends.

Something of this element of surprise which, as I say, is her most essential characteristic, is to be found even in her history. It is easy to believe in the Etruscan origins of Fiesole, of Cortona, of Perugia or Chiusi, but who without some real and intimate knowledge of Bologna would claim her as a city of that mysterious people who built with naked rocks and for Eternity? Yet such is her origin,[1] nor in that wonderful polity of which we know so little was she a mere outpost, rather was she the chief of the twelve cities which that people founded to the north of the Apennines.[2] Mantua was but a colony of hers. In those days her name was Felsina, and set as she was among the foothills of the Apennines where in later times the Roman road of Caius Flaminius from Arezzo first came down into the plain, it is possible that she held even in Etruscan times a path over the mountains from Arezzo and Perugia, of which latter city it is said she was a colony.

Felsina presently fell to the Boii when the Gauls came

[1] It is possible that Bologna is older than the Etruscans, that she was founded by the Liguri, and it is probable that she was later (about 800 B.C.) in the hands of the Umbri ; the Etruscans in this case rebuilt her about 600 B.C.

[2] We know certainly only the names of four of them : Felsina (Bologna), Mantua, Adria, Melpum. They were established by the twelve cities of the Etruscan League in Etruria south of the Apennines. Cf. Pliny, iii. 15–20.

over the Alps into the valley of the Po, and in 189 B.C. a Roman colony of three thousand with Latin rights was established there and Felsina became Bononia.[1] Two years later, in 187 B.C., the consul M. Æmilius Lepidus built the great road which still bears his name—the Via Emilia, through Cispadane Gaul from Rimini to Piacenza, upon which Bologna was one of the chief stations ; and about the same time the consul Caius Flaminius constructed a road, perhaps on an earlier trackway, across the Apennines from Arezzo to Bologna. Thus the city would seem to have been a place of considerable importance in the Roman occupation and administration of Cisalpine Gaul, but as a matter of fact we know absolutely nothing of her until the time of the Civil Wars when, during the siege of Mutina (Modena), in 43 B.C., Bologna was occupied by Mark Antony, and was the scene of Pansa's death after the battle of Mutina. This was the most famous moment in the Roman history of the city, for it was in this year that Octavianus, at the head of his army, met the combined forces of Antony and Lepidus and arranged the terms of the Second Triumvirate. The meeting is said to have taken place on a small island in the Reno, the river which flows by Bologna, and local tradition identifies this spot with La Crocetta del Trebbo, about two miles below the city in the plain, but without any real certainty.

As a Roman Colonia, to which rank Augustus raised it afresh after the battle of Actium, filling it with partisans of his own, for it had been especially under the patronage of the Antonine family, Bologna flourished exceedingly, and though it was almost burnt to the ground in A.D. 53, Claudius fully restored it, and it seems to have enjoyed a vigorous existence till the beginning of the decay of the Roman administrative system in the fourth century, when S. Ambrose, Archbishop of Milan, speaks of it as much declined.

---

[1] Livy speaks of Felsina as late as 196 B.C. The Romans seem to have called the place Bononia since it was in their time a city of the Boians.

5

It was, however, able in A.D. 410 to withstand the Goths when Alaric set up Attalus as Emperor after the second siege of Rome, and it had evidently played a great part in Stilicho's defence against the barbarian, and seems indeed to have been certainly a main, and perhaps the chief, Roman camp north of the Apennines. Indeed, the strategic position of Bologna was only second in its strength, there in the great plain, to that of Ravenna itself. Set as the city is, in full possession of the crossing of the Reno by the Via Emilia, a crucial point in the great plain, and at the north gate of the second Roman pass over the Apennines,[1] this situation gave her the command at the same time of the most fertile portion of Cisalpine Gaul and of the second gate thence into Italy, and its strategic and commercial importance was such that had at any time the consideration of the choice of a capital for Italy been only or even mainly economic, Bologna must have been chosen, in spite of its one serious disadvantage, its liability to flood.

In the Dark Age it seems really to have suffered comparatively little from the continual raids of the barbarians and the long periods of war. Indeed, in the seventh century Paulus Diaconus reckons it as a wealthy place, and from that time it only increased in riches and in strength. To-day, though it is a flourishing place, I do not think it deserves its ancient surname of *grassa* ; but it may still bear with honour its title of " Learned " and " Free."

And as I have tried to show, Bologna is still a city full of surprise, original and curious, and with much that is mediæval still about her, though this is almost never obvious to the superficial observer. She is, however, still a closed city, surrounded by a wall of brick about three and three-quarter miles in extent, in which there are still twelve gates, and within, as of old, she is divided into three parts, of the East, of the South, and of the West.

[1] The first and most important pass over the Apennines was the Furlo held by the fortress of Petra Pertusa but ultimately in the power of Ravenna. See my *Ravenna* (Dent, 1913).

When Paulus Diaconus wrote of her as so flourishing in the seventh century, she still formed part of the Exarchate of Ravenna, but in the following century she gave herself to Liutprand, king of the Lombards, and she remained within the Lombard power till the appearance of Charlemagne, who gave her to the Papacy as the heir of the Exarchate. From the Ottos, however, she obtained her freedom, and it was then she took for her device that dangerous but glorious word *Libertas*, which indeed she was never really to forfeit.

Her great distinction during the whole of the Middle Age was the pre-eminence of her University, which, though tracing its origin to very early times, may be said, as we understand such things, to have been founded in 1119, and is thus, save that of Salerno, the most ancient in Italy. Here by the labour of innumerable scholars, the greatest of which was perhaps Irnerius, Roman Law was restored to the world. For the " school " of Bologna consisted of a long line of jurisconsults who, during the twelfth and thirteenth centuries, here renewed by their lectures and writings the science of Roman Law, and thus exercised an immense influence not only on the study of Law, but upon legislation throughout the West.

In 1155, for instance, when Frederick Barbarossa held his great Diet on the plains of Roncaglia for the purpose of publishing a code of laws which should secure his own power in Italy, four professors were summoned from Bologna to assist him. In return they obtained from the Emperor those celebrated ordinances known as the *Habita*, in favour of their University, then certainly the first in the world.

Bologna, thus early famous for her learning, was politically devoted to securing her own independence. Therefore we find her eagerly making part of the Lombard League against Frederick Barbarossa. Nor was she less zealous in her hatred of Frederick II. Indeed the greatest achievement of the mediæval city was the defeat of the imperial forces in the famous battle of Fossalto upon 29th May 1249, when she took King Enzo, Frederick's natural son, prisoner, and placed him in an iron cage which held him fast till his death twenty-two years later. All through the Middle Age, Bologna was far more proud of this victory, and especially of her capture of King Enzo, than she was of her great University or anything else she was able to accomplish.

Not long after this, like almost every other city in Italy, she found herself torn in pieces by the anarchy of Guelf and Ghibelline, the two parties being led by the two families of Geremei and Lambertazzi. In their struggles a certain Taddeo de' Pepoli saw his chance, and in 1337 was able to seize the power in Bologna. But the rule of Taddeo and his son presently gave birth to two other factions, *Scacchesa* and *Maltraversa*, and the Pepoli in 1350 sold the city to the Visconti of Milan, who for value received restored it ten years later to the Pope.

But Bologna had known freedom ; in 1123 her commune had first been constituted, and it was not long before she revolted from the Papal government and recovered her liberty, to lose it at last to one of her own citizens, Giovanni Bentivoglio, who in 1401 made himself lord and in 1402 was killed in a rebellion. Again the Visconti stepped in, but after various struggles and disputes with the Papacy the Visconti found that once more a Bentivoglio had seized the power ; this in 1434. In the hands of the Bentivogli Bologna remained till 1506, when Pope Julius II drove that family out and brought Bologna once more under the Papal government, where it remained, save for the very pregnant incident of Napoleon, until 1860, when it became a part of the kingdom of United Italy.

II

There is not, I suppose, another city in Italy which bears so few obvious marks of her history as this curious city of Bologna, that in spite of her secrecy, nay, perhaps because of it, one soon comes to love so much. She is the least demonstrative city in the peninsula.

The centre of Bologna is to be found in the Piazza Maggiore, now called Piazza Vittorio Emmanuele, and the Piazza del Nettuno which opens out of it. In the former stands the greatest church in Bologna, S. Petronio, with the Palazzo dei Notai, dating from 1381, beside it. To the west rises the towered Palazzo Pubblico, to the east is the Portico dei Bianchi, the beautiful work of Vignola, while on the north stands the Palazzo del Podestà, between which and the Palazzo Pubblico in the Piazza del Nettuno is set the great and splendid Fountain of Neptune which names this smaller square.

This magnificent fountain, which is popularly called the Fontana del Gigante, was designed in the mass by Laureti of Palermo, who was sent to Florence to find a sculptor worthy of such a work. He chose Gian Bologna the Fleming who came to Bologna in 1563. He brought with him Zanobi Portigiani the celebrated founder. They set to work upon the colossal statue of Neptune, the four *putti* upon dolphins, the sirens and harpies, and the scrolls bearing the arms of Pope Pius IV, his Legate Carlo Borromeo, the Vicelegate Pier Donato Cesi, and of the Commune of Bologna; while Andrea della Porta and others finished the work in marble. The result was wholly successful, and indeed what we see is one of the most glorious works of the late Renaissance. The work was completed, Dr. Ricci tells us, in 1566. It bears the inscription upon its four sides : FORI ORNAMENTO—POPULI COMMODO—AERE PUBLICO—MDLXIIII.

The Piazza Maggiore is almost surrounded by buildings of the thirteenth and fourteenth centuries, lending it a noble aspect which is enhanced by its fine spaciousness. The oldest of these buildings is the Palazzo del Podestà, which dates from the beginning of the thirteenth century. In 1247 it was known as the *Palatium Vetus*, the Old Palace, to distinguish it from the *Palatium Novum*, then begun to the north. Here in 1249, after the battle of Fossalto in May, King Enzo of Sardinia, his father's vicar-general in Lombardy, was imprisoned, for twenty-two years, till his death in 1272. The great hall is still called the Sala del Re Enzo. Everything was done by the Emperor to win his son's release, he entreated and humbled himself and made vast promises. King Enzo himself offered to " gird the city with a ring of gold " as the price of his liberty ; but the Bolognese refused to listen to him. The capture of this golden-haired prince in the flower of his youth—in 1249 he was twenty-four years old—dazzled them, they regarded it as their greatest and most famous achievement and never ceased to boast of it. So King Enzo's youth withered away in his Bolognese prison, not we may think in utter misery, for he was a poet, and there was a lady who loved him, Lucia Vendagoli, who used to visit him in various disguises, and once nearly succeeded in rescuing him in a cask, but a lock of that golden hair of his escaping, betrayed him, and he spent the rest of his life in prison composing many verses, among the earliest of Italian poems. Who does not know those charming, pitiful lines *Dolori Amorosi*, or that Sonnet of recollection so wonderfully translated by Rossetti ?

> There is a time to mount ; to humble thee
> A time ; a time to talk, and hold thy peace ;
> A time to labour, and a time to cease ;
> A time to take thy measures patiently ;
> A time to watch what Time's next step may be ;
> A time to make light count of menaces.
> And to think over them, a time there is ;
> There is a time when to seem not to see.
> Wherefore I hold him well-advised and sage
> Who evermore keeps prudence facing him
> And lets his life slide with occasion ;
> And so comforts himself, through youth to age,
> That never any man at any time
> Can say, Not thus, but Thus thou shouldst have done.

The Old Palace was not known as the Palazzo del

Podestà till the fifteenth century. In the first years of that century, in 1410, the great hall of King Enzo was the scene of the Conclave which elected Pope John XXIII, Baldassare Cossa, who was enthroned in state in S. Petronio. In the last years of the century, however, the Palace was largely rebuilt in the Renaissance style as we see. The beautiful tower, however, remains, for the most part, a work of the thirteenth century, though it has suffered from restoration.

The vast Palazzo Pubblico to the north-west of the Piazza was begun about 1245, but was to a great extent also rebuilt in the fifteenth century, from which time the curious clock-tower dates, and has been very much restored in our time. Over the main entrance is a bronze statue of Pope Gregory XIII, placed there in 1580. But by far the finest ornament of the Palace is the splendid terra-cotta of the Madonna and Child by Niccolò dell' Arca, who, though like Niccolò Pisano of Apulian origin, may be called the greatest of the sculptors of Bologna. He was very strongly influenced by the work of Jacopo della Quercia, as is obvious in all his work, which is so glorious a treasure of this city and nowhere more to be loved than in this grand and ample relief of the Madonna and Child with its rich drapery. Niccolò died in 1494, and this relief dates from 1478.

Within the north-west court of the Palace is a fine staircase, attributed to Bramante, and dating from 1509, to the first floor, where in a spacious hall is a terra-cotta of Hercules by Alfonso Lombardi and a rather dim fresco painted by Francia in 1505, a votive Madonna del Terremoto, in which is a fine view of the city, which in that year had suffered from an earthquake. In a neighbouring hall, the Sala del Consiglio Provinciale, is a modern painting of Irnerius the jurisconsult by Luigi Serra, and another of the Return of the Bolognese after the battle of Fossalto.

The church of S. Petronio, built in honour of Bologna's patron saint, though not the Cathedral, is nevertheless the most important in the city. It is thought that it was

S. Apollinaris, the disciple of S. Peter and Bishop of Ravenna, who first preached the Gospel in Bologna, and it is said that her first Bishop was S. Zama. S. Petronio is of a later time than that, the greater part of his life certainly having passed in the first half of the fifth century. His condition was indeed very similar to that of S. Ambrose, with whom he is often represented. Gennedius in his *De Viris Illustribus*— our chief source of information about him—tells us that Petronius was of a noble family whose members had long occupied high posts at the Imperial Courts of Milan. His father, who also bore the name of Petronius, was, it seems, probably Prætorian Prefect in Gaul from 402–8, and the future saint in his youth seems to have been able to visit the Holy Places in Jerusalem, though whether or not as a pilgrim we do not know. About 432 he was elected Bishop of Bologna, where he erected the church or churches of S. Stephen in imitation of the shrines at Golgotha and the Holy Sepulchre. The first church built in his honour in Bologna dates from about 1141, when his relics were discovered, but this we see took its place in 1390.

S. Petronio is not only the largest church in Bologna, but had it been completed as it was planned it would have been the largest in the world. For, according to that plan, it was to have been a Latin cross of upwards of 700 feet in length with a transept of 460 feet and a dome 500 feet over the crossing.[1] This enormous building was never carried out, however ; what we see is a fragment consisting only of the nave and aisles, 384 feet long and 157 feet wide with a height of 132 feet. This was the work of Antonio Vincenzi with additions by Gerolamo Rinaldi in the seventeenth century, and a façade in its only completed lower part by Domenico da Varignana in the sixteenth century. The main door, however, has sculptures of an earlier time from the hand of Jacopo della Quercia (1425–38) consisting of

[1] S. Peter's in Rome, the largest church in the world, is 696 feet long with a transept of 450 feet and a dome of 435 feet over the crossing.

a very lovely Madonna and Child with SS. Petronio and
Ambrogio in the tympanum, with scenes from the life of
Christ on the door and from Genesis on either side. The
sculptures on the side doors are by Tribolo and Alfonso
Lombardi.

Within, the church is extremely beautiful and spacious,
and indeed it is one of the most successful " Gothic "
interiors in Italy. It is divided into three naves by ten
mighty pillars bearing the clerestory with its curious round
windows and the vault of the seventeenth century.

The first chapel on the left is the oldest in the church ;
here, upon 4th October 1392, was celebrated the first Mass.
Two spoilt pictures of the fifteenth century by Giovanni da
Modena are all that remain of antiquity there to-day.
But just outside this chapel, between it and the next, is an
old stone cross of the twelfth century found at the Porta
Ravegnana and placed here in the eighteenth century.
The two following chapels are without interest, but over the
pilasters beyond them is a huge fresco of S. Christopher by
Giovanni da Modena and beneath two very early clocks.

The next chapel—Cappella de' Bolognini—was built in
the first years of the fifteenth century, and, in 1408, adorned
with frescoes by order of Bartolomeo Bolognini. On the
left we see above, Paradise with the Coronation of the
Blessed Virgin, amid Angels and Saints, below stands S.
Michael with sword and balances, and beneath, the Inferno.[1]
It may well be that we have here the work of Giovanni da
Modena, who may be the author of the frescoes to the right
in which we see the story of the Magi, as well as of those in
which we have scenes from the life of S. Petronio. The
altar is interesting, the rich paliotto is formed of various
pieces, some from the church of S. Maria del Carrobbio.
The founder of the chapel, Bartolomeo Bolognini, is buried

---

[1] Vasari attributes these very Dantesque works to Buffalmacco,
but according to Vasari Buffalmacco died in 1340, whereas we
have documents to show that these frescoes were not painted
before 1408.

here beneath a tombstone bearing his effigy. Between
this chapel and the next is perhaps the most ancient
representation of S. Petronio left to us, a curious statue in
wood.

In the next chapel, which Donato Vaselli adorned in the
fifteenth century, is a fine picture in tempera of the martyrdom of S. Sebastian with Donato Vaselli, the donor, by
some unknown master of the Ferrarese school. On the side
walls are two other works, the Annunciation by Lorenzo
Costa, and the Twelve Apostles, perhaps by some scholar of
his. The pavement of this chapel is interesting and beautiful, made in 1487, probably in Faenza. The stalls are dated
1495 and are the work of Giacomo de' Marchi da Crema.

The sixth chapel is without interest, but in the seventh
is a very fine picture by Lorenzo Costa of the Madonna
enthroned with her little Son between S. Sebastian and
S. George, with S. James and S. Jerome sitting at her feet.
On the two curiously carved pillars of the throne are set two
figures representing the Annunciation. Above in the lunette
is a glory of angels from the same hand, as indeed is the
design of the windows. The other chapels upon this side
of the church are without interest.

Coming now to the high altar and the choir, we are reminded that it was here Charles v bought his coronation
as Emperor from the Medici Pope Clement VII, and here
upon 24th February 1530 he was crowned. The crowns of
Lombardy and of the Empire had been brought to Bologna
for the occasion, for neither Milan nor Rome, devastated by
the armies of the Empire, was in a fit state for the great
ceremony. In the Palazzo Pubblico, Charles placed the
Iron Crown upon his head, and later, here in S. Petronio, for
the last time in Italy, the Pope crowned an Emperor
Surrounded by Italian princes and Spanish generals.
Charles was not easily to be recognized as the successor of
Augustus and of Charlemagne, and while they shouted in
Bologna, Florence wept.

The first chapel from the altar in the right aisle is without

S. PETRONIO BOLOGNA

interest, but in the second is a fine balustrade of the fifteenth century, with very low reliefs that Dr. Ricci ascribes to Niccolò dell' Arca, that should not be missed.

The next chapel is S. Antony of Padua's. The statue of the Saint here is from the hand of Sansovino, the *chiaroscuro* paintings of his miracles by Girolamo da Treviso. The windows are attributed to Tibaldi. In the following chapel the fine stalls are by Fra Raffaele da Brescia and come from S. Michele in Bosco. The other chapels have little to interest us.

Before leaving S. Petronio the small Museo di S. Petronio, entered at the end of the left aisle, should be visited, if only for its designs by Peruzzi, Giulio Romano, Vignola, Palladio, Cristoforo Lombardo, and others for the façade of the church. Here, too, is a bust of Guido Pepoli, some beautiful reliefs of Joseph and Potiphar's wife, Potiphar's wife showing her husband the mantle of Joseph, Noah building the Ark, and the dream of Jacob. The second room contains vestments and various church vessels and choir books and a wooden model of the church.

After paying our respects to S. Petronio, the patron saint of Bologna, it is incumbent upon us, I think, as Englishmen to go a little out of our way to visit the church of S. Salvatore in the Via delle Asse behind the Palazzo Pubblico, and for this reason. Among the twelve thousand students that even in the twelfth century, it is said, flocked to the University of Bologna, were many Englishmen, and among these was Thomas Becket, who as S. Thomas of Canterbury became the patron of his countrymen who frequented the schools here. Now the favourite hostel of the English in S. Thomas's day and after, was the house of the Canons Regular, whose church was S. Salvatore. Immediately after the canonization of S. Thomas, an altar was set up in his honour in that church, and presently a chapel was dedicated to his name. It was maintained by the English scholars, and was indeed their chapel, for later we find them disputing its ownership with the Canons. This dispute was

settled, of course, by a compromise, in 1305.   In 1478,
however, S. Salvatore was demolished and the chapel with
it ; but in the new church a new altar was dedicated in
honour of S. Thomas, though by then the English scholars
had become very few at Bologna.   Nevertheless, the altar
was preserved till 1613, when the church was again pulled
down and rebuilt on a greater scale.   No new altar was then
dedicated in honour of our Saint, but the old altarpiece was
preserved and is to be seen to-day in the south transept
of S. Salvatore.   It is by Girolamo da Treviso and represents
the Presentation of the Blessed Virgin in the Temple with
S. Thomas of Canterbury.   Opposite is a rich ancona of the
end of the fourteenth century in many compartments,
representing the Coronation of Our Lady and many other
subjects ; it is the work of Cristofero da Bologna.

After returning from S. Salvatore into the Piazza Maggiore
one should pass right across the square into the Via Clava-
ture.   Here is the church of S. Maria della Vita, a building of
the fifteenth and seventeenth centuries.   To the right of
the choir is a curiously emotional and realistic group in
terra-cotta of the Maries weeping over the Dead Christ,
by Niccolò dell' Arca.

After returning once more to the Piazza one should turn
south into the Via Archiginesio, and follow it into the
Piazza Galvani past the beautiful sixteenth-century
Archiginesio Antico, where the University was newly housed
in 1563.   We shall find the old University buildings in
another part of the city, but it was here that the lady-
professors of the sixteenth and seventeenth centuries held
forth, one of them on account of her beauty being compelled
to lecture from behind a curtain !   And it was here that
Luigi Galvani made his discoveries in " galvanism."   The
fine porticoed buildings are the work of Francesco Terribilia.
Within, the cortile should be visited and the panelled
lecture-room built by Antonio Levanti.   The schools,
however, have departed to a newer building, and this is
used as the Biblioteca Comunale.

We turn to the left out of the Piazza Galvani and soon come past the Banca d'Italia to the Piazza Cavour, through which we pass by the Via Garibaldi into the Piazza S. Domenico, now Piazza Galileo. This is the most pictur-esque square in Bologna, its irregularity and its air of anti-quity, the two columns and the tomb which stand about it, adding to its charm and interest. The Gothic monument in the midst contains the dust of Rolandino Passeggieri (1300) the jurisconsult and others. The smaller tomb holds all that was mortal of Egidio Foscherari. The columns support statues of the Blessed Virgin and S. Dominic. Here is the church of the Dominicans, dedicated in honour of the founder of the Order, who died in Bologna in 1221.

As we see it, S. Domenico is almost entirely a building of the eighteenth century, but certainly before 1218 a church stood here dedicated in honour of S. Niccolò delle Vigne, which in that year passed into the hands of Blessed Reginald, S. Dominic's disciple.

The great treasure of the church is, of course, the body of the founder of the Order of Friars Preachers, and the glorious shrine in which it reposes in a chapel in the right aisle, originally the work of Niccolò Pisano. " In the year 1225," says Vasari, " Niccolò was entrusted with the execution of a tomb in marble for S. Domenico, the founder of the Order of Preaching Friars, who had then but recently died. Concerting his measures, therefore, with those who had the direction of the matter, Niccolò constructed the tomb with many figures still to be seen on it, finishing the whole in the year 1231, to the great extension of his fame, the work being then considered one of extraordinary merit and superior to anything of the kind that had been seen. He also prepared plans for the rebuilding of the church and of the greater part of the convent." Unfortunately but little reliance can be placed upon Vasari's dates. It is certain that when S. Dominic died in Bologna in 1221 his mortal remains were confined in a wooden bier, from which they were removed with considerable pomp twelve years later, on 23rd May 1233, in the presence of the Archbishop of Ravenna, then Metropolitan of the See, and the magistrates of Bologna. They were on this occasion enclosed in a simple urn of stone, and there they remained until the completion of the great sepulchre which had been entrusted to Niccolò Pisano. But Niccolò was bound by contract to Siena, where he had much work to do, and he seems to have contributed very little more than the design and the composition of the reliefs, which were only completed in 1267. The actual work was done by his pupil and assistant Fra Guglielmo, and upon 5th June 1267, in the presence of both masters, the tomb was placed in position. The very simple sarcophagus which then rested simply upon columns in the crypt was carved in relief with scenes from the life of S. Dominic and of his disciple, the Blessed Reginald of Orleans, with statuettes of the Madonna and Child and the Four Doctors of the Church. Thus the tomb remained till 1469, when Niccolo dell' Arca was employed to complete it with a cover. This sculptor also made the glorious kneeling angel on the left. The angel on the right is an early work of Michelangelo's (1494), to whom is due also the S. Petronio over the sarcophagus. Later still, in 1532, Alfonso Lombardi was employed to add a base to the tomb, and there he carved reliefs of the Birth of Our Lord, the Birth of S. Dominic, S. Dominic preaching, and his death. In the half dome over the tomb, Guido Reni has painted in fresco the apotheosis of the Saint. The chapel itself was rebuilt in 1596, and restored again in the eighteenth century.

S. Dominic's tomb, even though it were not one of the most beautiful shrines in Italy, would always form the chief interest in any church, but S. Domenico has other things to show us. There are the wonderful sixteenth-century stalls in the choir by Fra Damiano da Bergamo. In a chapel on the right there is a picture by Filippino Lippi, the Marriage of S. Catherine, with S. John Baptist, S. Peter, S. Benedict and S. Sebastian, painted in 1501; and then between the first and second chapels to the left of the choir is the tomb of King Enzo, who was for so long the unhappy prisoner of the Bolognesi. Opposite is a portrait of S. Thomas Aquinas by Simone da Bologna, said to be an authentic likeness, while in the adjoining chapel is the tomb of that great man Taddeo Pepoli, where we may see him meting out justice to his fellow-citizens. Here too is an altarpiece by Giacomo Francia.

In the left transept is the Chapel of the Relics which contains the head of S. Dominic in a silver reliquary. Here, too, lies the Blessed Jacobus of Ulm, a famous glass painter. To the right of the altar is a curious painting attributed to Vasari—the Eating of the Paschal lamb.

In the large chapel of the Rosary in the left aisle Guido Reni lies and beside him his pupil Elisabetta Sirani. And in the vestibule leading to the Piazza stands the very lovely Renaissance tomb, recalling that of Carlo Marsuppini in S. Croce in Florence, of Alessandro Tartagni of Imola (d. 1477), the famous jurisconsult, by Francesco di Simone. The Cloisters are interesting and contain some old tombs.

Following the Via Garibaldi out of Piazza Galileo we presently come into the Piazza dei Tribunali, before the Palazzo di Giustizia with a façade by some pupil of Andrea Palladio's. Thence we turn into the Via delle Tovaglie and come to the fifteenth-century church of Corpus Domini, built by S. Catherine Vigri, the Abbess of the Poor Clares in Bologna, where she was born in 1413. At twelve years of age she became maid of honour to the Princess Margarita d'Este, and two years later upon the marriage of her mistress she entered a community of devout ladies of the Third Order of S. Francis in Ferrara. This community presently adopted the austere rule of S. Clare. A new nunnery of Poor Clares being founded in Bologna, S. Catherine was chosen first prioress. An extraordinary mystic, she was favoured with the gifts of miracles and prophecy. She died on 9th March 1463, and was buried here in the church of her convent, where her body is still preserved entire and unde-cayed. A book of her prophecies was published in Bologna in 1511, but the most famous of her works is a mystical treatise entitled *The Seven Spiritual Arms*.

Close to the church of Corpus Domini in the Via d'Azeglio is the glorious Palazzo Bevilacqua, built in 1481, with a beautiful court and a fine doorway by Francesco di Simone. Here the Council of Trent sat in 1547.

Not far away, in the Via Urbana, is the Collegio di Spagna, originally built by Cardinal Albornoz, the General and Legate in Italy of the Pope in Avignon, built in 1365 and restored two centuries later. Thence we proceed down the Via Saragossa, turning at the unfinished Palazzo Albergati into the Via Nosadella, and so crossing at last into the Piazza Malpighi beside the church of S. Francesco.

Here are more Gothic tombs of Jurists, those of Accursius Odofredus and Rolandino dei Romanzi, all of the thirteenth century, all restored in 1892. They cannot keep us long from what, when all is said, is perhaps the most remarkable monument in Bologna. For the church of S. Francesco, dating from 1246, is the first Italian church built in three naves in the Gothic style, vaulted and buttressed. And yet it was allowed to be desecrated and used as a military magazine for many years and was only restored to sacred use in 1887. The desecration of the church spoiled it of almost everything that it had of precious or curious ; but at least the modern restoration has given us back the beautiful spacious church itself, full of the sun, as pleases me, and full of all the graciousness of the light and the sky. There remain, or have been placed here, however, two early Crucifixes of some beauty, and the altar reliefs are fine works of the fourteenth century by the brothers Massegne of Venice ; while in the left aisle is the tomb of Alexander v, who died in 1410, by Sperandio. On quitting the church the beautiful campanile should be noted.

From S. Francesco we pass by the Grand Hotel Brun into the busy Via Ugo Bassi, and following it till we come to the Piazza del Nettuno, turn there into the Via dell' Independenza on the left, to find at last the Cathedral of

Bologna, the church of S. Pietro. The first cathedral church of Bologna was that of S. Zama, now utterly lost to us ; the second was that of SS. Peter and Paul, now one of the sanctuaries of the sevenfold S. Stefano, as we shall see ; this was founded in the middle of the fourth century. The third was this church of S. Peter built in 910 ; but the building we see dates only from the seventeenth century, and is perhaps the least interesting sanctuary in the city.

We leave it at once to continue our way out of the Piazza Nettuno by the Via Rizzoli, which soon brings us to the strangest sight in Bologna, the Leaning Towers in the Piazza di Porta Ravegnana. The taller of these is the Torre Arimelli, and was built in 1109 by Gherardo degli Arimelli, perhaps as an eerie or a defence. It leans some four feet out of the perpendicular. The shorter tower, the Torre Garisenda, was begun in 1110 by Filippo and Ottone Garisenda ; it is almost exactly half as high as its companion, which rises to 320 feet, but it is just twice as far out of the perpendicular. Why these towers were built, and more especially why they lean, whether this be accidental or of set purpose, we do not know. As of everything else in Italy that was notable and strange, Dante has spoken of these towers also. In the Inferno he compares the giant Antaeus when he bends towards him to the Torre Garisenda when a cloud sails over it from the quarter to which it leans.

> . . . As appears
> The tower of Garisenda, from beneath
> Where it doth lean, if chance a passing cloud
> To sail across, that opposite it hangs ;
> Such then Antaeus seemed, as at mine ease
> I marked him stooping. . . .

These strange towers, which stand within twenty feet of one another in the small Piazza where seven ways meet, have a more lasting impression on the mind than anything else in the city.

To the right of the Piazza, where the Via S. Stefano and

6

the Via Castiglione meet, stands the Mercanzia, a fine
Gothic building of the fourteenth century added to in the
fifteenth and restored in our own day. It is well to follow
the Via Castiglione a little way to see the great castellated
Palazzo dei Pepoli, a building of 1344, with its fine court and
colonnade. Thence we shall turn into the Via dei Pepoli
which will bring us at once to the most interesting monument in this part of the city, the sevenfold church of
S. Stefano.

This extraordinary monument dates from very early
times, its nucleus being perhaps the old cathedral church of
SS. Pietro and Paolo ; to this S. Petronio is said to have
added other oratories, more particularly S. Stefano, in imitation of the sanctuary of the Holy Sepulchre. No certain
explanation of this strange group of buildings is, however, to
be had. As we see it to-day, the sevenfold church of S.
Stefano is entered first by the great door in the church of
the Crocifisso, which as we have it dates from 1637. To the
left of the great door, high in the wall, is a pulpit dating
from the twelfth century. From the Crocifisso we pass into
the church of the S. Sepolcro or Calvario, a building perhaps
originally a baptistery, dating possibly from the fourth
century, rebuilt in the sixth or seventh and again in the
tenth. In the twelfth century the tomb of S. Petronius
was placed here. From this sanctuary with its antique
columns we pass into the old Cathedral church of SS.
Peter and Paul, a Romanesque building of the early eleventh
century as we see it, with extensive restorations of our own
time. Here where the roof is borne by columns and pier
alternately, lie the great martyr of Bologna, S. Vitalis (d.
382), and the martyr Agricola, in two sarcophagi. Hence
we pass into an open court called the Atrio or Cortile di
Pilato, probably dating as we see it from the eighth century
but rebuilt in the eleventh. Upon the font here is the name
of King Liutprand, and its water is said to have been blessed
by S. Petronio. In a little chapel on the left is a Crucifixion
by Giacomo Francia.

From the Atrio di Pilato we pass into the church of the
S. Trinità, its vault upheld by pilasters and columns with
Romanesque capitals. In the third chapel on the right is a
group carved in wood dating from the thirteenth century,
of the Adoration of the Magi. From the same side of the
church we enter the Cappella della Consolazione with its
Renaissance tabernacle, and thence pass into the Romanesque Crypt dating from the eleventh century.

Such is the amazing group of churches, which it might
seem almost impossible to explain. No one who comes to
them should omit to visit the delicious Cloister of the
eleventh century, one of the loveliest works in all the
Romagna.

Not far from S. Stefano, across the Via Farini, stands on
its little hill the church of S. Giovanni in Monte, which,
like S. Stefano, is said to have been founded by S. Petronio.
Its oldest memories, however, carry us no farther than
1060, and even so it was entirely rebuilt in 1221, the
campanile dating from 1286, and the whole church was
rebuilt in 1407 and restored and enlarged in 1440. As for
the cupola, it dates from 1496, and was renewed in the
sixteenth century. Its main interest for us to-day lies in
the works of art it possesses. Over the main door is an
eagle in terra-cotta by Niccolò dell' Arca, and within, in the
third chapel on the Epistle side, are two works of Guercino,
the Infant Christ and S. Joseph and S. Jerome. In the
seventh chapel on this side and in the choir are two fine
works by Lorenzo Costa of the Madonna enthroned with
S. Agostino, S. Possidonio, S. Giovanni and S. Francesco,
and the Coronation of the Blessed Virgin with God the
Father above, Our Lord who crowns His Mother, and below
S. John Baptist, S. Victor, S. Augustine, S. John Evangelist,
S. Jerome and S. Sebastian. This is not so fine a work as
the other, which is one of the best pictures by Costa that
has come down to us. The fine stalls in the choir here
are by Paolo Sacca.

From S. Giovanni, we pass by the Guarazzi to the church

of S. Maria dei Servi, where there is over the sixth altar on the left an Annunciation by Innocenzo da Imola, and behind the choir the fine tomb of a cardinal. Here, too, the stalls are beautiful.

Hence passing through the Piazza Aldrovandi we come to the Palazzo Fantuzzi, which has a very lovely staircase, and then to S. Vitale, the crypt of which still remains, and which is said to have been consecrated by S. Petronio. In the church, in the chapel on the left, is a very interesting picture. In the midst is a Madonna and Child by Sano di Pietro of Siena and around Angels in a landscape by Francesco Francia.

From S. Vitale we turn into the Via S. Vitale westward, and taking the second turning on the right, Via Benedetto XIV, come into the Piazza Rossini, before the church of S. Giacomo Maggiore. This church, which was founded in 1267 and was given a fine portico in 1477, was unhappily altered in the first years of the sixteenth century. It contains some fine works of art.

In the seventh chapel on the right is a Marriage of S Catherine by Innocenzo da Imola. The eleventh chapel on this side is entirely decorated in fresco by Tibaldi ; while the third chapel on the left has a Coronation of the Virgin by Jacopo di Paolo (1420), and close by is a great painted fourteenth-century Crucifix by Simone de' Crocefissi. But in the Bentivoglio chapel, the sixth on this side of the church is the masterpiece of Francia, the Madonna and Child en throned on high with four angels and four saints. Above is the vision of S. John by Lorenzo Costa ; and at the side Costa has painted wonderful frescoes of the Triumphs of Life and Death after Petrarch, and the Madonna enthroned with her little Son surrounded by the Bentivogli family Above are other frescoes by local masters. To the right is an equestrian portrait in relief of Annibale Bentivoglio (1445) by Niccolò dell' Arca, and by the entrance to the chapel is a portrait in relief of Giovanni Bentivoglio (1477 In the ambulatory opposite is the monument of Antoni

Bentivoglio (1435) by the great master Jacopo della Quercia.

It was the Bentivoglio family who built this chapel and the beautiful Renaissance portico of the church. To this family is due also the little church of S. Cecilia and the frescoes there of Francia, Lorenzo Costa, and their pupils. They tell, though not so sweetly as an earlier age would have done, the story of S. Cecilia, her husband S. Valerian, and her brother S. Tiburtius. In the first, by Francia, we see the Marriage of S. Cecilia and the pagan noble Valerian whom S. Cecilia forbade her bed, saying she was loved by an angel, whom she would show him if he would seek out Pope Urban, " on Via Appia with the poor folks," and ask for baptism. In the second fresco, by Lorenzo Costa, we see Pope Urban instructing Valerian, and in the third, by Tamarocci, we see Valerian baptized. In the fourth, by Chiodarolo, we see Valerian returned home, the Angel appearing to him and S. Cecilia, and giving them the two crowns of roses and lilies, as Voragine relates in the *Golden Legend.* In the fifth fresco, by Aspertini, we see the Martyrdom of Valerian and his brother Tibertius, whom he had converted.

Upon the other wall we see the burial of these two Saints in another fresco by Aspertini. In the second on this side we see S. Cecilia before the Roman prefect, by Chiodarolo; in the third, her martyrdom, by Tamarocci; in the fourth, by Lorenzo Costa, half alive, half dead, she preaches to the poor; in the last, by Francia, she is buried—an exquisite picture.

From S. Cecilia we pass up the Via Marsala to the last church in Bologna that calls for our notice. This is the Carmelite church of S. Martino with a fourteenth-century façade rebuilt in our own time. Here are some more works by Francia, Lorenzo Costa and their pupils. The enthroned Madonna and Child with S. Roch, S. Bernardino, S. Anthony and S. Sebastian with a Pietà above, and below Christ bearing His Cross, in the first chapel on the left, is by

Francia ; while on the last altar upon this side is an Assumption of the Blessed Virgin, with, above, the Resurrection of Christ, in great part by Lorenzo Costa. Opposite to it on the other side of the church is a work by Aspertini, the Madonna and Child with S. Lucy and S. Nicholas.

These churches do not by any means exhaust the interest of Bologna, which has always and everywhere something surprising to show us ; they are but the more interesting sanctuaries of a city which before any other in Italy keeps her best for herself. Nor does she offer them to us as mere picture-galleries; they are churches first and last, and the beautiful things they possess are there for quite other reasons than to minister to our pleasure and curiosity. For this I think we should be constantly thankful. Too much, of course, here as elsewhere, has already passed from these living sanctuaries to the corridors of the museum and the gallery which spoil everything they possess. It is to these we turn last of all, and if we are wise, without too eager an expectation.

Of the school of Bologna, the school painting that is native to the city, as that term is to be understood in Florence, Siena, Venice, or Perugia, there can be nothing to say, for until very late times there was no tradition of art peculiar or proper to Bologna, which for the most part leant almost entirely upon Ferrara where painting was concerned, and upon foreigners from Italy proper in the matter of sculpture. We therefore learn without surprise that in the second half of the fifteenth century the Ferrarese Francesco Cossa established himself here in Bologna and was followed in 1483 by his countryman Lorenzo Costa. It was from them that the first Bolognese painter to show any sign of genius learnt his art. This man was Francesco di Marco Raibolini, whom all the world knows as Francia.

Francia was born in Bologna about 1450. He was trained first as a goldsmith, which art he is thought to have abandoned on the advice of Costa. Bologna is rich in his work, the Accademia possessing no less than nine of his works grouped together in a room at the far end of that long gallery which contains beside, the work of Guido Reni, the Caracci, Francia and Raphael. Here we see the beautiful Madonna and Child with Saints and Donor (78) painted in 1494, the Madonna and Child with the poet Casio (81) dated 1499, and the strange Immaculate Conception with four saints (371) dated 1500. Here, too, are another Immaculate Conception with Saints (79), a Madonna and Child with four saints (80), a charming predella with the Adoration of the Shepherds, the Holy Trinity and the Crucifixion (82), a Pietà (83), the Madonna and Child with S. Laurence and S. Jerome (372), and Christ on the Cross (373). The too refined and eclectic art of Francia cannot recompense us for the fact that the unself-conscious art of the fourteenth and early fifteenth century is not to be had in Bologna. Certainly these retouched pictures will not make us forget our loss, nor indeed will the work of Giacomo Francia, whose Holy Family with four saints (84) is the merest repetition, or of Aspertini, whose early Adoration of the Child is nevertheless not without charm, or even of Francia's best pupil Timoteo Viti, from whose hand there is here a Mary Magdalen (204) painted in 1508. By Francia's first masters there are two works in the Accademia ; by Cossa, a Madonna and Child with S. Petronio, S. John and the Donor (64), a masterpiece of the Ferrarese school painted in 1474 ; by Lorenzo Costa, S. Petronio with S. Francis and S. Thomas Aquinas (65) painted in 1502.

Through Timoteo Viti, who was, after Giovanni Santi, Raphael's first master, we reach Raphael, by whom there is here the famous S. Cecilia, from the church of S. Giovanni in Monte, where it adorned the altar dedicated in honour of Beata Cecilia Duglioli. There, as we know, S. Cecilia stands in the midst, a small organ reversed in her hands, her eyes lifted to heaven, her own music quite put out by the songs she hears of the angels. About her stand S. John, S. Augustine, and S. Paul and S. Mary Magdalen. The

picture has suffered greatly, and we are not sure how much
of it was ever due to Raphael himself, and this, I suppose,
must excuse our disappointment in it. Indeed we turn from
it with a real eagerness to that Madonna and Child in Glory
with S. Michael, S. John, S. Catherine and S. Apollonia (197)
by Perugino which hangs in this same room, and curiously
enough was painted for the same church, but in 1498,
whereas Raphael's picture is, I think, of 1516.

Here we turn aside for a moment into the corridor to
look at the beautiful Giottesque Polyptych (102) and the
Madonna enthroned with Saints (205) by Antonio and
Bartolommeo Vivarini.   What beside these are the works of
the Carracci and Guercino, or of Guido Reni either ? I have
nothing to say of them for they say nothing at all to me.
I turn from them puzzled by my forefathers' enthusiasm
for such things, to look at a lovelier work—a standard dating
from 1482 painted by Niccolò da Foligno, with the Adoration
of the Child and behind it the Annunciation (360).

The excellent Museo Civico is not so disappointing as the
Accademia for it does not promise so much. It contains,
too, what I suppose is one of the finest collections of
Etruscan antiquities in existence, but for me it holds but
two things of real delight, I mean the two reliefs of Jacopo
della Quercia, the first a relief of the Birth of the Virgin
in Sala xv, the other a relief of the Madonna and Child in
Sala xvi. For these in their beauty no words are good
enough, nor may one ever really forget them.

CHAPTER V

IMOLA, FAENZA, FORLÌ AND CESENA

I LEFT Bologna one spring morning by the Porta Mazzini to follow the great Roman road, the Via Emilia, straight as a ruled line across the plain at the very foot of the great mountains. I was soon weary. To follow a road afoot so straight and so broad as this is no light matter, for one misses the enchantment of the by-ways and all that is unexpected and unforeseen ; one tramps in the wake and the dust of the armies of two thousand years and is soon overwhelmed by the mere persistence of a way which stretches before one without hope or hesitation for ever and ever in a continually sharpening vista of weariness. Nothing in the world is stronger or more formidable than this ever-lasting road ; not the mountains in whose shadows it runs ; fair and delectable though they be, they have not the power to uplift the heart from the heaviness of the way ; not the plain, though all heaven leans over it with love, for the road is master and has conquered them both. It is only an army, that can break the way with its songs, that is master of the road, and for such this Way was made, and its directness and strength are part of its service. But for us who would linger and loiter here and there, who are alone and cannot fill that mighty breadth with a lonely voice, the Via Emilia is a tyranny and a curse, the most damnable iteration of miles in all our Christendom.

So I was easily weary. I rested at S. Lazzaro, I lingered at Ozzano, at Castel S. Pietro I gave in and took to the byways. But there in that delightful stronghold beside the Sìllaro I was reconciled with the Way ; and there, where something still remains in the rosy brick of the old Rocca, half-covered with ivy and trees, to remind you of the old fortress it was, founded by the Bolognese in the end of the twelfth century to hold the passage of the Sìllaro where the great road crossed that stream, I threw off the tyranny of the Way and began to enjoy it. I lingered there amid the old churches and I lingered in Dozza, lovelier by far, lovely with vines and olives and mighty cypresses, a true castello of the hills, with a great Rocca very well preserved, which the Bolognesi and the Imolesi constantly disputed, and that in 1470 Galeazzo Maria Sforza took from Taddeo Manfredi to give as dowry to Caterina his daughter, the promised bride of Girolamo Riario. In 1528, however, when Clement VII was in secure possession of all this country he gave the fortress of Dozza and its territory to Cardinal Campeggi of Bologna, who adorned it with much care and thought. It is to him perhaps is due the fine double cortile. The Rocca is, however, apart from its own natural beauty, all Dozza. The church is uninteresting, though a lunette in the wall strangely carved with the Madonna and Child enthroned between a saint and one who offers a gift to the divine Child, should be noted.

Coming down from Dozza to the great road again and going on my way into Imola, I presently came to the Santuario della Madonna del Piratello, a famous shrine of the Blessed Virgin to which the people of Imola make pilgrimage in the month of Roses, for, as I heard the tale, it was not only a Rose—Rosa Mystica—in whose honour this shrine was built, but it was a rose which was in part the means of founding it.

For it seems that in the year 1483, upon the twenty-seventh day of April, the sky being grey and the road deep with snow, there came by a pilgrim who stopped in this place before a rude pillar upon the top of which was set an image of the Madonna with her little Son in her arms ; but there was no shelter for the image save that afforded by a

THE VIA EMILIA

little pear tree, whose branches were so laden with snow that it seemed in full blossom.

The pilgrim knelt to say a prayer, and, caught by the sweetness of Madonna's face, lighted in the snow a little candle which he had in his knapsack for use at the inn ; and this he did in honour of the Mother of our dear Lord. But no sooner had he lighted this candle than out it went. And sadly, half doubting, he asked wherefore the north wind had so little respect for that flame, seeing in whose honour he had lighted it. And the Madonna smiled, and suddenly he was aware of two fair angels who picked up the little candle and relighted it and held it while Madonna said : " Rise and go to the Governor of Imola and tell what thou hast seen— how I stay here in the wind and the cold with only this poor pear tree for a protection." And the pilgrim wept : " Che Tu sii benedetta," said he. " If they doubt your words," Madonna continued, " you have a sign ; in your breast you will find a rose. It is this you will show to them as you have shown it me."

Then the pilgrim went into Imola through the snow and sought the governor and told him all things. But none believed him. Then he opened the bosom of his cloak, and lo, a white rose nestled there full of sweetness ; and they that saw this wonder believed his word. And they sent in haste to the lord Girolamo Riario and to Madonna Caterina, his wife, and soon over that image by the wayside and the sheltering poor pear tree there rose a temple, a fine tower, the work it is said of Bramante, with other things also which we may see to this day, and thither, as is meet, the people of Imola came forth in the month of Roses to lay roses at Madonna's feet.

Now when I had heard all this and had reverently beheld the image, the glorious tabernacle, the roses and some fine fifteenth-century glass, and had seen with my eyes that it was but the truth I had been told, for a traveller does well to accept nothing upon hearsay, I came over the Santerno into Imola, a little city of charming palaces and churches defended of old by a mighty Rocca which still remains, but in ruin.

Imola was the Roman Forum Cornelii, and though it was no doubt a considerable town of Cisalpine Gaul, we know little of it.   Octavian went into winter quarters there in the Civil War, and Martial composed the third book of his Epigrams there, if we may rightly interpret what he says :

> Romam vade, liber ; si veneris unde, requiret,
> Æmiliae dices de regione viæ.
> Si, quibus in terris, qua simus in urbe, rogabit :
> Corneli referas me licet esse foro. . . .

The name of Imola comes to it, according to Paulus Diaconus, from its citadel, which was called Imoles.   It was, of course, a town of the Exarchate, and with that province passed to the Holy See in the eighth century.   In the ninth it bravely defended itself under Fausto Alidosi, against the Saracens, and in the tenth and following centuries was constantly at war with Ravenna, Faenza, and Bologna, as well as distracted by internal discords.   Then rose the Commune.   Imola was generally upon the Imperial, and later upon the Ghibelline side in the great quarrel of Pope and Emperor, though even so it found it convenient at times to side with the Papal party.   By the end of the thirteenth century the Alidosi had made themselves lords, and though, notably in 1295 by Maghinardo Pagano, their rule was disputed, they retained their power as pontifical vicars till 1424, when Angelo della Pergola, Filippo Maria Visconti's captain, gained the supremacy.   Two years later, however, Imola was restored to the Holy See, and the famous Capranica, not yet Cardinal, as Legate set up a new form of government. This did not endure, and in 1434 Imola passed into the hands of the Sforza.   Forty years later Pope Sixtus IV bought the town from that family, then in possession of the Duchy of Milan, for his nephew Girolamo Riario together with the hand of Caterina Sforza, the Duke's illegitimate daughter. A little later the people of Forlì, weary of the tyranny of the Ordelaffi, put themselves under the protection of the

Pope, who sent Girolamo to occupy that city and thus add Forlì to Imola. It is to this time that Imola owes the beautiful palaces and churches which she still boasts. Girolamo Riario, however, according to the chroniclers, was a second Nero, and it is therefore not surprising that in 1488 he was murdered by three of his bodyguard in Forlì.

The rule of the Riarii was indeed to be brief. Alexander VI was as eager as Sixtus IV had been for a lordship for his family. The first cities he thought of were those of Imola and Forli, which Caterina held for Girolamo's son, Ottaviano Riario.

When Cesare Borgia appeared in November 1499 before Imola, it opened its gates ; Forlì, however, held out bravely till the following January. With the death of Alexander VI and the flight of Cesare the Riarii attempted to regain their lordship, but without success, and in 1504 Imola submitted to Julius II, to remain in Papal hands till the establishment of the modern kingdom of United Italy.

Imola is chiefly notable to-day on account of its fine palaces, the work for the most part of the Riarii: the Palazzo Sforza, commonly called Palazzo Paterlini, in Via Cavour, where Caterina Sforza dwelt ; the Palazzo Sersanti in Piazzo Vittorio Emanuele, one of the noblest buildings in Romagna, built in 1482 by Giorgio Fiorentino for Girolamo Riario and Caterina Sforza; the Palazzo della Volpe, another Sforza palace, in Via Umberto I, really the Via Emilia which runs quite through the city ; and the Palazzo del Pozzo in the same street, built for the same Signori, and adorned with a very beautiful cortile. More ancient than these is the Palazzo Municipale, which the Alidosi are said to have built, but which is now a rebuilding of a later time.

Of the churches, S. Cassiano is chief. It was begun in 1187 and finished in 1271, but as we see it, alas, it is wholly a rebuilding of the nineteenth century ; among its more precious possessions must be named the noble thirteenth-century Crucifix sculptured in wood, the beautiful paten called of S. Pietro Crisologo, and the Chapel of SS. Cosma e

Damiano with its cenotaphs to two of the Alidosi. In the crypt, as it is said, lie S. Pietro Crisologo, the famous Bishop of Ravenna, who died at Imola, *c.* 450.

S. Cassiano is not the only church in Imola which is worth a visit by any means. One of the most ancient foundations in Romagna is the church of S. Maria in Regola, once Benedictine, which is said to have been founded by Galla Placidia, and where upon the high altar is a famous relic of the Madonna, a piece of her veil, presented to the monks by the patrician Longinus of Ravenna in 577. Under another altar here is an ancient sarcophagus, carved in the fourteenth century, in which lies the body of S. Sigismund, King of Burgundy, the patron, as we shall see, of Sigismondo Malatesta of Rimini. Nor should the church of the Osservanza be missed. It is to be found a few steps outside the Porta Montanara, and, apart from its own delight and beauty, it boasts a notable and beautiful fresco of the Madonna of Mercy. The Virgin stands, her gorgeous cloak outspread over a host of kneeling people, and on either side are two Franciscan saints, perhaps S. Francis and S. Bernardino. This delightful work, attributed to the Vivarini, was painted to celebrate the peace established in 1472 between Taddeo Manfredi and his son Guidazzo. In the Piazza beside the church is a ruined shrine attributed to Bramante, in which are the remains of a fresco of the Madonna. It is known as the Tribuna di Giulio II, because it was built in honour of that Pope, who spent twenty days in Imola in 1506.

Quite as charming as the Osservanza is the church of S. Domenico, with its noble Gothic doorway, its fine panel by Giovanni da Riolo of the Madonna and Child enthroned, and its Giottesque frescoes in the fine old Campanile. Nor must I forget to mention the ruined Rocca of Girolamo Riario and Caterina Sforza, with its cortile attributed to Bramante.

But whatever else the traveller misses in Imola, there is one thing above all he must not fail to see. I mean the

pictures in the Biblioteca Comunale. The noblest of these
is the Madonna della Pietra, a work of the fifteenth century,
in which we see the Blessed Virgin kneeling on the ground,
her arms outspread over the people of Imola, protecting
them from the shafts and arrows of pestilence, aimed at
them from the sky, a most noble and lovely piece of work.
Here, too, is a picture of the Madonna enthroned with her
little Son between S. Pietro Crisologo and S. Cassiano,
attributed to Innocenzo da Imola, and, if from his hand,
the only picture by him remaining in the city.

Many delightful days may be spent in or about Imola,
wandering in the valley of the Santerno or on the plain that
stretches away to the east of the Via Emilia, and boasts
such delights as Castel Guelfo and Mordano.

But the road calls,—that long indomitable Roman way at
the foot of the great mountains, a way in its straightness
and its dust so hard to follow.

That way under the beautiful mountains brings you
some four miles out of Imola to Castel Bolognese, where in
1434 the hired forces of Milan and Florence met in a great
battle, for once decisive. The army of the Milanese was
captained by that great commander Niccolò Piccinino, that
of Florence by Gattamelata and Niccolò da Tolentino.
Piccinino was victorious, Tolentino, Orsini, and Astorre
Manfredi, lord of Faenza, were taken prisoners with the whole
of the Florentine forces, save a thousand horse which, with
Gattamelata, managed to escape. They left, however, only
four dead upon the field and some thirty wounded. Such
was the warfare of the condottieri; it prophesied of
Fornovo.

It was already evening, when, in the beautiful twilight
in which the mountains stood up like spectres against the
west, I entered Faenza, the Roman Faventia, and of this
city I cannot say enough. It is a quiet and delightful little
place, full of antiquity, and many a pleasant day may be
spent among its churches, palaces and pictures and in
wandering about its old-world streets. In Roman times it

was chiefly notable as the source of Ravenna's water supply, an aqueduct stretching between the two cities, and as the starting-place of a road across the Apennines which connected Faesula and Florentia with the Via Emilia. With the rest of the cities of the Exarchate, when the Imperial power failed at last in the eighth century, Faenza passed under the authority of the Holy See. We hear of it as a Commune in the eleventh century, and in the twelfth as governed by the Counts of Modigliana. In the great quarrel it first took the Imperial side, but joined the Guelf League, and in 1241 the Emperor took possession of it after an eight months' siege. In the thirteenth century it was the scene of bitter internal struggles in which the families of Accarisi, Manfredi, Lambertazzi, Nordigli and others disputed its possession, but from 1294 the Manfredi became masters and their whole ambition seems to have been to make themselves independent of their overlord, the Pope. Thus in 1328 Cardinal Bertrando Poggetto, in 1356 Cardinal Albornoz, were sent to summon them to render service as vassals of the Holy See.

But the one really tragic event which befell Faenza in the Middle Ages was the sack of 1376, when she was almost destroyed by the English condottiere, Sir John Hawkwood. This fine soldier was at that time in the service of Pope Gregory XI ; he took Faenza in March, and not only pillaged it, but is said to have butchered some four thousand persons. The Manfredi, however, were not thus to be disposed of. When, more than a hundred years later, Cesare Borgia made his famous raid into the Romagna in search of a kingdom, he found Astorre Manfredi in Faenza, and, unlike Pandolfo Malatesta at Rimini and Giovanni Sforza at Pesaro, ready to resist him. From the autumn of 1500 to April 1501, Faenza, under its gallant young lord, held out. By the terms of the capitulation, which was made at last on April 20, Astorre Manfredi was to go free, but he was detained in Cesare's camp and presently taken to Rome, confined in S. Angelo, and at last drowned in the Tiber. On the death

f Cesare, Francesco the brother of Astorre attempted to
eturn, but Venice was then in possession of the city, which
ight years later was brought back into the Papal power by
ulius II, never to leave it till our own time.

Faenza, *la città di Lamone*, as Dante calls it, is one of the
ayest of these little cities upon the Via Emilia, in the
hadow of the great mountains. The great road runs clean
hrough it, as it does through Imola, opening out, as it were,
n the midst of the city into the fine Piazza Maggiore, now
amed after Vittorio Emanuele, about which are grouped
he Duomo, the Palazzo del Comune, and the Torre dell'
)rologio. The Duomo is a noble building dedicated in
onour of S. Pietro, begun in 1474 by the great Florentine
naster, Giuliano da Maiano. It is a basilica in the early
Renaissance style of Brunelleschi, consisting of nave and
isles surmounted by a demi-cupola. Within, its chief
oast is the work of Benedetto da Maiano in the altars, and
specially in the monumental tomb founded by Giovanni
Manfredi in 1468, of S. Savino, the first Bishop of Faenza
313). The sarcophagus stands upon pilasters in a round-
rched niche and is carved with six scenes from the life
f the saint. Above are two exquisite statuettes of the
3lessed Virgin and Archangel Gabriel. The whole is a
vonderfully charming and virile work, among the best
xecuted by this master. Over the fourth altar on the
ight is a fine picture of the Blessed Virgin with Our Lord
nd S. John Baptist and SS. Peter, Joseph, Anna and
'aul, by Innocenzo da Imola. Over the fifth altar on
his side are three reliefs by Agostino di Duccio the exile,
vhom we shall meet again in Rimini, of scenes in the life of
. Terenzio. Here, too, is a fine sixteenth-century tomb by
'ietro Barilotto.

Faenza is full of charming buildings. Among these I
vould note especially the façades of S. Michele and of the
'alazzo of the Manfredi, opposite. Among the churches
vhich should be visited beside the Cathedral are those of
he Chiesa della Commenda and S. Maglorio, both of which

7

contain an altarpiece by Girolamo da Udine, and the former has a fine fresco by Girolamo da Treviso of the Madonna with Our Lord and S. John Baptist with S. Mary Magdalen and S. Catherine and, above, God the Father in heaven.

But if it be pictures we desire, we shall find all that is best worth seeing here gathered in the ex-convent of S. Maria dell' Angelo, where, upon the first floor, the Pinacoteca has been established. Here are five good pictures by that Umbro-Romagnol master Palmezzano, the pupil of Melozzo da Forlì, who came a little under the influence of Rondinelli. The best of these fine works is that of the Madonna and Saints with God the Father above in the lunette, painted in 1498. The others represent Christ bearing His Cross, Tobias and the Angel, S. Jerome and S. Austin.

Palmezzano's pupil, the Romagnol-Ferrarese Francesco Zaganelli da Cotignola, has one picture here, a Dead Christ with saints, and below a view of Faenza ; while a very different master, Bertucci of the Umbro-Romagnol school, is represented here by eight works : the Madonna and Child with four saints painted in 1511, an altarpiece in four compartments, painted in 1506, a Nativity, an Adoration of the Magi, a Noli me Tangere and three pictures of Saints.

But when all is said, by far the most interesting picture in Faenza is the work of a curious follower of Cossa, who came under the influence of Botticelli. He was a pure Romagnol and his name was Scaletti. The only pictures we have surely from his hand are here in Faenza. They are two, and consist of an altarpiece of the Madonna and Child with Saints painted in 1484 and a portrait of the young Astorre Manfredi kneeling before S. Bernardino da Feltre. They are quite delightful and astonishing and worthy of study. Here, too, is a delightful bust of S. John Baptist by Donatello, and a statue in wood of S. Jerome attributed to the same master

Delightful as Faenza is, it will not keep anyone too long from the persevering road and the most mediæval of all these little cities upon the Emilian Way, Forlì.

Forlì, with its narrow, cobbled streets, dark palace and

ASTORRE MANFREDI. BY LEONARDO SCALETTI
Pinacoteca Faenza

almost threatening houses, is still the city of Catherine
Sforza and of that noble great defence she made in her most
tragic hour against the lightning that was Cesare. It is a
town of very ancient lineage, well known to the Romans,
who called it Forum Livii, though we know nothing of it at
all till suddenly in the fifth century it appears as the scene
of the betrothal or the marriage of Galla Placidia with
Ataulfus, the king of the Goths. Three hundred years
later, with the rest of the Exarchate, it passed to the Papacy,
and appears in the beginning of the Middle Ages as a city
of Ghibelline sympathies, ruled in the thirteenth century
by various lords in turn—Simone Mestaguerra, Maghinardo
Pagano, Uguccione della Faggiuola, and others, till in 1302
the Ordelaffi came into power. We see this family continually trying to establish their independence of the Holy
See, their overlord, and suffering the usual vicissitudes there-
for, in 1327 and in 1359, when Cardinal Albornoz appeared
to avenge the majesty of the Popes. In 1480 Forlì was seized
by Girolamo Riario, and in 1488 he was murdered by three
conspirators while he sat after supper in the palace here, his
body being thrown into the street and dragged round the
walls by the populace. Catherine Sforza, his wife, and
her children were seized—indeed, only the commander of
the fortress of Ravaldino remained faithful, refusing to surrender unless Catherine in person commanded it. She was
accordingly allowed to enter the fortress ; then suddenly
she gave orders to shut the gates and to die rather than
surrender. She was pregnant at the time, but quite
undaunted she mounted the ramparts and faced the rebels,
haranguing them and shouting over the din that they might
if they would kill the children she had left with them as
hostages, for she had still a son safe in Imola and another
already quick in her womb. Her courage inspired the
whole garrison to resist to the end, and, in spite of the Papal
reinforcements which the rebels received, the fortress held
out till relieved by the troops of the Duke of Milan, sent
down the great road to defend his relative ; and Catherine's

young son Ottaviano became lord of Forlì with his mother as regent. In 1499, however, Forlì fell to Cesare Borgia in spite of Catherine, who, however, fought him tower by tower, retreating round the ramparts till she was taken at last and sent a prisoner to Rome. After Cesare's death Forlì became directly subject to the Holy See.

The heroic act of Catherine Sforza, the dark days of that rebellion, and of the tragic apparition of Cesare, who took the dauntless princess prisoner and lodged her in the Vatican, are recalled at every step in Forlì, as much, I think, by the aspect and atmosphere of the place as by the ruined ramparts and the Rocca, which was originally built by Cardinal Albornoz. Forlì is indeed a tragic city, relieved in our thoughts of her by the memory of her smiling churches and the pictures they contain. These are for the most part works by Palmezzano and his pupils.

In the church of S. Mercuriale, in the Piazza, upon the third altar on the right is a magnificent work, a picture of the Madonna in glory with saints and donor worshipping a Crucifix. Over the fifth altar in the same church is a Madonna enthroned between S. Mary Magdalen and S. John Baptist. Again in SS. Biagio e Girolamo in the first chapel on the right are frescoes of Prophets and of the Martyrdom of S. James, early works from the same hand. And in the fourth chapel on the same side of the church is a triptych of the Madonna and Child with saints and donors. In the cupola are frescoes of the Madonna and Child with Cherubim by the same master. All these works are from the hand of Marco Palmezzano, the pupil of Melozzo da Forlì, whose hand we seem to see in these early works in the first chapel on the right in SS. Biagio e Girolamo.

This church can boast of other treasures also in the lovely tomb of Barbara Manfredi, made by Francesco di Simone in 1466, and in the curious picture of the Immaculate Conception by Guido Reni in the third chapel on the right.

It is true that Melozzo da Forlì, by whom there is, here in

his native city, only a solitary work in the Pinacoteca, was the master of Palmezzano, but that prolific painter was certainly influenced to some extent by Rondinelli. By this great man, happily, certain works remain here ; among these are two in the Duomo, one at the end of the right transept, a S. Sebastian, and the other a Visitation in the Sacristy. The Duomo, apart from Rondinelli's work, is, unhappily, without interest for us, since, with the exception of the chapels in the transepts, it is a rebuilding of 1844.

We turn now to what, when all is said, is the most interesting collection of pictures south of Bologna on all this road, the Pinacoteca of Forlì in the Ginnasio Comunale in Piazza Morgagni, not omitting to notice on our way up the staircase the noble sarcophagus of S. Mercuriale by Antonio Rossellino.

Here is the famous *Pesta Pepe*, by Melozzo da Forlì, the pupil of that great master Piero della Francesca. It is an heroic figure, full of the joy of life and health, an apothecary pounding herbs, a noble thing taken directly from life, of which, of the joy of which, it seems to have captured so much. We pass from it to the fourteen works of Palmezzano with an inevitable disappointment, and yet with gratitude too ; for though they have not the energy of Melozzo, they have a real and sometimes an innocent delight. Far dearer to us, however, is the charming Madonna and Child by Niccolò Rondinelli, the ever-charming pupil of Giovanni Bellini. With him we touch the greater schools of Italy, to find here to our joy a lovely Adoration of the Child (103), and Christ upon the Mount of Olives (104), of the Florentine school of the fifteenth century, a beautiful Crucifixion (76) by some Sienese master of the fourteenth century, and a portrait by none other than Lorenzo di Credi (130). By Guercino, too, there is an Annunciation (86), and by Francia a Nativity (98). In the small rooms are some fine medals and a good fifteenth-century bust of Pino Ordelaffi.

Beyond Forlì, still keeping to the great road which the railway has followed all the way from Bologna, one crosses the wide valleys of the Montone and the Ronco, passes through Forimpopoli, the ancient Forum Popilii under Bertinoro of the Malatesta on the hills to the south, and comes over the Savio into the city of Cesena. The way is perhaps a little monotonous for a traveller on foot, but is not without beauty and interest. Bertinoro should be visited, if only for the sake of the wonderful view it offers of all the great plain to the north and east, and he who has time and goodwill may care to search out Polenta in the hills still farther to the south, whence came the famous family of Ravenna.

As for Cesena, it is the first hill city of our journey, a delicious and beautiful little town which no one should miss. Cesena has had a notable career, both in ancient and in mediæval times. A flourishing town in the time of the Empire, it was a strong fortress in the time of Belisarius and played no inconsiderable part in the Gothic war; but its most dramatic period of history lies in the Middle Ages, when it was in the hands of the Ordelaffi. The wife of Francesco Ordelaffi held it against Cardinal Albornoz, but after a bitter defence was forced to surrender it. In 1377 it was sacked by Robert of Geneva, afterwards anti-pope. Indeed, one still seems to see that appalling figure, a figure, as it were, out of the Inferno of Dante, stumbling over the dead, yelling as he goes " Blood, Blood, I will have more blood, I will kill ! " Later it came into the hands of the Malatesta of Rimini, and in the famous years of Sigismondo Malatesta was held by his brother Novello, of whom Pisanello made so lovely a medal. He greatly embellished it with palaces and a glorious library; but after his death, when the Malatesta fell, it came into the hands of the Pope.

Its chief glory remains the library, with its fifty thousand volumes and four hundred manuscripts, most of the latter having been made for Malatesta Novello, who was in his own way as enthusiastic a humanist as his greater brother.

At his death this library, which has always been famous
—indeed, Aldus Manutius knew it well—came into the hands
of the Franciscans. The building is of considerable beauty,
with two fine doorways sculptured with the Malatesta
badge, a noble hall upheld by columns and fine fifteenth-
century furniture. Here, too, is a good Francia, the
Presentation in the Temple.

Nor should the Duomo be missed. This is a good brick
building, with a noble doorway of the fourteenth century,
and within two beautiful altars of marble, the work of the
Lombardi in the early part of the sixteenth century.

Cesena claims two Popes among her sons, Pius VI and
Pius VII. The latter, who was to be the victim of Napoleon,
entered the Benedictine order in the monastery of S. Maria
del Monte, about a mile to the north-east of Cesena. The
glorious church, which stands nobly on a hill, is a fine land-
mark and offers a splendid view of the sea. It is said to be
the work of Bramante, and is certainly worthy of such a
master.

I confess, when I set out from Cesena early one fair morning
for Rimini, my whole intention was to find and identify
the Rubicon. Three streams have been called by that
famous name, and I crossed the first of these, the Pisciatello,
perhaps three miles out of Cesena. A few miles farther on
I crossed the Rigossa, and this too has been called the
Rubicon. Moreover, close by stands a column which
Montesquieu considered a genuine piece of antiquity, forbidding in noble Latin anyone to cross the great boundary
marked by the little river with a legion or cohort. Neither
of these streams quite convinced me, however, and as for
the column I knew from books that it was a forgery. I
came into Savignano about midday, with the abrupt cliff of
the Republic of S. Marino rising up before me, by the
great noble Roman bridge over the Fiumicino, which again,
and with far more reason, for it is twelve miles from Rimini,
has been called the Rubicon. No one, however, that I
questioned seemed to know what I meant. It was very

different when, coming out of Savignano, I presently crossed by another great Roman bridge over the Uso just before I came to S. Arcangelo. There I found a beggar lying along the parapet in the sun, and when I asked the name of the stream he told me at once *Il Rubicone*, and I was satisfied. This was the stream upon whose bank Cæsar halted with the thirteenth legion and many times considered in his heart whether he would go on or not into Italy in defiance of the law of the Republic. He went on, as we know, lured by that heavenly messenger who sounded the advance upon a trumpet snatched from the hand of a trumpeter, and in three months was master of all Italy. I was delighted to learn from the priest of S. Arcangelo that my opinion about the Rubicon has Papal authority behind it, a Papal Bull having been issued in 1769 pronouncing once and for all in favour of the Uso. It was only when I got home that I found the bull was Clement XIV's. Now Clement XIV was born in S. Arcangelo.

S. Arcangelo is a lofty and picturesque fortress of the Malatesta, well worth a visit on account of its ruined Rocca of the fifteenth century, and offering you the most picturesque way into the Republic of S. Marino. I refused it and went on to Rimini in the twilight, for I was weary, and the Ave Maria had long since rung from the grave campanile when I entered that lean, unforgettable town over the mighty bridge of Augustus Cæsar.

CHAPTER VI

RIMINI

F OR all its dark and forbidding aspect Rimini remain one of the most interesting and even delightful cities in the Marches of Italy. As the gate of the Marches, a province of an extraordinary and virile beauty too little known to travellers, it has much to offer us : a great hill country violent in gesture, but mild and delicious in its generous humanity, stark and yet smiling withal, where upon every height little isolated towns of rain-beaten brick and stone shine and glitter and beckon across profound valleys too wide for their streams ; a sea-coast, lean and very desolate but strangely beautiful, where, upon the edge of that uncertain and shallow sea, hosts of white sea-birds gather and call and pass in great flocks and clouds of darkness and of light, ever restless in a loneliness that is bitter and tragic, that seems to be haunted by some great and terrible event. Upon this country of mountain and sea-coast, in the narrow marsh between them, upon the rushing and forbidding Marecchia, Rimini is set like a seal guarding its secret.

Her story is an old one. As Ariminum she was, long before the Empire appeared, a famous place. In her heart met the two great roads that traversed Italy and Cisalpine Gaul, the Via Flaminia and the Via Emilia, the northern highways of the Romans. Every conquest, from that of the Gauls to that of the Britons, which came northward from Rome, surged into Rimini, halted there, and surged out again, along that mighty road we have traversed, to cross

the Po at Placentia and the Alps by the great S. Bernard.
Rimini was the most important of all the stations upon
these roads, and they were the most important highways
within the Imperial administration. There was this, too,
that Rimini, in whose heart these two great highways met,
was set in the very mouth of the narrow pass between the
Apennines and the Adriatic, which was the natural gate of
the peninsula. This I have already tried to explain in
speaking of Ravenna, for it is more important in connection
with the history of that city than of Rimini, because, whenever the pass was in dispute the command of it passed from
Rimini to Ravenna, Rimini being hard to defend but
Ravenna impregnable. But we see Rimini playing an
important part in every war waged by the Romans for the
conquest and the holding of Cisalpine Gaul and the north.
In 225 B.C. it was occupied by a Roman army during the
Gaulish war ; in 218 B.C. Sempronius directed his legions
upon it in order to oppose Hannibal on the Cisalpine plain ;
throughout the Second Punic war, indeed, it played a great
part and was nearly always the headquarters of a considerable Roman army. In the final Gallic war that followed the retreat of Hannibal, as in the Civil Wars of Marius
and Sulla, it played much the same part, and it was, as we
have seen, the first business of Cæsar to seize it when he
crossed the Rubicon. Nor is it less conspicuous in the wars
of Octavian and Antony, of Vitellius and Vespasian, nor
hundreds of years later in the long contests between
Belisarius and the Goths. It was a very important place,
and when Augustus established Ravenna as his great naval
port upon the Adriatic he did not neglect Rimini, but
adorned her with many splendid public works, some of
which we may still see, for he realized that in the era of
peace which he had inaugurated its importance would
not be diminished, but changed, and that its position
so valuable for an army would be equally valuable
for merchants, as indeed proved to be the case, for
through all the years of the Empire Rimini appears

SIGISMONDO MALATESTA. BY PIERO DELLA FRANCESCA
Tempio Malatestiano Rimini

as one of the richest and most flourishing cities of
Italy.

But few travellers, I suppose, are drawn to consider such
facts as these when they visit Rimini to-day, for a later
interest, and above all a great personallty, stand between
us and them and absorb all, or almost all, our thoughts
there. As we pass to and fro in those curiously mean and
restless streets to-day, between us and antiquity there rises
the appalling and yet compelling figure of Sigismondo
Malatesta, the tyrant and humanist. It is his face that
stares at us from the walls of the great church of the place; it
is his love that lies buried in that unrivalled mausoleum; it is
his courage and achievement and cruelty that fills the place
with a lean and virile beauty, that haunts the ruins of the
degraded Rocca and seems to interpret for us the violence
of that shrunken smiling river, hurling itself into the
shallow sea under the great Roman bridge across which the
Via Emilia still staggers northward. Here in Rimini he
has obliterated the memory of Rome.

It is often the case that one finds in some provincial
achievement a more perfect expression of the soul of a great
national movement than in anything to be found in the
capital. It is so, for instance, with that great style of
architecture in England which we call the Early English.
Nothing in London sums it up so completely or so perfectly
expresses it as does the Cathedral of Salisbury, which is
perhaps the most completely English thing in England. In
the same way the strange confusion of reminiscence which
we have come to call the Italian Renaissance is perhaps more
completely summed up and more perfectly expressed in the
figure, the personality, the achievement and the failure of
Sigismondo Malatesta than it is in the life of Lorenzo de'
Medici or the work of Leonardo or of Raphael. It is this, I
think, which lends such force to his legend.

The city of Rimini, in the first years of the Lombard
invasion, came to be the nucleus of a new province, the
Pentapolis, and no longer to make one of the cities of

Flaminia, the débris of which with parts of Emilia was re-grouped about the fortress of Ravenna and known as the Exarchate. With the failure of the Exarchate in the eighth century the Pentapolis, as we have seen, came, as did the Exarchate itself, directly into the power of the Holy See. Its government during the four hundred ensuing years is obscure and doubtful; but apparently at some time during the twelfth century the Malatesta, originally of Penna Billi in Montefeltro among the Apennines, obtained power in Rimini, coming in first as Podestà and remaining as tyrants or lords. Two Malatesta, Ugo and Giovanni of Penna Billi, are known to us in the twelfth century, but it is another Giovanni whom we must reckon with as the first ancestor of Sigismondo. In the year 1216 this Giovanni was called into Rimini by Ottone da Mendola, the Podestà, to defend Rimini against Cesena. This he did so well that in 1237 he was himself appointed Podestà, and before he died in 1247 he had made himself master and lord. Giovanni married a daughter of Pietro degli Onesti of Ravenna, and had by her as heir Malatesta da Verrucchio, born in 1212. He who may be called the founder of the house married three times and had four sons—Giovanni, surnamed *lo sciancato*, for he was a cripple, born in 1245; Paolo, born in 1252, surnamed *il bello*, for he was very fair; Malatestino, surnamed *dell' occhio*, for he was blinded in one eye by the Greek fire while still a boy one day of battle in Ravenna; and Pandolfo, afterwards lord. The famous and tragic love story which involved Giovanni *lo sciancato* and Paolo *il bello* with Francesca da Polenta, the wife of the former, is known to every reader of Dante and Byron. It was but the first, if it was the first, of those evil chances which dogged the steps of every member of this house to the latest generation.

Verrucchio died, it is said, in 1313, at the age of one hundred years, and was succeeded by Malatestino. He ruled five years and was followed in the lordship, which had then been much increased, by Pandolfo. This man had two sons—Pandolfo, born in 1295, and Galeotto, born in 1302.

The latter it was who faced Cardinal Albornoz when he came into the Marches to re-establish the real suzerainty of the Holy See then in Avignon. He obtained, however, from the Pope, investiture as vicar of Rimini, while his brother Pandolfo likewise obtained Pesaro. He married late in life and had four sons and four daughters, of whom only Carlo, born in 1364, and Pandolfo, born in 1370, have any interest for us ; the one was lord of Rimini and Imola, the other lord of Fano and father of Sigismondo Malatesta.

Sigismondo was born on June 19, 1417, and succeeded his uncle, who was childless, while still a mere boy, in 1432, and in the following year was betrothed to Ginevra, the daughter of Niccolò d'Este of Ferrara. In the same year he was knighted, with his brother Novello, afterwards lord of Cesena, by the Emperor Sigismund, on his way back to Germany after his coronation in Rome ; and soon afterwards he brought Ginevra to Rimini as his bride. He was already a soldier of some note, and had secured himself in Rimini, where possibly, with the help of Roberto Valturio, the engineer, he had begun to build himself the most formidable fortress or Rocca in all the March, and was famous for his courage and daring, when in 1435 he took service with the Pope as condottiere. It was the age of Niccolò Piccinino, Gattamelata, Francesco Sforza and a host of adventurers, who with their hired armies, in the service first of one great city and then of another, were marching about Italy looking for lordships. Not all were as successful as Sforza, who at last made himself master of Milan, but it was a time in which rewards were certain, a time of perpetual though not severe fighting, and among the familiar names of those professional leaders known as condottieri Sigismondo's was one of the most respectable and by no means the least to be feared. A chronicler of the time places him indeed third upon the list of great soldiers after Sforza and Gattamelata, but before Piccinino and Federigo of Urbino. In the service of the Pope, of the Visconti, of Florence, of Venice, of Naples, and in his own behalf, Sigismondo wrote his name as a soldier across the confused history of his time, and would no doubt appear to us much as Niccolò Piccinino does but for the fact that he was something more representative of his time than a soldier could be, in the fifteenth century, at any rate, and in such a country as Italy then was.

I have said that Sigismondo was a great humanist, and there have always been many to add, and among them was Pope Pius II, that he was also a great criminal.   As a soldier he was violent, cunning, rash, brave and unfortunate ; nothing succeeded with him, and it is perhaps in his failure we may find the root of the accusation against him.   If nothing succeeds like success, nothing fails like failure. However that may be, the accusations that were brought against Sigismondo, and at last and with most force by his greatest enemy, Pope Pius II, who bore him a grudge because, as he believed, Sigismondo had betrayed Siena, are many and serious.

It is asserted that he murdered his three wives ; but as soon as we begin to sift the evidence we find that there is not enough to hang a dog.   Yet upon this evidence and because he hated him, Pope Pius had Sigismondo burnt in effigy in Rome.   Let us, however, consider the matter.

Sigismondo was married three times, was a bad husband, and all his life was in love with Isotta degli Atti, a beautiful and learned lady of Rimini, whom at last he married.   His first wife was Ginevra d'Este, who died, it seems, of fever when Sigismondo was absent from Rimini ; nor did her death break his close relations with her family, the famous house of Ferrara.   As his second wife he married Polisenna Sforza, the sister of the future Duke of Milan, who also died mysteriously, but without any real suspicion falling upon Sigismondo, at any rate in Rimini.   His third wife was that Isotta degli Atti, whom he had loved all his life, and in whose arms he died, for she outlived him.   At any rate, the accusations against Sigismondo are false then in the letter ; we may well ask what purpose he gained or might have hoped to gain by the murder of his wives. To that we can make no answer. The friendship of the Estensi was always his greatest mainstay; the death of Polisenna endangered his friendship with the most successful soldier of the time. Far from gaining anything by the death of his wives he lost enormously. Perhaps it will be said that he murdered one or both of his wives to marry Isotta, his mistress, but in fact, when they died, whether by his hand or by misadventure, he did not marry her. Let it be far from us to "whitewash" Sigismondo or to attribute to him the virtues or the sentimentality of our own time. He himself could write

> Porto le corne che ognuno le vede
> E tal le porta che non se lo crede

and he was cynical and vicious; but we need not believe that so cunning and sinister a soldier was a fool, nor must we take the malice of Pope Pius II too seriously. That great man was the overlord of the Malatesta and he had an unruly vassal. He wanted Sigismondo's lordship, and it was not long before his successor obtained it; he hated him too for his supposed betrayal of Siena in the service of Alfonso of Aragon. Both politically as Pope, and personally as a Sienese, Pius was prejudiced against Sigismondo, and his prejudice makes his evidence at least suspicious. The worst accusation brought against Sigismondo, however, is not the murder of his wives, but the violent rape and murder of a stranger, a great German lady on her way back from Rome, where she had been for the Jubilee of 1450. Concerning this we do not know whether the tale be true or not. The accuser is Pius II. Battaglini in his Life of Sigismondo absolutely denies it, adding that the murderer could not be found, and it is certain that Pope Nicholas V, who visited Sigismondo in Rimini immediately after he is supposed to have committed this appalling outrage, did not believe it.

By this defence of Sigismondo I do not mean to claim

that he was a good or a virtuous man. He was a man of his time, the mirror of his age, corrupt, powerful, full of force, a splendid nature divided against itself ; in him, as in his age, a barbarian fought with a god and was often, perhaps finally, victorious. If, after all, he was guilty of these foul murders, that was the barbarian in him. Let us turn now to the god.

Of his fine generalship and soldierly qualities, of the great and famous fortress he built in Rimini, I have already spoken, but he was also a poet of considerable achievement and some distinction, and, above all, he was a noble humanist. As a friend and patron of art, and especially of letters in his own day, he is not behind Lorenzo de' Medici in his enthusiasm. Lorenzo had better opportunities, but he was perhaps not capable of the personal devotion and service which Sigismondo gladly gave to the cause he had at heart. And of course he was the victim of his passion. A host of pedants settled at Rimini and lived upon him, dictated to him in matters of taste, and can only have succeeded in not enraging him because of the purity of his enthusiasm. Porcellio, Basinio, Trebanio, their very names seem to tell us what they were. But four men at least he knew and loved who were worthy of his friendship—Valturio, the engineer, who built the Rocca ; Leon Alberti, who built the Tempio, a vast mausoleum of marble contrived out of the old Gothic brick church of S. Francesco and the spoil of S. Apollinare in Classe ; Piero della Francesca, who painted him there kneeling before S. Sigismund of Burgundy ; and Vittore Pisano, who struck medals in his honour. The work of these men, the compelling figure of Isotta, and his own astonishing personality, have won him a foremost place in the records of that age in Italy we call the Renaissance.

But Sigismondo's enthusiasm for letters did not end with the patronage of scholars and poets and the building of his famous Tempio. Towards the end of his life he found himself, a condottiere in the service of Venice, upon the sacred soil of Greece. Around him were scattered the riches of our museums, the marbles, the vases, the inscriptions, which seem to us the noblest and most beautiful things in the world. Yet he left them all untouched, and brought back as loot the body of a " saint of scholarship, the authentic bones of the great Platonist, Gemisthus Pletho," and these he defended with his life and laid at last in a stone sarcophagus outside his Tempio in Rimini ; you may find them there to this day. Others contended for a costly prize : for him there was the crown of wild olive.

The end of his life was characteristic in its passionate failure. Having lost everything but Isotta and the city of Rimini, having been burnt in effigy in Rome and pressed to surrender to the Holy See even the city of his ancestors, which he had loved and glorified his whole life long, he turned as a rat turns and faced his foe. Taking with him only Gasparre Broglio, his lieutenant and biographer, and a few trusted followers, he set out on horseback, suddenly, for Rome to meet the Pope—Paul II it was—face to face, a dagger hidden in his bosom. He obtained audience, though only after some delay ; but the Pope had had word of his intent, for when he received him it was in the midst of his cardinals, and when Sigismondo, coming before him, suddenly drew his dagger, their swords flashed out from under their scarlet robes. He flung the dagger at the Pope's feet, falling on his knees.

Paul II spared him, but he returned to Rimini none the less broken-hearted, a dying man. Winter came and spring and summer, and still he was only weary, till at last, on October 7, 1468, he breathed his last in the arms of Isotta, whom he had so much loved.

In Rimini to-day it is only the strange and tragic personality of Sigismondo, its lord, that touches us. The work of the Romans, the noble bridge over the Marecchia by which the Via Emilia leaves the town, the curious Forum in which that great road meets the Via Flaminia, the glorious arch of Augustus under which that great way comes in from Rome, can scarcely draw us away from the miserable ruin of the mighty Rocca which Sigismondo built by the

8

hands of Valturio, and the Tempio Malatestiano, which he
contrived out of the old church of Francesco by the hand of
Leon Alberti.   This, at any rate, remains actually as he left
it, unfinished but perhaps more interesting on that account.

The church of S. Francesco was originally a Gothic
building of brick; this Sigismondo did not destroy, but contrived to cover inside and out with marble after the design
of Alberti in the style of the early Renaissance.   The
façade, which is unfinished, is very noble indeed and is
adapted from the arch of Augustus which doubtless im-
pressed Alberti, eager as he was to appreciate every fragment
of antiquity.   On either side of the old church he built a
vast arcade of marble with round arches, behind which the
pointed windows of the old church shine, and under which
are placed great stone sarcophagi in which repose the dust
of pedants and poets, the bones of Valturio and of the
Platonist Gemisthus Pletho which Sigismondo, with so
many pains, brought back with him from Greece.   Upon
the plinth are the arms of Sigismondo and his emblem and
Isotta's, the elephant and the rose.   The dome, which,
according to Alberti, was to have surmounted the whole,
was never built.   The choir, as we see it, is a restoration of
the old church done in 1709, for Leon Alberti's design had
only been applied to the nave and body of the church when
Sigismondo came to ruin.

Within, the church is strange, lovely, and, above all
significant of the age and of the man who contrived and of
the man who built it.   Pope Pius II asserted that it resembled
a Pagan temple rather than a Christian church; but then
as we have seen, he was Sigismondo's enemy and wanted an
excuse to burn him in effigy in Rome.   The effect is rich
and noble, and, rightly understood, is no more reminiscent
of a Pagan temple than is S. Peter's.

As one comes into the church, on the right, built into
the wall, Sigismondo has caused his own tomb to be made.
It was to have been after the design of Leon Alberti, but
that was never carried out, what we see being the work

of Bernardo Ciuffagni. On the sarcophagus is graven in antique letters this inscription : SUM . SIGISMUNDUS . MALATESTE . E . SANGUINE . GENTIS . PANDULFUS . GENITOR . PATRIA . FLAMINIA . EST. Later was carved in small letters the date of his death.

Of the chapels, that first on the right is dedicated to S. Sigismund of Burgundy. Over the altar is the statue of the saint seated on the elephant of Sigismondo between two pillars of Greek marble, over which on the architrave is a frieze of children's heads and flowers, and above, in the arch, the shield of Sigismondo—all by Bernardo Ciuffagni ; while on either side is carved his shield bearing his monogram or cipher. This monogram has been generally supposed to represent " the entwined names of Sigismondo and Isotta," but this is very doubtful. It would seem to be merely the first two letters of Sigismondo's name, and as a monogram to be in keeping with the traditions and practice of his family. The rose, which is everywhere scattered through the church, may perhaps be Isotta's emblem, but is more likely to refer to the gift of the golden rose which Sigismondo received from Nicholas V.

On the walls of the chapel are great winged angels holding a canopy. Under that, to the left, was of old a beautiful bronze grille by Maso di Bartolommeo, through which one looked into the Chapel of the Relics. The balustrade consists of three pillars, on which *putti* stand with the shield of Sigismondo and a marvellous screen of intertwined garlands, and above, on one side, the emblem of the rose, and on the other the cipher of Sigismondo. The piers which divide this chapel from the next are covered with reliefs of the theological and cardinal Virtues by Ciuffagni.

The next chapel is that of the Relics. It is closed by a wall so that it cannot be seen from the church. In this wall Matteo da Pasti has built a door, one of the loveliest in Italy. On either side of the doorway he has carved three prophets, and between them medallions and coats, while above, on the lintel, he has made in a medallion an allegory

of *Virtù*, Force seated on two elephants breaking a column
as in the medals he made for Sigismondo. In the triangles
formed by the arch he has carved two *putti* astride dolphins,
and below the shield of Sigismondo. Within, in 1451,
Piero della Francesca painted Sigismondo kneeling before
S. Sigismund of Burgundy, his patron saint, in fresco.
Behind the figure of Sigismondo are his two greyhounds,
and in a medallion within the picture we see the famous
Rocca.

We now come to the chapel of S. Michael the Archangel,
really the mausoleum of Isotta, first the mistress and then
the wife of Sigismondo. The figure of the Archangel over
the altar by Ciuffagni is a portrait of Isotta, and the whole
chapel is decorated in her honour, the tomb being upon the
wall on the left, a beautiful sarcophagus, supported by
elephants with the shield of Sigismondo over it, and above
two elephants' heads, very splendid. There we read :
TEMPUS LOQUENDI, TEMPUS TACENDI ; and on the tomb
itself Sigismondo carved her name : DIVAE ISOTTAE
ARIMINENSI, B.M. SACRUM MCCCCL. The decorations of this
chapel are very splendid. Upon the pillars we see eighteen
bas-reliefs by Sperandio, illustrating, as I think, a poem by
Sigismondo in honour of Isotta. What we see is a whole
company of angels, playing instruments of music, organs
horns, tambours, viols, harps, cymbals and flutes ; some are
seated, some are dancing ; here two sing lustily together
clashing the cymbals ; there one shouts in welcome with
uplifted hand, proffering the rose.

This joyful company of children is but the herald, as it
were, of a whole world of glad immortal creatures, gods
and heroes that Simone Fiorentini and Agostino di Duccio
have carved for the pillars of the next chapel, that of S
Girolamo, and for those two on the other side of the nave
the Cappella della Madonna dell' Acqua and the Cappella
del Beato Galeotto. In the chapel of S. Girolamo we seem
to come upon the very gods themselves, but they are but
the signs of the zodiac, the planets and constellations in

which indeed the gods still remain to us. Here is Diana on her high triumphal car, drawn by beautiful horses, the crescent moon in her immortal hand. Here is Mercurius, all plumed, holding the snaky Caduceus, a viol in his hand, and under his strange Eastern head-dress his gold locks tumble on his shoulders. Here Venus Aphrodite comes over the sea naked and beautiful, drawn by swans in her car of silver, and in her hand is a shell from the foam of Cypris. There Saturn stands with a sickle in his hand about to kill his own son ; here Mars, on a great scythed chariot drawn by horses, with uplifted sword, threatens the world ; while great Jove, the eagle crouched on his serene head, for ever forbears to hurl the ready thunderbolt. Nor is this all, for here come three lesser gods, the Heavenly Twins, Cancer the Crab, Scorpio and the rest, among them a great Goat and Eolus, the wind, and there is the elephant of Sigismondo, and the city of Rimini, for this was the heavenly sign under which Sigismondo was born. All these subjects, like those in the Cappella di S. Michele, are taken from one of Sigismondo's poems and refer to the signs of heaven, not to the Pagan gods ; but these were the works which doubtless offended Pope Pius II. About the chapel is a gracious frieze of *putti* running and bearing garlands, supporting now the shield of Sigismondo, now his cipher.

Opposite this chapel, which is the richest in the whole Tempio, is the chapel of S. Gaudenzio. There, on the pillars, Agostino di Duccio has carved eighteen bas-reliefs of the arts and sciences, and some of these are as lovely as anything of the kind in Italy.

In the next chapel, that of Beato Galeotto, the holy dust of this saint of the Malatesta family was laid, and there, too, Sigismondo buried his two wives, Ginevra d'Este and Polissena Sforza. Simone Fiorentino has carved here, on the pillars, eighteen bas-reliefs of children playing, delightful things ; for in one place they dance around a gushing fountain, laughing at one another, and again they play together in the sea or ride on dolphins, and there they play with the rose, and here they hide behind the letters of Sigismondo's name.

The next chapel, like the Chapel of the Relics opposite to it, is closed. The carvings, however, are very good, representing Samson and Saul, David and Joshua, with the escutcheon and the portrait of Sigismondo crowned with laurels.

In the last chapel, the chapel of the Madonna dell' Acqua, Sigismondo gathered the dust of all those of his race who were before him in the lordship of Rimini and laid it in a sarcophagus made for him by Agostino di Duccio, of Greek marble and nobly carved with two bas-reliefs, one representing Pallas in her temple, surrounded by the race of the Malatesta, where before all, his sword in his hand, stands Sigismondo himself, the other representing his Triumph. The Triumphal Car, drawn by horses and decked with captives, passes under a Roman arch decorated with roses and hung with shields bearing his cipher. Upon the car, enthroned, rides Sigismondo, and far away in the distance rises the fortress of Rocca Contrada, which he captured—his greatest victory. Between the two reliefs we read : SIGISMUNDUS . PANDULFUS . MALATESTA . PANDULFI . F. INGENTIBUS . MERITIS . PROBITATIS. FORTITUDINIS . QUE ILLUSTRI . GENERIS . SUO . MAJORIBUS . POSTERISQUE."

Such was the Temple Sigismondo raised to God in his own honour and in honour of his mistress, Isotta. In its astonishing beauty and representative significance there is nothing to compare with it in Italy or in the world.

But little remains in Rimini that is not connected with Sigismondo, but among that little is the Library in the Via Gambalunga, founded by the jurist Gambalunga in 1617 ; the Picture Gallery in the Municipio, where there is a very lovely early work, a Pietà by Giovanni Bellini, which was perhaps painted for Sigismondo, a fine Ghirlandaio, and a medallion portrait of Augustus, which certainly was. A charming little chapel in the Piazza Giulio Cesare upon the spot where S. Anthony once preached, which may well be due to

Sigismondo, and the pictures by Paolo Veronese, a large altarpiece of the Martyrdom of S. Giuliano in the church of that name near the Ponte d'Augusto. But Rimini remains worth visiting because of that curiously sinister and yet compelling figure who was her lord in the middle of the fifteenth century.

CHAPTER VII

THE REPUBLIC OF SAN MARINO

THERE is one excursion, most conveniently made from Rimini, which no one who is interested in the curious things of Europe will omit, I mean the journey into the Republic of S. Marino, that little state of some thirty-eight square miles, with a population of about ten thousand souls, which here, in the midst of Italy, still retains its independence. It is a pleasant thing, and a salutary thing, to remind oneself now and then of such a little state as this, which, in spite of the greed and aggression and vulgar ambition of the great nations, has been able, partly, it is true, by good luck, but with a sturdiness we must all admire, to maintain its own character, its liberty and its right to live. Not one of the Germanic nations, though each was infinitely stronger, richer and more populous, than this little republic, has been able to save itself alive; but this little Latin people have been able to accomplish it, and it is significant that its only fellow is the Gallo-Iberian Republic of Andorra upon the confines of France and Spain. A straw will show which way the wind blows, and I think in these days, when the second-rate efficiency of the Teuton threatens to engulf everything that is vital and characteristic in Europe, we should be eager to encourage and consider such little states as those of Andorra and S. Marino. Not that they can in any way help to stem the flood of mud that rolls over us all from the Germanies, but that in their happiness and sturdy independence they serve as examples of all that we should lose by a Germanic domination, under which all

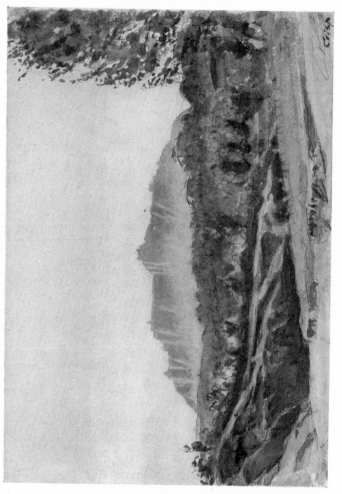

SAN MARINO

that is most divine in us, most characteristic and genuine, would be smothered by the most accursed mediocrity that has ever appeared in Europe, and would be crushed out of existence by a system, a training and a tradition essentially barbarous, atheistic and hopeless.

The road into the Republic leaves Rimini by the Porta Montanara. For the first few miles the way is dull enough and would be monotonous but for the gay country people coming into the city in their jolly carts, red and blue, and painted with all manner of flowers, drawn by noble white oxen which labour slowly along the road. Presently, however, the great grey cliff, triple-towered, upon which S. Marino stands, rears into the sky—a glorious and rugged outline—rendered impregnable by nature, one might think, against the invader. The road climbs slowly through all the twelve miles of the way, through vineyards and olive gardens, with nothing in view but the gaunt and yet noble face of the Republic, till under the eastern front of the great cliff upon which the capital is set we have a fine view to the north of Verucchio, whence came the Malatesta, of Scorticata and Montebello, with its Rocca behind Verucchio over the lean and pallid valley, wide and almost empty of water, of the Marecchia, which flows by Rimini to the sea.

At the Borgo, under Monte Titano, as this rugged grey rock which towers over everything and commands a world as marvellous in its noble beauty as is to be had in Italy, is called, it is best to leave your carriage, if you have one, and to climb into the city of S. Marino afoot as one did of old.

For myself, having known S. Marino so long, I always pass first quite through the little city with its rude churches and its old houses and gardens and by-ways, straight up to the Rocca, whence I may look over the mountains and the sea, and recall the history of Europe and all that past out of which have come two things so alike and yet so different as England and S. Marino. Lying there on the great tower and hearing in the stillness of the hot summer afternoon the steel shoes of the asses a thousand feet below on the white road, I look westward towards the vast mass of Monte Carpegna, with S. Leo, the brother of S. Marino, like a fortress to the north, and to the south all the dear hills and mountains of the March, and to the east the wideness of the sea. Then it is that I like to recall the story of S. Marino.

For it seems that, as long ago as the fourth century of our era, there were in Dalmatia, whose mountains one may just see at dawn from this very place, two stone-masons, by name Marinus and Leo, who were Christians, and who, because they loved Our Lord, set out from home to come to Rimini to repair the walls of that city which had been destroyed, and to succour the Christians there who were sorely persecuted. But when they had been a little while in Rimini they found that the fate of the Christians within the city was not so hard as that of those in the country places, wherefore they set out, Marinus for Monte Titano, Leo for Monte Feliciano, to do what they could, and there they established hermitages and succoured the peasants round about.

Now Monte Titano then belonged to a certain noble Riminese lady, by name Felicissima, who at her death bequeathed it to Marinus and his companions, for many had come to him from the cities round about ; and she recommended only this in making her gift—that they should always remain united and apart.

What was the fate of S. Marino during the barbarian invasion we have no means of knowing, but when the Lombards had established themselves in Italy, it appears, first as a part of the Exarchate, and then as an appurtenance of the Lombard duchy of Spoleto. By then a monastery had been founded there, whose abbots in the tenth century would seem to have been subject to the civil government, but they soon contrived to regain their independence and to establish S. Marino as a free commune, whose complete independence was recognized by the Papacy in 1291. In the hurly-burly, here in the March, of the fourteenth and fifteenth centuries that independence was very often in grave danger, first from the Montefeltri and then from the Malatesta of Rimini, and especially from Sigismondo, who for a time made himself master there, but the Sammarinesi learned how to play off one tyrant against another, and the Pope against them all. To get rid of the Malatesta they placed themselves under the protection of the Counts and Dukes of Urbino, and eagerly aided Pope Pius II against Sigismondo, in reward receiving some of his castles. A more relentless foe, however, appeared in the person of Cesare Borgia, who had expelled the Duke from Urbino, and under the protection of the Pope was acquiring a state in the March. He seized the Republic in 1503 and held it, though only for a few months. When Pope Urban III in 1631 took possession of the Duchy of Urbino he was not wise or just or generous enough to recognize the independence of S. Marino, which the Duchy had really maintained since the middle of the thirteenth century. Nevertheless, just a century later, S. Marino nearly fell by reason of a conspiracy within her gates. This failed, but the attempt upon her liberty was renewed in 1739 by the Cardinal Alberoni, Papal Legate of Ravenna, though, it is said, contrary to the orders of Pope Clement XII. He invaded the Republic, imposed a new constitution upon the people, and attempted to force them to submit to his government.

Not quite sixty years later, in 1797, the great soldier of the Revolution doffed his hat to her and offered to enlarge her territory, but she was wise enough to refuse. In the great reorganization of Italy which he attempted, he, respecting her sturdy independence and her littleness, re-fused to destroy a thing so old and so noble by incorporating it in any greater state. " Let us keep S. Marino," said he, " as a model of the Republic." And it was so. When the reaction came, and with the defeat of Napoleon the " kings crept out again to feel the sun," S. Marino, independent still, returned under the protection of the Papacy, and although attempts were made both in 1825 and in 1853 against her liberty, Victor Emmanuel and the kingdom of United Italy respected it, and by an Act of March 22, 1862, recognized the independence of the Republic, and ever since Italy has maintained friendly relations with it.

The government thus guaranteed might seem to be a model for a small state.   It is administered by two *Capitani Reggenti*, elected for six months from the General Council, which is composed of sixty members elected for life and chosen from the nobles, burgesses and rural landowners in equal numbers.   This is no servile state with a large proletariat, but an agricultural commune, such as England happily remained till modern times.   The Council thus chosen has legislative powers, a Council of twelve being chosen from its members to form the Supreme Court, and altogether there is no happier or better governed community of people in Europe.   Every one is patriotic and ready to serve in the national militia which guards the Republic of the Three Hills.   This militia is composed of nine companies —thirty-eight officers and nine hundred and fifty men, and the whole population is properly proud of it.

Height—it is that which everywhere strikes the mind in S. Marino—dizzy, perilous height, with a sheer fall into the world a thousand feet, or ten thousand feet, for all one knows, below.   One feels this most, of course, on the tower of the Rocca, chiefly because the houses protect one all the way up.   Lying there on the top of the great tower on a summer afternoon in the scanty shadow of the bastions one reminds oneself slowly of all those things of which I have spoken, looking out across that great and beautiful world over which S. Marino hovers like a hawk or an eagle.   Before one lie the two other towers that with this of the Rocca crown the triple hill, the Torre della Fratta and the Torre del Montale, and far away one descries the brood of houses that is Urbino, and the great wedge of rock that is S. Leo, the road up to which Dante knew as he knew all this country, and found so steep that he uses it as a likeness to the mountain road of Purgatory :

Who travels on S. Leo's road . . .
Must use his feet.

Surely it was from some such height as this that that
eagle mind saw and considered Italy, and told us of it in
words of bronze, as when he speaks of the Malatesta :

The old mastiff of Verucchio and the young
That tore Montagna in their wrath still make
Where they are wont an auger of their fangs. . . .

or of Faenza and Imola, now far away, of the turncoat
Pagani and of Cesena :

Lamone's city and Santerno's range,
Under the lion of the snowy lair,
Inconstant partisan that changeth sides
Or ever summer yields to winter's frost.
And she whose flank is washed by Savio's wave,
As 'twixt the level and the steep she lies,
Lives so 'twixt tyrant power and liberty.

As our eyes linger, however, on that almost brutally up-
reared cliff that is S. Leo, one thinks of a very different man
from Dante—one thinks of Cagliostro, for he died there in
prison in 1795.   The charlatan that was Giuseppe Balsamo
and called himself Count Alessandro di Cagliostro had, I
suppose, a career as amazing as any man ever had.   One
runs over it, gazing at his prison and his grave.   Born at
Palermo of poor parents in 1743, he ran away from school
at thirteen, and was then sent to a monastery where he
became assistant to the apothecary.   It was here he picked
up what he knew of chemistry.   But he soon tired of a
monastery, as the monastery did of him, and after a loose
life in Palermo, in 1767, he set out to see the world and seek
his fortune in the company of a Greek philosopher, one
Alhotas.   With him he is supposed to have visited Greece,
Egypt and Asia Minor.   When at last he returned to Italy,
it was Rome he made for, and there he married a very pretty
woman, Lorenza Feliciani, whom he used as his accomplice
in the extraordinary career of fraud he now determined to

engage upon. In 1771 he and his wife set out to visit the
capitals of Europe, from Warsaw to London. Cagliostro
posed as physician, philosopher, alchemist, necromancer
and spiritualist, as best served his purposes, making a fortune
out of his " Elixir of Immortal Youth," and founding lodges
of " Egyptian freemasons." In Paris he was mixed up in
the affair of the Diamond Necklace and spent some time in
the Bastille in consequence. In 1789 he returned to Rome.
There the Inquisition caught him founding " some feeble
ghost of an Egyptian lodge." He was imprisoned and condemned to death for freemasonry, but his sentence was never
carried out. Instead he spent the rest of his life, some six
years, in the fortress of S. Leo. His wife meantime became
a nun and ended her days in a convent.

The Rocca of San Marino cannot boast of so strange a
prisoner as that, but in spite of its silence, now so fierce
even in its quietness, the old fortress need not fear to out-
face San Leo. It defied, for how long, Sigismondo Malatesta
the most cunning, though not the most successful, soldier of
his day ; it received, though reluctantly, the caress of
Cesare Borgia, who doubtless, from the very place where
I lay considering all this, mapped out his campaign and
enjoyed his principality ; and it remains to entertain you
from America, or me from England, and to receive us as
the fortress of a sovereign-state.

Indeed, for all its aspect of peace, this little Republic
must be a very fierce and terrible thing. It has escaped,
though Tripoli cannot match its fruitfulness—it and its ten
thousand happy people. Truly one notes as one wanders
up and down the old steep ways hewn out of the rock
between the houses that seem part of the very mountain,
how proud the Sammarinesi are of their country and their
liberty. Libertas, that glorious and dangerous word—it
is their motto—you see it everywhere, as you may in Siena,
only here it is engraved too in the hearts of these moun-
taineers who may so lordly look down upon the rest of the
world.

Dear and simple people, may they ever enjoy the " rights of man " and breathe their mountain air as free-men ! Indeed, that is your prayer, or should be, in every little church you enter in the rugged little country, and especially in S. Francesco. For S. Francesco is old, and one can pray there, whereas the Duomo was built, unfortun-ately, in 1836. San Francesco, however, is old and humble and contains, too, more than one precious thing—precious at least in San Marino, such as the fine sepulchral stone carved in relief with the figure of the dead it hides, the Bishop Madroni, a famous personage. There, too, are pictures by Girolamo da Cotignola ; a curious altarpiece of the Immaculate Conception in which we see Madonna kneeling in prayer, a Bishop on either side, while God the Father appears in heaven surrounded by the Cherubim, who bear the legend : NON EST PRO TE SED PRO OMNIBUS HEC LEX CONSTITUTA EST. In the other picture we see Madonna enthroned with her little Son, surrounded by S. John Baptist, S. Francis, S. Marino and perhaps Felicissima. On the steps of the throne are two music-making angels.

Even these things, however, so rare in such a place as this, are not the rarest in S. Francesco. For we may still see there, though sadly damaged, the work of Niccolò da Foligno, four figures of Franciscan saints—of S. Celestino, and S. Francesco, and S. Bonaventura, and S. Antony of Padua. At least one could when I was last in S. Marino, but I see Mr. Berenson catalogues them as in the Municipio. There, indeed, is the big polyptych by Giulio Romano, cheek by jowl with Pompeo Batini's picture of S. Marino himself in the act of founding the Republic.

The grave and tomb of S. Marino are in the Cathedral, and are the only reason why one should pay it a visit.

When all is said, however, even when one has counted the old houses that are so picturesque a feature in this little city, the Casa Braschi, for instance, the Casa Tonnini, the Portico of S. Chiara and the fine old convent, the Casa Gozi and the wonderful streets all of old steps and stone stairways, the great gates and even the beautiful church and convent of the Cappuccini, what remains most interesting in S. Marino is the Sammarinesi and the views they have, from every part of their city and indeed from all over the Republic, but best from the fierce old Rocca, over the world. It is these which bring one to San Marino again and again and again, and make the long road out from Rimini, or the hard but glorious way from S. Arcangelo, seem nothing to pay for the joy of seeing them once more.

CHAPTER VIII

PESARO AND GRADARA

IT was a rainy morning when I left Rimini at last, and by train on account of the weather, for Pesaro ; but I had not been in that delightful little city—one of the pleasant-st in all the Marches—more than a few hours when the un shone out again and Pesaro showed me a smiling face, as ndeed I cannot but think she does to every one who enters er gates. I do not rightly know what it is in Pesaro that aakes me feel always so happy there ; whether it be the harm of her wide Piazza with its beautiful Palazzo della 'refettura, or the kindness and hospitality of her citizens, nd not least of these who keep the inn, the Albergo Zongo, hat noble old palace once a cardinal's, dark and forbidding t first, but always to be remembered with pleasure and ratitude, or whether, after all, one's pleasure lies not so uch in Pesaro herself as in the delight of the country in vhich she lies. Perhaps the happiness and lightness of eart that always come to me in this little city by that miling morning sea is the result of all these charming things, or once to be had altogether and enjoyed without an fterthought.

For you may spend your morning pottering about the old own where there is nothing very serious to see, but where verything that meets your eye is graceful and charming. 'our afternoon you may spend in the delightful rooms, ardens and terraces of the Villa Imperiale, where that eonora, whom it is said Titian painted as Venus, as you aay see in the Uffizi Gallery to this day, will seem to pass

9

and repass, waiting the return of Francesco Maria of Urbino or you may drive out to the great Rocca of Gradara, which the Malatesta built and held so long where there are two priceless treasures that certainly Pesaro cannot match On your return from either villa or fortress, towards sunset you may linger by the Porto, where there is so much sleepy movement, the sound of ships and of the sea and a light and a colour that, till one has found them there, have seemed merely fabulous, too good to be true, too precious to be seen by these mortal eyes.   And for the evening, one strolls out of the great shadowy rooms of the Albergo Zongo down the rough way into the Piazza and sits at the *caffe* under the arches of the Prefettura, listening to a country song, watching the people and catching now and then the tinkle of a mandolin, the throb of a guitar. All one's days and nights in Pesaro are full of melodies, of form and colour and sound and no one can be the least surprised to learn that Rossini was born there, for the whole city and the hills and woods about it are full of music, to which the sea continually beats a grave and sober accompaniment, gently breaking in a line of foam along the shore.

The city, so enchanting in its simple beauty and quietness to-day, has a long history. Situated in Umbrian territory later occupied by the Gauls, it seems to have become a Roman colony as early as 184 B.C., if indeed the town was not then first founded. Its position upon the Flaminian Way, which runs quite through it, ensured it a good measure of prosperity, as long as the Roman administration lasted and of this good fortune we hear much in the letters of Cicero, but beyond that we know nothing of it before the fall of the Empire. In the Gothic Wars of Belisarius it suffered a memorable siege and was destroyed by Vitiges, but when the Exarchate had been established it rose again to prosperity as one would expect, and it appears as one of the five cities of the maritime Pentapolis. In that destruction, however, all its antiquities perished, and, in the town we know, nothing of Roman times remains to us.

What we have in Pesaro is a city of the Middle Age and the Renaissance. It came to the Pope with the rest of the Pentapolis, but in the appalling confusion of the tenth century we find it boasting a count of its own, one Alberic. We know little or nothing of it till suddenly the Malatesta appear as Podestà there, the famous or infamous Giovanni *o sciancato*, the husband and murderer of Francesca da Rimini, filling that office in 1285. He was then in possession of the Rocca of Gradara, and the stronghold so close to the little city by the sea enabled him to make himself master of Pesaro. He was succeeded apparently by his brother, Pandolfo, whom the Pope turned out, but he returned, and presently, when Malatestino, the brother who had succeeded to Rimini on *lo sciancato's* death, came to die, he added Senigallia, Fano and Fossombrone to his lordship and would have added more still but that Clement V, fearing for his states, sent Bertrand de Got against him. However, Pandolfo managed to hold his own, or what he claimed as his own, and was invested in his lordship in 1325 by a bull of Pope John XXII. This Pandolfo had two sons, Pendolfo Guastafamiglia and Galeotto. These two faced the great warrior, Cardinal Albornoz, with varying success, and at last the Papacy, far away in Avignon, invested Galeotto with the lordship of Rimini, and Guastafamiglia with that of Pesaro. From this man are the Malatesta of Pesaro descended.

The branch of the Malatesta stock descended from Guastafamiglia held Pesaro till the year 1435, when Galeazzo Malatesta, having quarrelled with Sigismondo of Rimini, called in the great enemy of the latter Federigo of Montefeltro to his assistance. Ten years later Galeazzo sold the city for 20,000 florins to Francesco Sforza, on the understanding that it would be handed over to Alessandro Sforza, the great Francesco's brother, who had married a niece of Galeazzo's. It remained with the Sforza till, in 1500, Cesare Borgia came down and took it. Giovanni Sforza, who then held it, had flattered himself that the hurricane which was Cesare would pass him by, for he was under the protection of Venice, and he had been the husband of Lucrezia Borgia.[1] He found out his mistake in time, however, and remembering the fate of the Riarii, fled to Venice.

Cesare entered Pesaro in October " with an imposing display of luxurious military equipments." We read of men at arms in sumptuous liveries of red and yellow, worn over richly chased cuirasses, their belts studded with serpents' heads. But Cesare happily, or unhappily, was soon done with, and Giovanni Sforza returned in 1504. He died, however, in 1510, leaving an only son, Costanzo, then a child. His natural brother, Galeazzo, ruled in Pesaro as regent, but Costanzo died in 1512, and Galeazzo had so completely won the goodwill of the people that they proclaimed him lord. This, however, did not accord with the desires of the Pope. The investiture of Pesaro had legally lapsed with Costanzo's death, and Julius II claimed it as overlord. Sforza resisted the claim, and Julius immediately sent the Duke of Urbino against him. After a brief resistance, Galeazzo surrendered the citadel and quitted Pesaro, attended, it is said, by nearly the whole population. They accompanied him as far as La Cattolica, on the road to Rimini ; there he left them to go to Milan and to die in the following year.

Pesaro was now governed by the Cardinal-Legate Sigismondo Gonzaga. The Pope had boasted that he would bring all the fiefs of the Marches under the direct authority of the Holy See, but he was not a Rovere for nothing. He had already made an exception in favour of Urbino, where his nephew was Duke, and now one of his last acts was to invest the same lord with Pesaro to be held in vicariat for the annual payment of a silver vase, one pound in weight. The Bull was dated February 16, 1513 ; less than a week

[1] The betrothal had been celebrated in 1493 by a ball in Pesaro, from which the guests issued forth in couples, dancing through the streets a sort of polonaise led by the Papal ambassador. The marriage was annulled by the Pope in 1497.

later the Pope was dead. Nevertheless, three weeks later the Duke and Duchess of Urbino entered Pesaro in state.

It was some eight years later, however, that Pesaro became for a time the permanent residence of the Ducal household, and in 1529, during the absence of the Duke at the wars, the Duchess Leonora received Pope Clement VII there, on his way to crown Charles V at Bologna. Later, Clement VIII, Titian and Tasso were entertained there.

The Dukes of Urbino held Pesaro till the end, when, on the death of the last of them, the more than half-crazy Francesco Maria, in 1631, the whole Duchy, with Pesaro, passed directly into the hands of the Holy See, where it remained till modern times.

Partly, maybe, on account of the conservative administration of the Popes, but partly too because the Pesaresi are themselves proud of their traditions, Pesaro everywhere reminds you of her origins. In what remains of the beautiful church of S. Domenico, we see the work of one who laboured in the service : " *Magnifici et Excellentissimi Domini Malatestæ nati quondam recolendæ memoriæ Domini Pandulphi de Malatesta.*" The church dates indeed from about 1390, and is one of the first buildings most of us see in the city, for it stands at the entrance to the Piazza Maggiore, close to the Albergo Zongo. The most lovely door of the church, adorned with sculptures of God the Father, S. John Baptist and S. Mark in the tympanum, and with seven other saints set upon the pilasters and the arch in niches, is said to be the work of a local master.

From this door of S. Domenico it is but a step into the noble Piazza Maggiore, the centre of the city, where upon one side rises the splendid Palazzo della Prefettura, built by Laurana, it is said, in the middle of the fifteenth century for the Sforza, and completed by Girolamo Genga and his son for the Duke of Urbino in the following century. The great hall within was the ball-room in which Lucrezia Borgia danced in 1493. Before that, however, it had been the scene of the marriage of Costenzo Sforza in 1475 with

Camilla of Aragon. The ceiling is of later date and is due to the Rovere, a work of the sixteenth century.

Passing in front of the Prefettura, one goes down the Via Rossini past that master's house on the right, to the Duomo Vecchio with its great façade of brick. The church has been restored out of all recognition, but I happened there on the feast of its dedication in October, the feast of S. Terenziano, nor shall I ever forget it, for I demanded of an aged woman in the crowd in the nave what feast was celebrated there on that day with so noisy a cacophany of unruly voices within sound of Rossini's house, to be answered : " *Signore, c'è la Festa di San Terenziano nostro protettore.*" May he protect them for ever and ever.

The church of S. Francesco, which till lately has been used as the cathedral, is a far more interesting church if only on account of its very glorious portal, where in the arch is a fine sculpture of the Madonna and Child between S. Francis and, I think, S. Peter. Above, on either side, is an Annunciation, and on the apex of the arch the Madonna with a saint below on either side. This beautiful doorway should be compared with that of S. Domenico which I have tried to describe, and with that of S. Agostino in the Corso, with its strangely elaborate pinnacles, a later work.

A few other buildings remain of some interest : the Rocca, built by Giovanni Sforza, not far from S. Francesco ; the Rocchetta, on the other side of the city ; and the church of S. Giovanni Battista, begun by Girolamo Genga (1540). Nor should anyone fail to visit the Orto Giulio, if only for the delicious view it offers of the river and the port.

But in sights, as apart from mere pleasure, the pleasure to be had in any old city in Italy, reverend by reason of its age and the love men have borne it, Pesaro is not very rich. Yet it can offer more than one notable picture, and, I suppose, the finest collection of Italian majolica in the world.

To begin with the pictures. In the ex-church of S. Ubaldo is an altarpiece by Giovanni Bellini, once in S.

Francesco, a Coronation of the Blessed Virgin with four saints and many charming predella scenes, a curious work most unfortunately damaged. The predella scenes are especially lovely.

In the Museo Mosca, opposite Rossini's house in the Via Rossini, are several charming minor works ; a Madonna and Child by Rondani ; a notable cornice of the seventeenth century ; a fine Tuscan portrait of Guicciardini the historian ; a charming Raffaellino del Colle, an Adoration of the Shepherds with a fine landscape, in which one seems to see the castle of Gradara ; and a Madonna and Child with S. Francis and three other saints, an interesting picture, perhaps by Catena.

In the Ateneo Pesarese, in the Palazzo Almerici, in the Via Mazza are some really fine works ; a head of S. John Baptist, by Marco Zoppo, and a curious Pietà from the same hand ; a strangely mystical picture in which we seem to see Madonna—or is it S. Anne ?—asleep, and in her sleep she sees a vision of the Garden of Eden where the Tree of the Knowledge of Good and Evil rises, bearing Our Lord stretched as upon a cross, the serpent curled about its trunk, and Adam and Eve eating of its forbidden fruit. Here, too, is a very lovely fourteenth-century triptych, a Florentine work, in which we see the Madonna and Child enthroned with an angel on either side, and beside them S. Michael and S. Francis. In the predella are four Franciscan saints, and in the midst the Flagellation, between S. John Baptist and S. John the Evangelist. A curious picture of S. Jerome in his study looks like a Venetian work, as does the really glorious picture of God the Father in heaven, while Simone da Bologna is the painter of a rather charming Coronation of the Virgin. The noble S. Ambrose comes out of the central marches and is of the school of Allegretto Nuzi ; and to Giovanni Francesco da Rimini is due the delightful Dominican picture of the Supper served by Angels. Six little panels of the Entry of Christ into Jerusalem, the Pentecost, the Woman of Samaria, Christ in Hades, the

Conversion of S. Paul, and Gethsemane are early fourteenth-century works from Tuscany. Lastly a picture of S. Bartholomew and the Emperor Constantine is a curious early work of Jacopo di Paolo.

But the Ateneo does not only boast of pictures, but of sculpture—you may see here good reliefs of Federigo of Montefeltro and Battista Sforza, perhaps by Laurana—and, as I have said, of the finest collection of majolica to be found anywhere. It consists of nearly six hundred pieces from Pesaro, Urbino, Castel Durante, and Gubbio, some of which are from the hand of the immortal Maestro Giorgio. It is impossible to describe such things ; they must be seen with the Italian sun upon them to give up all their delight.

Pesaro is thus not devoid of treasures, and yet, after all, she herself is better than all of them together, not excepting even so fair and wonderful a thing as the Villa Imperiale.

This glorious pleasure-house, built for love, is set on the hill to the north-west of the city and more than a mile from the gate. The villa is now the property of Principe Albani, who is kind enough to allow us to enjoy it if we provide ourselves with a permit at his palace in the Via Mazza (No. 5).

It was Alessandro Sforza, the first of that house to hold Pesaro, who first built a villa here, and it was an Emperor who laid the foundation stone for him—Frederick III, in 1469. But it was Eleonora Gonzaga, Francesco Maria's Duchess and perhaps Titian's Venus who caused Girolamo Genga to build, beside the old villa of the Sforza, a palace of delight, as a surprise for her husband, *a bellis redeunti animi ejus causa*. She never finished it, perhaps Francesco Maria returned too soon, but even as it is, what can one say of it, but that beyond anything of the sort in Urbino, or, indeed, in Italy, it brings back to us that age of pleasure which was to end in so appalling a catastrophe, so long a captivity. Here is a paradise of courts, hanging gardens, terraces, loggias, and above all a *bosco*, whence you may see Urbino, S. Marino, Monte Cònero and, above all, the sea, with the great heights of the central Apennines from Monte Carpegna southward, in the distance.

As for the two villas and their rooms, how may I describe them ? One treads there tiptoe, as it were following a ghost, the ghost of Titian's Venus, through the rooms which Girolamo Genga, Camillo Mantovano, Dosso Dossi, Angelo Bronzino and Raffaellino del Colle helped to decorate in honour of Duke Francesco Maria, his triumphs, his appointments, his glories, his vindications. Titian's Venus might seem indeed to have no place at all there. Yet indeed, when you come to think of it, there is no one there but she. For she lives for ever in Titian's canvases and trips lightly out of those heavy frames in the Uffizi and the Pitti palaces, tired of the tourists, to lead one through these empty faded rooms which she has loved, out into the *bosco* within sight of her own sea ; but who shall remember Duke Francesco Maria or anything that ever he did ?

Before leaving Pesaro for good, there is one journey to be made ; it will fill a spring day or a long afternoon in early summer, to the castle, about which is grouped the little town of Gradara. It is a drive of six miles perhaps, and though the road is a little dull the first sight of Gradara catches the breath, it is so splendid, and far away S. Marino shines. Quite apart from the interest to be found in this great ruined and half-empty Rocca which Giovanni Sforza built so splendidly in 1493, with its open court lined with the *stemme* of the Sforza, we shall find there more than one work of art of high importance and infinite charm and delight, for instance, a fine altarpiece by Giovanno della Robbia, and two fine pictures, one of them by Giovanni Santi of Urbino.

The Robbia altarpiece is in a little desecrated chapel half-way up the Rocca. There we see the Madonna and Child with S. Jerome and Mary Magdalen, S. Catherine and S. Bonaventura, and beneath, in the predella, three scenes —S. Francis receiving the Stigmata, the Annunciation, and S. Mary Magdalen in the desert communicated by an angel.

The main piece is all in blue and white, but the predella is in blue and white and green.

The pictures are in the Municipio. The work by Giovanni Santi shows us the Madonna and Child enthroned with S. Stefano, S. Sophia with her church, S. Michele and S. Giovanni Battista. Over the Madonna's head are three Cherubs, and the whole is in a lovely landscape. Upon the foot of the throne we read the following inscription : GRADARIE · SPECTĂDA · FUIT · ĪMPENSA · ET · IDUSTRIA · VIRI · D · DOMINICI · DE · DOMINICIS · VICARII · ANNO · DMCCCCLXXXIIII · DIE · X · APRILIS · ET · PER · DUOS · PRIUS · TEMPORE · D · IO · CANO · PI · RECTORIS · ECCLIE · S · SUPHIE · IONNES · SAN · URB · PINXIT. The picture is in a bad condition and getting rapidly worse.

Another work, a Madonna of Mercy with the Holy Child in a mandorla in her bosom, and at her feet a crowd of children, has this inscription : MCCCC°LXXXXIIII ADI XL DE DICEMBRE. The painter is unknown, but it is signed with a vine leaf.

CHAPTER IX

FANO AND SENIGALLIA

FROM Pesaro it is a matter of some seven miles southward along the Via Flaminia to Fano, once the city
of Fortune and now of Fortunatus. There is no one who
tramps this road but will be glad of Fano, for it is both
interesting and charming, a place to enjoy, a place to linger
in and wander about contentedly, passing in and out of the
old churches there, from pictures by Santi to others by
Perugino, from a masterpiece by Leon Alberti to the ever-
delightful statue of Fortune herself on the public fountain
in the Piazza, from the great Roman arch of Augustus to
the splendid Palazzo della Ragione and Palazzo dei Malatesta ; and then there are always the sea and the fishing-
boats like strange multi-coloured birds on the opal water
against the faint beauty of the evening sky.

Fano, Fanum Fortunæ, has been a place of considerable
importance certainly since Caius Flaminius, the Censor,
about 220 B.C. drove the Via Flaminia from Rome to
Rimini, for it was, and is, at Fano that that great highway
comes down from the mountains to the sea out of the great
pass of the Furlo by the valley of the Metauro, to turn
suddenly northward along the coast to meet the Via
Emilia in the Forum of Rimini. In Fano, too, the road
from Ancona along the coast met the Via Flaminia ; and
so, quite apart from its port, a by no means negligible
advantage, Fano was an important market in Roman times.
So important was it even in Cæsar's day that that great
soldier hastened to occupy it with a cohort of that single

Legion with which he had crossed the Rubicon and invaded
Italy. It formed, as it were, a second and inner gate to
Italy from Cisalpine Gaul, the first and main gate being, as
I have tried to show, Ravenna. For it held the eastern end
of the Furlo pass, the most difficult mountain passage upon
the Flaminian Way, and was like Ravenna, based upon the
sea. Therefore we find every soldier who came by this
way anxious about it, Cæsar first and then in A.D. 69 the
Generals of Vespasian.

Fano was of colonial rank and had the title, Colonia
Julia Fanum Fortunæ. It was famous everywhere, it
appears, for its great temple of Fortune, of which nothing
but the memory remains. That, however, endures in a
very remarkable way, for if Fortuna was the patron of
Fano in Pagan times, S. Fortunatus inherited the ob-
ligation when Christianity triumphed, and has not foregone
his duty even yet, so that we find to-day in Fano, in place
of the Temple of Fortune, the Cathedral of S. Fortunatus.
The city, too, in the time of Augustus was adorned with a
Basilica which Vitruvius tells he himself built. To this
period belongs also the great triumphal arch of white
marble, now silver grey, erected in honour of Augustus,
which still forms the northern gate of Fano by which the
Via Flaminia leaves the city.

With the fall of the Empire, Fano fell upon evil days,
like every other city in Italy ; but it was well defended by
the walls which Augustus had given it. These, however,
Vitiges the Ostrogoth, whom Belisarius broke at last,
destroyed, and Fano was twice reconquered by the Imperialists. It formed one of the five cities of the maritime
Pentapolis, and though often at the mercy of the Lombard,
survived that appalling flood, and came, by the gift of
Pepin, at last into the hands of the Pope in 754. Its
fortune thenceforth, until the opening of the Middle Age,
is vague and obscure. It certainly became a commune
and was not less than its neighbours at the mercy of the
merciless factions which distracted every city in Italy, but

ARCH OF AUGUSTUS, FANO

THE CATHEDRAL, ANCONA

is not till the Malatesta appear that we get any very clear idea of its story. It was Malatestino, the younger brother of *lo sciancato*, who first brought Fano into the Malatesta dominion, and by treachery. Dante records how he invited the two worthiest citizens of Fano, Angiolotto da Carignano and Guido del Cassaro, to a conference at La Cattolica and there treacherously drowned them off the headland of Focara. It will be remembered that this notable family divided into two branches, when, after Cardinal Albornoz had appeared as the Papal champion in the Marches, Galeotto Malatesta was invested with Rimini, and Fano and Guastafamiglia with Pesaro. In the lordship of Galeotto Fano ranked second immediately after Rimini. Thus it was that when Galeotto died, his two elder sons Carlo and Pandolfo succeeded the one to Rimini, but the other to Fano. Pandolfo, who was the father of Sigismondo Malatesta, after great adventures and success in Lombardy, returned to Fano, and there he died and was buried. His elder brother outlived him, but died childless, and therefore Sigismondo succeeded him as lord of Rimini, Fano and Cesena, and was confirmed in this lordship by Pope Eugenius IV. Cesena he gave later to his younger brother Novello, but Rimini and Fano he held and defended as long as he could, that is to say, until in 1463 the hatred Pope Pius II bore him was able to deprive him of Fano, though not of Rimini, by means of Federigo of Urbino. From that time, with sundry intervals, Fano has remained in the hands of the Papacy, and owes to Pope Julius II the establishment of the first printing-press with movable Arabic type within its walls ; to Pope Paul V the restoration of its port.

The centre of Fano, and it is a beautiful centre, is the Piazza Maggiore, with its glorious sixteenth-century fountain crowned by a lovely nude figure of Fortune which turns with every wind that blows. The name of the builder of the Fountain has not come down to us ; it was completed in 1575, but the statue of bronze is the work of Donnino

Ambrosi of Urbino, who cast it in Senigallia in 1593. The
Papal Government, however—it was the time of the Catholic
Reaction and the Protestant heresy—when it was pre
sented with this noble work, found the figure too naked
for its taste. Therefore it was placed in a niche
upon the staircase of the Residenza dei Magistrati. But
in 1614 a wiser counsel prevailed and the beautiful figure
was placed upon the Fountain for which it had been
designed.

Behind the lovely Fountain to the left stands the
Palazzo della Ragione, the most important mediæval
building in the city. It was built in 1299, in the time of
Boniface VIII, when a certain Barnabò Lando of Piacenza
was Podestà, and indeed the palace recalls the noble Palazzo
del Comune of that city, though it is without battlements
and certainly loses nothing in repose and beauty on that
account. It was built by a certain Magister Paulutius to
the order, as an inscription upon a pilaster towards the
Corte Malatestiana tells us, of Andrea de Giambattista della
Mano and Angelotto de Piero d'Angelo. It is in the Lom
bard style and has even without suffered a little from
restoration; within, it has, of course, been completely
transformed. Under the second window of the main
façade are figures of the three protectors of Fano. The
beautiful tower, which closes the angle of the Palace towards
the Piazza, is a work of the eighteenth century; it replaced
a tower of the early part of the fifteenth century ruined in a
storm in 1569.

Beyond the Palazzo della Ragione, passing under an arch
attributed to Bramante (1491) in the angle of the Piazza
we come to the Palazzo dei Malatesta so largely ruined. It
was built by Pandolfo, the father of Sigismondo Malatesta
between 1413 and 1421. What we see, however, is a com
posite building, the part to the right dating from the
sixteenth century and only that to the left from the time of
Pandolfo. The architect of the latter is unknown, but the
loggia of the former is attributed to Sansovino. Within is a

mall museum containing a few Roman remains. Under
he portico are two slabs of Carrara marble, upon which are
nscribed the terzine of the Divine Comedy (*Inferno*,
xviii), which refer to Fano and the fate of her two worthiest
t the hands of the one-eyed Malatestino.

> . . . Instruct the twain whom Fano boasts
> Her worthiest sons, Guido and Angelo,
> That if 'tis given us here to scan aright
> The future, they out of life's tenement
> Shall be cast forth, and whelmed under the waves
> Near to Cattolica, through perfidy
> Of a fell tyrant. 'Twixt the Cyprian isle
> And Balearic, ne'er hath Neptune seen
> An injury so foul, by pirates done
> Or Argive crew of old. That one-eyed traitor
> (Whose realm, there is a spirit here were fain
> His eye had still lacked sight of) them shall bring
> To conference with him, then so shape his end
> That they shall need not 'gainst Focara's wind
> Offer up vow nor prayer.

Returning now to the Piazza, across the base of which the
oad to Ancona passes on its way to meet the Via Flaminia
n Piazza Amiani, one follows the great Way to the right
until one comes to the Via Arco d'Augusto. Turning there
nd passing the Duomo, with its fine portal of the thirteenth
entury, fine windows and noble tower, the lower part of
vhich is circular, with an octagonal upper story, upon
vhich is a lovely octagonal Gothic lantern, one comes
resently to the great arch of Augustus under which the
Roman road passes out of the city. This glorious triumphal
urch was erected in honour of the first of the Emperors and
eceived in the fourth century a second story in honour of
he first Christian among them—Constantine the Great.
What it was in its virginal beauty we may see from a relief
upon the façade to the right of the fine Renaissance door
with its statue of S. Michele. It then possessed three
entrances with seven arches over them.

Just inside this great Roman arch is the Scuola di S.

Michele, partly built in 1475 from the stones of the arch, with a charming double loggia. Upon one of its capitals is another, but small, relief of the Arch of Augustus.

From the Arch of Augustus one turns back along the Via Arco d'Augusto, and taking the first turning on the right into the Via Montevecchio, following it to the left, and then again taking the first on the right on to the Via Bonaccorsi, comes to the porticoed church of S. Maria Nuova. S. Maria Nuova, originally S. Salvatore, is the church of the Franciscans in Fano, who left S. Lazzaro without the walls, to build a convent here, in 1519. To this date the Portico belongs ; though so late it bears some resemblance in style to the Porta di S. Michele, but it is not so lovely. The church within has suffered from a restoration in the seventeenth century. It consists of a single nave and is not now a very interesting building. The treasure of the church, however, lies in its pictures.

Over the third altar upon the right is a magnificent altarpiece, by Perugino, of the Madonna enthroned with her little Son between S. John, S. Francis, S. Peter, S. Paul, S. Mary Magdalen and perhaps S. Bonaventura. Above, in the lunette, is a Pietà with four saints, while below in the predella are five scenes from the life of the Blessed Virgin : the Birth, Presentation, Marriage, Annunciation and Assumption ; in the latter we see Madonna presenting her girdle to S. Thomas. The inscription, which is mutilated, would seem to tell us that the picture was painted in 1497.

In the second chapel on the other side of the nave is another picture by the same master representing the Annunciation. Under a beautiful Renaissance pergola in a lovely landscape among Umbrian hills at evening, S. Gabriel Archangel suddenly kneels before Our Lady, who would leave him in her bewilderment. Above, God the Father, amid the Cherubim, blesses her, while the Holy Spirit descends to her in the form of a dove. The mutilated inscription hides the date.

THE VIRGIN AND CHILD WITH FOUR SAINTS.   BY GIOVANNI SANTI
S. Croce, Fano

In the first chapel on this side of the church is a beautiful picture of the Visitation, by Giovanni Santi, the father of Raphael. There we see, in a landscape harder and more rugged than Perugino shows us, Madonna meet Elizabeth, while on either side stand their friends, behind Elizabeth a lady and her servant, behind Madonna I suppose S. Joseph and two women, one of whom may well be S. Anna.

From all this loveliness it is hard to drag oneself away, and yet something at least as wonderful awaits us in the fourteenth-century church, rebuilt in the seventeenth and now abandoned, of the Hospital of S. Croce. Here we have one of Santi's loveliest works. In a fair country we see Madonna enthroned, as it were, by the wayside, with Our Lord in her arms. Two cherubs support behind her a long curtain on a rod, and about her stand S. Helena, a marvellously lovely crowned figure with the Cross, a holy father with a crucifix, S. Sebastian and S. Roch. We shall see nothing fairer than this in all the length of the Marches.

In the same street, Via Nolfi, is the church of S. Pietro in Valle, which for so long has been closed, but is now open again. This was built in the beginning of the seventeenth century, but is of very ancient foundation. Within, in the first chapel on the left, is an Annunciation by Guido Reni ; but with Perugino in our minds we have little taste for this, nor for the Marriage of the Virgin, by Guercino in S. Paterniano, a church with a noble tower attributed to Sansovino, nor, except for Browning's sake, for the same master's Guardian Angel in S. Agostino. Browning's verses are worth all the Guercinos in the world.

> Dear and great Angel, wouldst thou only leave
>   That child, when thou hast done with him, for me !
> Let me sit all the day here, that when eve
>   Shall find performed thy special ministry,
> And time come for departure, thou suspending
>   Thy flight, mayst see another child for tending,
>   Another still to quiet and retrieve.

10

The church of S. Domenico is more interesting, with its recently uncovered frescoes by Ottaviano Nelli, and there is still one church that no one must omit to visit if he would know and understand Fano. I mean the church of S. Francesco, where Pandolfo Malatesta and his wife, Paola Bianca, are buried. Pandolfo's monument was made perhaps by Leon Alberti, and certainly to the order of his son, Sigismondo of Rimini. Paolo Bianca's monument was erected much earlier in 1413, not by order of Sigismondo, but probably of Pandolfo, and is by Tagliapietra.

Something, too, beside these tombs and the mutilated Palazzo Malatestiano is left of that notorious family in Fano. This is to be found in the Rocca Malatestiana at the western end of the Via Nolfi. It was begun in 1438 by Sigismondo, but the glorious tower was built only in 1452 by the Fanese, Matteo Nuti. Many a rebuff this fortress gave to Sigismondo's enemies, but Roberto, his son, surrendered it after three days' siege in 1463 to Federigo of Urbino, who had, as I have told, come against it at the order of Pope Pius II. Federigo came down from Macerata in the time of the harvest, and first he reaped the fields and gathered all he could, awaiting the Pope's troops, and in July the siege was begun. Fano was, it must be confessed, not ordained by Nature to withstand a siege, but Sigismondo had made it as strong as he could, and still had the upper hand so far as the sea was concerned, with the help of Venice. The city was, however, in terror, and soon opened its gates. Roberto retired into the Rocca with his mother and sisters. These ladies presently induced him to surrender, as he did on the third day, not a shot having been fired during the siege of the Rocca. When Roberto and his womenfolk presented themselves to Federigo, he escorted them himself to the place of their embarkation for Rimini. Pius, we read in his own account of the affair, rose from table when he had the news, for he was dining, and " spread his hands toward heaven, and poured forth thanks to the Almighty, who thus loaded him with benefits.

After which he said apart : There is now nothing to keep me at home ; God calls me to the Crusade, and lays open the way ; there is no reason for longer delay." Well might he rejoice ; yet with this in his mind, that had Sigismondo been in Fano, it is likely that Federigo of Urbino would have had a less pleasant news to send.

At Fano on the way southward along the coast to Senigallia and Ancona one leaves the Via Flaminia for a road only less notable in the history of Europe. It was by this way that Narses came on his great march southward from Ravenna to search out Totila and to kill him. He followed the Via Flaminia along the coast all the way from Rimini, where he had suddenly broken the barbarian Usdrilas, to Fano. At Fano he was compelled to leave the Flaminian Way, for the passage of the Apennines, by that road, was in the hands of the Goths, who held Petra Pertusa, that is to say, the Furlo pass. It was necessary to outflank this fortress, since it was too strong to be easily or quickly taken. Therefore the great eunuch marched out of Fano by the southern road along the coast, probably till he came to the wide valley of the Cesano. There he left the highway for a byroad up the left bank of the river, which presently brought him again into the Flaminian Way to the south of the great fortress. He encamped at Scheggia just under the main range of the Apennines upon their western side, and presently marched on to meet Totila at Gualdo Tadino, and to destroy him in a battle, which finally decided the fate of the Goths in Italy.

The way of Narses, however, glorious as it is, was not for me. My road lay straight along the coast over that so narrow strip of plain between the mountain and the sea to Senigallia.

This very ancient but not very interesting or picturesque place is famous in history as the scene of perhaps the most real and certainly the most appalling of the many crimes which have been laid at the door of Cesare Borgia.

Senigallia, the Sena Gallica of the Romans, was originally a Gaulish town, as its name implies, but of this we know nothing. A Roman colony seems to have been placed there as early as 289 B.C., immediately after the final subjection of the Senones. It figures now and again in Roman history, but most famously in the Civil Wars of Marius and Sulla, when it was taken and plundered by Sulla's lieutenant, Pompey, in 82 B.C. Thenceforward we hear little of it except as a station upon the Roman Way from Fanum Fortunae to Ancona. It continued obscurely throughout the barbarian invasions, and appears as one of the cities of the maritime Pentapolis when that province was handed to the Pope by Pepin. Thenceforth it seems to have decayed, and Dante speaks of it in his day as almost deserted.

> . . . Mark Luni ; Urbisaglia mark ;
> How they are gone ; and after them how go
> Chiusi and Senigallia ; and 'twill seem
> No longer new or strange to thee to hear
> That families fail, when cities have their end.
> All things that appertain to ye, like yourselves
> Are mortal ; but mortality in some
> Ye mark not ; they endure so long, and you
> Pass by so suddenly.

The city revived, however, and in the fourteenth century came into the hands of the Malatesta of Rimini, from whom it was wrested by Cardinal Albornoz. Sigismondo, however, repossessed himself of it but pledged it, in 1459, to Pope Pius II, and lost it for ever in 1463, when Federigo of Urbino took it without a blow. It remained in the direct control of the Holy See for eleven years, and then in 1474 Sixtus IV conferred it on his nephew, Giovanni della Rovere, when he married the daughter of Federigo of Urbino. To commemorate the event an oak tree—the badge of the Rovere—was planted in the Piazza, to which the motto, "Long may it endure," was attached. A tournament and a ball were held, during which Giovanni made himself popular by freely mixing with the people. The rule of the Rovere house certainly brought many benefits to the rather obscure town. Giovanni opened new streets, we read, and paved them, built palaces, churches, convents, and a hospital, constructed a harbour, a citadel, and fortifications, and established a great fair, which was probably more beneficial to the town than anything else he did. All went merrily enough, till suddenly Cesare Borgia appeared in the March, seized Urbino, drove out the Duke, and began to make himself master of the country. In this extraordinary campaign Senigallia played a great part. With Urbino in his hands Cesare proposed at once to move on the little city, the garrison of which was commanded by the famous Andrea Doria who, excluded from Genoa, had adopted the career of a condottiere, and was now in the service of Giovanni della Rovere. Cesare immediately dispatched his allies, Paolo Orsini, the Duke of Gravina, Vitellozzo and Liverotto against Senigallia, which made, in spite of Andrea Doria, but a feeble resistance. The citadel, however, held out, though without any hope of success. As soon as Cesare heard of the success of his allies he appeared on the scene with two thousand cavalry and ten thousand foot. His allies seeing so great a force assembled for so small a business began to wonder what he would be at. They were not long left in doubt. Cesare at once requested their attendance outside the gates to receive his congratulations. He received them with cordiality and distinction, but when he withdrew for a moment, one of his agents, Don Michelotto, entered with a company armed, arrested the four of them with their gentlemen, and before morning Vitelozzo and Liverotto were strangled with a violin string and a wrench-pin before Cesare's eyes. Machiavelli tells us that their deaths were cowardly, especially that of the wolf Liverotto. Their bodies were dragged round the Piazza and exposed for three days before burial.

Thus Cesare dealt with those who had done him a service

it would have been awkward to repay. On the same night he attacked the army of the allies, slaughtering and plundering them with the same barbarity they had used to the citizens of Senigallia. And each night he had one of the remaining lords, the Duke of Gravina and Paolo Orsini, brought out and cruelly put to death before his eyes. " Thus did he by a dexterous stroke of the most refined duplicity turn the tools of his ambition into victims of his vengeance."

Nothing in the history of the time is more in accordance with its spirit than this act of relentless common sense. Machiavelli, as an artist and a statesman, approved of it and described the massacre as " *il bellissimo inganno di Sinigaglia,*" and Cesare himself seems to have regarded it as a mere act of prudence such as was to be expected from a Prince who knew his business. It is perhaps needless to add that now as then, whatever immediate success such acts may achieve, time will reward them as they deserve. Certainly this was so with Cesare, when at the first crisis his dominion fell utterly to pieces and he found himself a fugitive. As for Senigallia, it returned into the hands of the Rovere under Pope Julius II, and remained in their dominion, till, with everything they had, in 1617, it came again into the direct power of the Holy See to remain there till modern times.

There are but two notable things to be had at Senigallia, and neither of them is in the city. Both will be found in the Franciscan church of S. Maria delle Grazie, some two miles to the west, where in the choir is a fine work of Perugino's, and over the third altar on the right a small picture by Piero della Francesca.

The Perugino altarpiece is almost a replica of the noble work at Fano. There we see the Madonna enthroned with Our Lord in her arms ; about her stand S. John Baptist, S. Louis of France, S. Francis, S. Peter, S. John and S. Andrew in a fair landscape. Perugino was at Fano in 1497 and 1498 ; and it was probably then this picture was painted.

The picture by Piero della Francesca is more notable; indeed, in its statuesque weight, it is, though not among the more pleasing, certainly one of the most remarkable, of the master's works. There we see the Madonna standing with her Son on her arm. He blesses us, and on either side, a little behind, in a quiet room, stand the donors, their arms crossed on their breasts.

With these two things in our hearts the long way to Ancona seems fairer than it is, for they chime with the sea that breaks all the way beside us upon the harsh beach, while before us shines the height of Monte Cònero.

CHAPTER X

ANCONA AND OSIMO

ANCONA in all the rose of sunrise, in all the gold of sunset, shining there aloft on its great cliff in all the burning heat of midday, and at night filled with impenetrable shadows, is not like an Italian city at all. More than anything else in Italy it reminds you of Spain, not only in its aspect so virile and affirmative and yet fateful, a city of the Orient, lean as a Moor with the ennui of the sunlight, but in its moods too, its lack of gaiety, its feverish and yet sleepy delight, its bitter disillusion. It is a city hard to approach with contentment, having something tragic in its composition ; but harder still to leave and to forget. It haunts you ever in less definite places and fills you with a curiously inverted sense of home-sickness ; inverted because no one has ever been happy in Ancona, only restless, resigned, or disquieted. It is a place where every one seems to have just arrived or to be about to go away, not a city, but a port wedded to all the restless sea, and that sea the gate between east and west, a place built round an old harbour, towering over it, thrusting long arms out into it, beautiful and yet full of the bitterness, involved in all the business, of great waters. The ships, hundreds of them, fishing-boats, cargo-boats, steamers of all kinds, loading and unloading, are crammed against its wharves, creaking and jostling one another, filling the whole city with their rumour and sound and smell. And with all this there comes into the strange, sleepy restlessness of the city something noble and full of distinction, which is, I suppose, the spirit of the sea to which

ANCONA

ncona seems actually to belong in a way quite different
om Genoa or Naples or Barcelona or even Cadiz.

You feel this quite as much in the brutal alleys, as sordid
s anything in London, of the lower town, as you do in
e climbing, narrow, steep ways of the upper city whose
own is that great Cathedral which looks out like a Pharos
r a fortress far across the sea. It is the one thing which
ves this city, so bitterly and strangely divided against
self, a real unity, for it is a powerful as well as a noble thing,
nd to it everything that is merely accidental, that has no
ot in it, must give way. You feel that, even though you
nnot understand or explain it. It is only in sight of the
ea that Ancona is alive or has a being. Apart from the sea
e is nothing, or rather she is two utterly different and
pposed things. The noble city upon the great hill
ustered about the Cathedral is what worlds away from
at crouching, leering, noisy modern thing that lurks and
hines and pours its bestial crowds like a flood of sewage
bout the base of that great cliff! Up there you see the
omen at sundown slowly pass along the half-deserted
veliness of the old by-ways bearing great vases of water on
eir heads as they go homeward from the fountain in all
e quietness of the evening. Below, in all the modern
rutality, of the Corso and its purlieus, trams shriek and all
e vampires and rascaldom of the modern world push or
ink homeward to their jerry-built flats in the glare of the
rc lamps, amid the appalling noise and vulgarity they call
ivilization. Up there the Ave Maria rings, and little
umble people bow their heads and doff their hats and
emember that Christ was born in Bethlehem; down in the
ity the sirens of a roundabout, the ding-dong of the tram
ongs, the howling of the vendors of stale newspapers or
dulterated drinks have long since not only silenced any-
hing which would recall to the modern world its appalling
estiny, but have obliterated the memory of anything that
appened not merely before 1860, but on the day before
esterday.

If the traveller would taste all the amazing contrasts tha[t] meet in Ancona, let him come into the place by train Let him after nightfall arrive in all the clanging misery the sordid vile ugliness of the railway station; let hin drive in a cab to his Albergo across a network of railwa[y] lines amid the stunning noise of shunting vans, up and dow[n] and in and out by reeking wharves and sheds where ther[e] is no real road, but only tramway lines; let him spend hi[s] evening in all the flare and vulgarity of the Corso; and the[n] on the morrow let him climb out of all this litter of yesterda[y] up through the older city to the Cathedral, to make up hi[s] mind, if he can, upon what he thinks of the modern worl[d] It is a salutary thing to examine the conscience. Here i[n] Ancona is an opportunity of coming to a just conclusion.

Though one may never really forget the modern encamp ment at the foot of the Monte Guasco, one can there by th[e] Duomo, with the great arc of the bay, so vast a stretch [of] sea, and the noble church, before one, put it out of one'[s] mind for a moment, and remember the noble antiquit[y] of that Ancona which for so many ages has towered an[d] hung upon this promontory which forms so wonderful a[n] angle with the coast. ’Αγκών, elbow, angle, it was from tha[t] word the Greeks derived her name, for Ancona was origi[n] ally a Greek colony, the only one on this part of the coas[t] founded about 530 B.C. by Syracusan exiles, “who fle[d] hither to avoid the tyranny of the elder Dionysius,” Strab[o] tells us. So Juvenal calls it Dorica Ancon, and thoug[h] we know nothing of its early history it seems that it earl[y] became a place of importance on account of its exceller natural harbour. The period at which Ancona became [a] Roman city is uncertain, but it is probable it came t[o] Rome with the rest of the cities of Picenum; at any rat[e] in 178 B.C. we find her using it as a naval station. I[ts] importance, like that of Ravenna, was made clear b[y] Cæsar, who marched straight upon it after he had crosse[d] the Rubicon. What Augustus did for it is uncertai[n] but Trajan built there in the harbour on the south

ew mole, to the vast improvement of the port, and
he city in his honour erected thereon a magnificent
ciumphal arch of Parian marble, a light and very graceful
vork, one of the best Roman works of the kind that have
ome down to us, for both this arch and the mole remain
o this day.

We hear among other Roman buildings in Ancona of
n amphitheatre, of which some remains have been traced,
nd of a temple to Venus, of which both Juvenal and
Catullus sing, the latter in his *Carmen*, xxxvi.

> Nunc, o caeruleo creata ponto,
> Quae sanctum Idalium, Syrosque apertos,
> Quaeque Ancona, Cnidumque arundinosam
> Colis, quaeque Amathunta quaeque Golgos
> Quaeque Dyrrhachium Adriae tabernam,
> Acceptum face, redditumque votum,
> Si non illepidum, neque invenustum est.

Nothing, not a stone of this Temple, unhappily remains.
It seems probable that it occupied the site of the Cathedral
on the summit of the great promontory which commands
he whole bay and the city within it. We know so little of
Ancona in the time of the Empire that we are tempted to
ay that its most important days were those of the Ostro-
gothic wars of Belisarius and Narses. At any rate, it then
played a considerable part. During the first part of that
great war (536–40) it was held by the Imperialists, but was
always in a state of siege owing to the fact that almost
until the end the fortress of Osimo was in the hands of
he Goths. Osimo, which was the only stronghold the
Goths held to the east of the Via Flaminia, commanded
Ancona, or at any rate greatly threatened it, and Belisarius
was always fearful of the fall of the city, and on this account
he was angered when his lieutenant, John, pushed forward
from Ancona to Rimini. This rash act, in the opinion of
he great General, endangered Ancona, and he hastily dispatched Ildiger and Martin to recall John from the more
northern city. John refused to obey, apparently because

he was aware, though Belisarius was not, that he migh
expect reinforcements from Byzantium. These presentl
arrived, with Narses at their head. Ancona was relieve
just in time. For a moment the conduct, or at any rat
the plan, of the war was in the hands of Narses. Agains
Belisarius' judgment he determined to relieve Rimini. A
screen of a hundred men was placed before Osimo, and
partly in ships by sea, and partly by the great coast road
the Imperialists set out from Ancona, and were completel
successful. Nevertheless, when Milan fell, owing to divide
councils, Narses was rightly recalled by Justinian. Belisariu
continued the campaign, and one of the last things he di
before formally marching upon Ravenna, the citadel o
the Gothic, as it was later to be of the Roman, defence, wa
to reduce Osimo, so that he left no enemy behind him.

Ancona in the Lombard invasion appears as the secon
city of the maritime Pentapolis and, as might be expected
was plundered by those barbarians. They governed it b
an officer with the title of Marquis. This title, it is said
gave its name to the whole of the country, which was a
that time the always uncertain March between Lombard
proper and the Roman territory. With the rest of th
Pentapolis in 754 it passed to the Papacy.

Its position in the ninth century was very insecure b
reason of the raids of the Saracens. They seem to hav
burnt it in 839, and it reappears as a free city, able i
1058 to join the Normans against the Pope and to face bot
Empire and Papacy. In order to keep its independence i
placed itself under the Eastern Empire in 1143, and, conse
quently, incurred the anger of Barbarossa and endure
many a siege from the Imperialists. It ceased to have an
relations with Constantinople, however, after the peace o
Constance (1183). It then returned to its allegiance to th
Pope, who appointed first a Podestà and then a Marquis t
rule there and govern the March, of which it was now
the capital. The first Marquis was Azzo vi, of Este (c. 1212)
In the thirteenth century it was continually at war wit

the Ghibellines of Osimo, and in 1245 it lost both its *car-roccio* and its leader, Marcelino Peto, Bishop of Arezzo, whom the people of Osimo first imprisoned and then hanged. Their bishopric was, in consequence, abolished by the Pope. But when the Pope was in exile in Avignon, Ancona, like most of the other cities of the March, rebelled, and the Malatesta appeared as lords until Cardinal Albornoz regained the March for the Pope in 1355. He was received, almost it might seem with thankfulness, in Ancona, and refortified the city with the present citadel, which he built upon the ruin of the Malatesta fortress of S. Cataldo. Urban V and Gregory XI knew the place well, but of all the Popes it is Pius II whom we most think of there, for on the eve of his death it was on the height in front of the Cathedral he would sit for hours day after day eagerly expecting the Venetian fleet which never came to carry him and his armies on that last crusade.

Ancona, which had for so long been really an independent city, failed at last in 1532, when it was surprised by Gonzaga, the General of Clement VII, who by a cowardly stratagem possessed himself of the city, expelled the senators and nobles, and brought Ancona under the direct dominion of the Holy See, in whose hands it remained until the modern kingdom of United Italy was formed in 1860.

That long and notable history is not perhaps very obvious in the city of Ancona as we see it to-day. The harbour remains the great spectacle and splendour, and both the ancient and mediæval Greek domination there is perhaps recalled for us any morning we care to pick our way along those littered quays by the spectacle, truly amazing to northern eyes, of such a legend as this upon the stern of some creaking hull : ΔΙΟΝΥΣΙΟΣ ΣΤΟΘΑΤΟΣ : ΙΘΑΚΗΣ. Ulysses own gaunt Ithaca ! how those storm-beaten cliffs leap to the mind at the word ! Time and space are annihilated, and suddenly between two heart-beats we feel ourselves in the waist of the ship tossing on these grey waters, while out of the mist looms up : " Ithaca

which lies low farthest up the sea-line towards the darkness
others face the dawning of the sun ; a gaunt isle but
good nurse of noble youths ; and for myself I can se
nought beside sweeter than a man's own country."

Every one who comes to Ancona should visit the por
potter about on the quays, talk to the sailors, smell the ships
and watch the tar frizzling in the sun. Fortunately it i
impossible to see the Triumphal Arch of Trajan withou
coming into the harbour. This arch, as I have said, wa
erected by the people of Ancona in honour of the Emperor
who had built them the great mole, upon which indeed i
stands lofty over the water. A continuation of this mol
was built by Clement XII, and again to him a Triumpha
Arch was erected, designed by Vanvitelli. It cannot, o
course, compare with the Roman work. The lighthouse wa
erected by Pope Pius VI. At the other end of the Banchin
stands the Lazzaretto, built in 1732. It is a pentagona
stronghold with a drawbridge, and is now used as a suga
warehouse.

Standing on the ramparts in front of the Cathedral yo
may see the whole harbour, moving in its appeal to th
imagination, as such a thing always is with its curious crie
and business and air of adventure, of hazard and safet
That view which gives you so much more than that, is,
suppose, among the finest upon this coast, but not mor
astonishing or really more beautiful than that of th
Cathedral behind you.

This wonderful church is built in mixed Byzantine
Lombard style, in the form of a Greek cross under a twelve
sided dome, completed in 1189. The façade, however, wit
its exquisite Gothic portico is attributed to Magheriton
of Arezzo. There is nothing lovelier in all the Pentapoli
than this glorious golden church standing so magnificentl
over the sea. It is said to occupy the site of the Temple c
Venus, of which Catullus speaks, and according to som
writers it actually contains ten of its columns.

Within the church is a museum, and though it ha

THE MOLE ANCONA

ffered from restoration, much that is very lovely has been
ft to us. In the right transept, for instance, the pillars
ill retain their Byzantine capitals, and the choir screens
ere date from the twelfth century. But it is in the
uthern crypt that most of what is very old will be found.
ere amid twelfth, thirteenth, fourteenth and fifteenth
ntury sculptures are many notable tombs: the sarcophagus
f Flavius Gorgonius, Praetor of Ancona, sumptuously
ecorated with reliefs of Christ and the Apostles, and
orgonius and his wife kneeling at Our Lord's feet, the
doration of the Magi, the Baptism of Christ, the Sacrifice
f Isaac, the Magi before Herod, and figures of Moses,
avid, and Goliath, and I know not what else. It dates
om the fourth century, and is maybe the oldest thing in
ne church, unless, indeed, that Roman bust close by is
der. Here, too, is the noble sarcophagus of S. Liberius.

From the left transept, too, we enter another crypt, and
ere is the tomb of S. Cyriacus, who was, it seems, originally
uried in the same sarcophagus as S. Liberius. S. Cyriacus
as the first bishop of Ancona, and is the patron of the
hurch.

There are many winding ways down from the Cathedral
nto the old city. The chief of these brings you presently
o the fine Palazzo del Comune of the thirteenth century,
esigned by Magheritone of Arezzo, but restored by Fran-
esco di Giorgio in the end of the fifteenth century, and
otally spoilt in 1647. We may see something, mere relics,
f the original building in the reliefs of Adam and Eve in
he façade; while within is the fourteenth-century statue
f Marco de' Rossi the legist.

Still following the steep way downwards, the Strada
elle Scuole, one passes on the left the church of S. Fran-
esco with its elaborate portal, a Gothic work of the fifteenth
entury, and presently comes into the great Piazza del
Plebiscito, at the top of which is the church of S. Domenico.
Iere in the third chapel on the right is a spoilt, but still
oble, work by Titian, the Madonna with S. Francis and

S. Blasius, with donor. This altarpiece was ordered k
Luigi of Ragusa for the church of S. Francesco, and is date
1520. The Madonna, all in golden light, is enthroned on
great bank of cloud, holding her little Son in her lap. H
full of eagerness, bends gently down to the earth, whi
angels play about Him, and two offer wreaths to Mar
Beneath is a wide and gracious view of hill and vale in whic
rises a church tower. On either side stand S. Francis an
S. Blasius, the latter pointing towards heaven, with a fir
gesture of joyful assurance directing the gaze of the kneelir
Luigi of Ragusa, whose uplifted hands are much like tho
of the monk in the Pitti *Concert*. The picture is inscribed
ALOYXIUS GOTIUS RAGUSINUS FECIT FIERI MDXX, TIT
ANUS CADORINUS PINSIT.

Adjoining the church is the Museum and Picture Galler
The Museum contains nothing of great interest, but th
Gallery has a few fine pictures, among them anoth
Titian, a Christ on the Cross painted about 1560, a lat
work which once stood over the high altar of S. Domenic
There we see the Saviour on the Cross, S. Dominic kneelin
at His feet, to the left the Blessed Virgin lost in grief, t
the right S. John spreading out his arms as though l
would lift his Lord from off that bitter tree, gazing upwar
in an agony of sorrow. A few clouds drift across th
gloomy sky, from which a ray of sunshine is about to bur
as after a storm.

Here, too, are a lovely picture of the Madonna and Chil
by Crivelli, three pieces by Guercino, and two by Lorenz
Lotto, an Assumption painted in 1550, and a Madonn
enthroned with four saints—the last a very lovely pictur

Several late Gothic or Renaissance buildings remain i
Ancona, but save the Loggia dei Mercanti, with its painting
by Tibaldi, I don't know that they are worth much troubl
to see. Certainly they are not worth the time a hurrie
traveller must spend to find them, away from the port an
the great views the Cathedral offers him, of which I a
least can never have enough.

And yet I don't know ; it is certain at any rate that
no one has ever been really sorry to leave Ancona, to say
goodbye to all that noise and meanness heaped in the
lower city, the vulgar brutality of the place and its
shrieking trams and confusion. And I, too, was glad at
last when the day came—and very early in the morning
it was—for me to set out for Osimo.

I went by a by-way, not knowing whither I went, but I
found a road which took me out to Monte Cònero, where
I found a monastery of S. Romuald, and the day I spent
there was one of the happiest of my life, for I had mountain
and sea together and great views over land and moving
water, under a sun that smiled out of a pure heaven in
which now and then great white clouds, islanded in the
blue, came as it were out of the hills.

Towards evening I went down to Sirolo and next day
in the diligence up to Osimo, winking and shining on a
great hill-top many miles from the sea. There, too, and
all the way thither, a landscape such as one sees rarely
in dreams, was spread out before me, and I thought indeed
I had come into Paradise without passing that dread portal
we all must pass ; and so it was.

We talk of Tuscany and call it the garden of the world,
and cannot find words enough to praise it or to tell how
much we love it all. And indeed no one has praised it
enough. And yet, fair as Tuscany is, here is a country
between the great mountains and the Adriatic to the
south of Ancona as fair every bit, though not perhaps
so obviously blessed ; but there has been no one to say a
word for it, no one to bid those, who find Perugia something
to remember, to go to Camerino and be satisfied, or to say
to such as care for S. Gemignano, Go you to Osimo.

And yet Camerino is nothing like Perugia, for all the
landscapes that lie at Perugia's feet are but little beside
that wide country of mountain and valley, almost terrible
in its beauty, that stretches out before the traveller from
the gate of Camerino. And as for Osimo, it is nothing

at all like S. Gemignano ; but it is not harder to find, and certainly, as I see it, it has more to offer, a greater and a more virile picture of this world, which from the Alps to Scylla and Charybdis is all blessed, something indeed without which we should perish.

All that Ancona refused you, Osimo will heap upon you—quietness, a country dignity, an ancient peace. As for antiquity, certainly it can look Ancona in the face and not be ashamed. For it was a Roman town in 174 B.C. when the Censors caused its walls to be built, and part of those walls remain. In 157 B.C. it became a Roman colony, and it played its part, strong as it was, in the Social Wars, and in the Civil War declared in favour of Cæsar and opened its gates to him. Nor did it fail to hold its own through the great years of the Empire ; and after, does not Procopius call it the chief city of all Picenum? Did it not, as we have seen, play a great part in the wars of Belisarius, who reduced it at last almost at the price of his life ?

It is of these things one thinks in Osimo, and not of the Middle Age or the Renaissance.[1] Those Roman walls, those inscriptions and statues in the Palazzo Pubblico, and the great world that lies at one's feet are what one turns to again and again, to the neglect perhaps of the churches and even of the Cathedral with its fine sculptures of the thirteenth century. It was always a place which was able to decide in great affairs what the issue should be, or at least its part in that issue. Thus it opened its gates to Cæsar and gave him half Picenum, though the partisans of Pompey had already seized it when Cæsar came down the long road to Ancona from Ravenna. In the hands of the Goths it faced Belisarius for years, threatened its everlasting enemy Ancona, and held up its head though it

[1] Till yesterday there was to be seen here in Osimo a fine picture of the Madonna and Child with angels by Lorenzo Lotto. But this has been stolen. There may still be seen in the Palazzo Pubblico an altarpiece by Bartolommeo Vivarini, a charming picture.

was the only city in Picenum that the Goths then possessed. As it was then, so it is to-day.

Not six miles from Osimo, in a place which bears a name so splendid as Castelfidardo, was decided in the year 1860 who was to be master in the March, Victor Emanuel or the Pope.

Cialdini had taken Pesaro and Senigallia without difficulty, while Rocca had stormed Perugia for Victor Emanuel; and Spoleto was being brilliantly defended for the Pope by O'Reilly's Irish, when, before Rocca could come to his assistance, Cialdini forced La Moricière, already retreating upon Ancona, to give him battle here in the hills and utterly defeated him. It is true that Italy has little to boast of in that victory of the 18th of September. Cialdini had thirteen thousand men with which to face La Morcière's badly armed and demoralized remnant. The honour of the engagement indeed, such as it was, lies all with the Papal volunteers, who, hopeless as the fight was, made a fine dash upon the Italian lines. The Swiss, however, failed, as did the almost untrained artillery, and La Morcière escaped to Ancona with a handful of troops, while the greater part of his force surrendered at discretion. In a country where many noble things are happily uncommemorated by statues, this pathetic and miserable affair, which every other people would have been glad to forget, has been represented in sculpture lest men should forget it. It is true that it may be claimed that the victory of Castelfidardo, followed as it was by the capitulation of Ancona, gave Victor Emanuel the Marches, yet it is not victories but great deeds which should be always remembered, and surely there is something both ridiculous and ignoble in reminding the world how, in the year 1860, thirteen thousand troops, well armed and fed, defeated five thousand badly armed and demoralized men where Cæsar and Belisarius have contended.

CHAPTER XI

LORETO

LORETO, which all the world has sought these many centuries, is not only one of the holiest, but one of the most beautiful places in Italy. The most sacred shrine of the Blessed Virgin in the West, though not the only one which professes to hold something in the nature of a relic of the Mother of God, it is set most gloriously on its olive-clad hill looking eastward over the sea. It was on a summer afternoon that I came from Osimo to the golden house of Our Lady so strangely to be found in this little town of the March. From afar Loreto had seemed indeed to consist of little more than the great sixteenth-century church, which, rising out of the silver of the olive gardens, crowns the hill on which it stands with so wonderful a crown of gold; and though, as I soon found, the city, spread over the hillside behind the great sanctuary, is by no means small, the impression I had received from afar proved to be a true one, for Loreto is really nothing but a shrine about which a vast church, splendid courts, a huge college and a great palace have been built, and under whose shadow lies the little city, a pilgrim as it were come to do reverence. The whole place has an aspect of serenity and reserve, an almost ceremonious air of peace which chimes very happily with the smiling countryside—a veritable paradise—in which it stands.

The fact that Loreto is a shrine, one of the most famous sanctuaries in Europe, often stands, I think, in the way of any fair judgment in regard to it. For instance, more

ROSARY STALLS LORETO

than once I was warned, and by Italians, not to go to Loreto, because, being a shrine, it necessarily swarmed with beggars whose mutilations and importunity made a visit there a nuisance and an agony. Even had such a warning been true, the fact that one will be a little worried for alms is a mighty poor excuse for avoiding anything beautiful, curious, or holy. Fortunately, I knew Assisi, and remembering the happy days I had spent there among the halt, the maim and the afflicted, I plucked up courage enough to disregard all the kindly attempts to prevent my pilgrimage with prejudice, and having seen Castelfidardo, a shrine of modern Italy, I felt bound to go on a visit to Loreto, which is a shrine of the older Italy which I love, and of the whole world.

I had not been three hours in Loreto before I knew how false were all those prophecies of unhappiness. And I will here state at once that during the whole of my visit to that famous and beautiful place I was not once annoyed in any way, nor importuned at all ; no alms were asked of me at all save at the church doors, and this annoyed me, for it looked as though one of those meddlesome societies that are so busy nowadays forbidding this and that all over the world had been at work here. However that may be, I, the merest stranger, was everywhere received by every sort of person with kindness, hospitality and the courtesy that Italy had long since taught me to expect ; and as the business I was on—for I had come to Loreto for a special purpose—necessitated a stay of some duration and brought me into relations with people of all classes, I think my experience was fairly conclusive.

But what is this shrine of the Blessed Virgin which is established here with so noble a magnificence and about which the whole world has busied itself for so many ages ? The Santa Casa of Loreto is the house in which the Blessed Virgin was born in Nazareth, miraculously transported hither by angels in the thirteenth century ; since when it has been one of the major places of pilgrimage in Europe.

If we inquire into the history of this amazement we shall come upon some such story as this. Upon the 20th of May, in the year of Our Lord 1291, Nicholas IV being Pope in Rome, the last Crusade having failed, Acre having fallen to the Soldan, and the Christians having departed out of Syria, the people of Rauniza, a little town near the seashore of Dalmatia between Tersatto and Fiume, suddenly beheld a marvellous spectacle ; for as they returned from the fields at evening they saw upon the summit of the Colle di Tersatto a little building of curious form standing where before there had been nothing. A vast multitude from all the neighbouring villages quickly gathered to see this wonder, and when they approached they found the building was a little house of brick, four-square, set lightly on the hill-top, and standing firmly there without foundations or indeed any visible support at all. A door opened on one side, giving access to this mysterious dwelling ; to the right was a window; and within, the roof was painted with the story of the life of Christ, and at one end stood an altar of stone, over which shone a painted Crucifix. Beside the altar was a small cupboard, and here and there a vase of rosy terra-cotta; opposite the cupboard was the hearth, and there, over it, in a niche, a wonderful statue of cedar-wood representing the Madonna with Our Lord in her arms.

Now it so happened that the bishop of that diocese, a holy man, one Alessandro di Modruria, had long been ill ; and lying on his bed he had a vision, and in this vision the Blessed Virgin appeared to him and announced that her little house at Nazareth was come hither into his diocese, with her statue made of the wood of Lebanon and a painted Crucifix, to seek refuge there from the Saracens. Her words are said to have been these, or like these, which follow : " My house in Nazareth is come hither into this land. It is that in which the Word became flesh ; the altar is that which was erected by the Apostle Peter ; the statue of cedar is my authentic likeness carved by Luke the Evangelist. Rise up, then, from thy bed of sorrow, for I give thee back thy health, because I wish the miracle of thy healing to fortify the faith of the people in what thou wilt relate to them." And Alessandro the bishop rose from his bed healed and well, to the astonishment of his people, who thought him dying, and going to the Santa Casa he announced to all what he had seen and heard. For this was, it seemed, the very house to which Gabriel came, and in which, as Madonna said, the Word was made flesh, which Mary had inherited from her parents, and which the Empress Helena visited when she came on pilgrimage to Nazareth and found whole and perfect amid the ruins, and knew it " by the poor naked walls, by the small hearth, by the few articles of household use, and the poor array of domestic furniture, but much more by a certain sacred awe which she felt as she entered." She it was who built over it a magnificent temple where a long succession of saints had worshipped, and among them S. Louis of France.

Through the world went the story of this miraculous translation, and wherever it was told, there pilgrims set out to see this wonder. Even Niccolò Frangipani, the governor of Dalmatia, we hear, though he was then fighting beside the Emperor Rudolph, returned immediately when he heard the news. At first he could not believe, but when the four wise men he sent to Nazareth, to examine the place whence the Santa Casa was come, returned and told him that the house of the Blessed Virgin was no longer to be found there, but only its foundations, whose measurements corresponded exactly with those of the little house on the hill-top, his doubts disappeared, and he too proclaimed the truth of the Translation. All through the country the news spread, and whole populations from the provinces of Bosnia, Albania, Croatia and Servia flocked to the shrine of Mary on the eastern shore of the Adriatic.

Three years and seven months later, upon the 10th of December 1294, the people of Tersatto and Rauniza awoke to find the little house gone. All day they searched for it in vain. About ten o'clock in the evening of that day certain shepherds of Recanati, here upon the western shore of the Adriatic, noticed a strange light coming from a laurel wood near the shore. Entering the wood, they were suddenly terrified to find the little house of Nazareth about which the whole world was talking.

It is said that this wonderful translation of the House of Mary from Nazareth into Italy was foreseen and foretold by three persons : first by a hermit of Montorso, then by S. Francis when he was at Sirolo, and lastly by S. Niccolò da Tolentino when he was at Recanati.

The Santa Casa had been wafted away from Nazareth to save it, it seems, from the Saracens ; for a similar reason it had been carried again by the angels from Tersatto to the laurel wood on the shore near Recanati. But there, too, as soon appeared, it was not safe, for the place was lonely, and now, when all the world was on the way thither, it presently became infested with robbers. So the angels, at the bidding of Mary, once more took up the little house and bore it in their arms out of that place and set it on the hill-top near where it still stands. That happened eight months after it had first come to Italy, but even then it was not safe or at peace, for it stood on ground owned by two brothers, who, seeing an immense profit in its advent, immediately began to quarrel as to which of them really owned the holy thing. And so presently once again the angels came down and bore the house away from their hatred and set it down in the very midst of the highway not far off, in the spot where it has remained ever since.

But even to-day, it is said, the dismay of the Dalmatians at their loss is by no means appeased. Numbers of them, we are told, still come to Loreto, and, dragging themselves into the church on their knees, licking the pavement with their tongues, they crawl to the sanctuary, or remain night after night before the doors when the church is shut after the evening Ave Maria, praying and crying out in their uncouth tongue : " Return ! Return to us, O Maria ! Return to Tersatto, Maria, O Maria ! "

The Santa Casa had no sooner come to rest at last upon he hill-top where it still stands than Boniface VIII, who hen sat on the throne of Peter, placed the Holy House in he care of the Bishop of Recanati, and again sent to the Holy Land a deputation to verify the prodigy.

Meantime vast multitudes of pilgrims from all over Europe poured into Loreto, and especially from Dalmatia and the cities of the March. Men and women, young and old, children and greybeards, sick and well, with banners and music, came down the long roads all day and all night in winter and summer alike, in the merciless sun, in the pitiless rain, half-distracted in their eager enthusiasm to see, to touch, to pray in the House of the Virgin, their Mother. Far from diminishing with time, the enthusiasm grew, and the people of Recanati in whose care the Santa Casa had been placed by the Pope, began to fear that the walls of brick, without foundation of any kind, would be too weak to withstand so many caresses, so many kisses, and the tears and cries of such multitudes. Therefore they built walls about it on secure foundations to support it in the winter storms and to withstand the pressure of the enormous crowds. And upon these walls they caused to be painted by the best masters of that time the story of the Holy House and all its journeying. But the Blessed Virgin showed that she had no need of man's assistance ; for no sooner was all finished than she caused the new wall to be removed several paces from the walls of the Holy House.

Such is the charming and poetic legend of the House of Mary, the Santa Casa of Loreto, famous through the world. The pilgrims still come to it from all lands and in all seasons ; not a week passes in the year but some kneel there who perhaps during their whole lives have dreamed of little else but the journey and the great sight at the end of it—the House of Her who is the Mother of God, the Mother of us all. Many there are who weep there where suddenly life falls away from them and for a moment they actually feel the arms of One about them by whom alone they are not too wretched to be loved. Many pray there hour after hour and at last are comforted. It is a place for tears, and if there be any consolation here you will find it. For in its universal human appeal, it resolves all the bitterness of life for a moment into sweetness, all its pettiness into an act of worship, all its insecurity into security, all its doubt and hatred into assurance and love.

Superstition, let us admit it, appears in all ages and in many forms, some beautiful, some ugly, some good in their results, some infinitely vile and bad. It is by the fruits of a superstition that it should be judged, for by their fruits ye shall know them. The Holy House of Loreto, if you choose to regard it as a superstition, must be one of that human and kindly sort which in every age has refreshed the weary, for its fruits have been altogether noble. It has produced a series of great works of art by some of the greatest masters of a great time, it has produced the Litany of the Blessed Virgin, than which nothing lovelier was ever sung in heaven, and all over the world it has brought men together in love, and has comforted millions who were without consolation. Let the remembrance of this appease him whose undue sense of right makes him righteous over much.

Such, then, is the legend : that many not inconsiderable people have believed it, is certain. We read, for instance, of a great number of saints who visited and testified their belief in, and devotion to, the Santa Casa ; among others S. Ignatius, S. Francis de Sales, S. Francis Xavier, and not least S. Carlo Borromeo, who came twenty miles on foot to Loreto, insisted on administering the Communion to a vast crowd of pilgrims assembled there on the feast of the Nativity of the Blessed Virgin, and begged to be allowed to pass the night in the Holy House, which he was permitted to do. It is evident that a mind and spirit so fine as Cardinal Borromeo's found no difficulty in accepting the miracle. On the other hand, many of the most sympathetic and learned inquirers of to-day refuse it. We may ignore the merely vulgar, but even Signor Arduino Colasanti, whose beautiful book on Loreto should be in every traveller's hand, gently disposes, or tries to dispose of the legend by proving among other things that there was in Loreto a sanctuary of the Madonna anterior to the period in which the Santa Casa is said to have been translated hither from Dalmatia. Whatever we may care to think about the Santa Casa, however, we cannot question its enormous and really universal appeal to the world during some six hundred years.

A shelter, as we have seen, had speedily been built about the Holy House when it finally came to rest in the place where it still stands. The first building was erected about 1300, Boniface VIII being Pope. According to the legend, it consisted of walls in support of the little building, and these walls were, as we are told, miraculously removed a certain distance away, by the Madonna. This building seems to have been roofed and repaired in the fourteenth century, and then in 1468 Giuliano da Romano built a magnificent church over the Holy House. This was decorated by the greatest masters of the time, among them Domenico Veneziano, Piero della Francesca, and Signorelli; but in or about 1550 Giuliano da Sangallo was called in, and he began the church we see, using what he could of his predecessors' building, which had, it seems, fallen or seemed likely to fall. In 1526 Antonio da Sangallo finished the interior of the present church, and in 1563, in the time of Sixtus V, whose statue stands on the flight of steps before the church, the façade was begun and completed four years later.

Long before then, in 1510, in fact, the Collegio and still unfinished Palazzo Apostolico about the Piazza before the church had been begun by Bramante and continued by Andrea Sansovino and Antonio da Sangallo.

The church has the appearance of a fortress or bastioned wall crowned by Giuliano da Sangallo's dome built about the sanctuary of the Holy House. The façade of the church is disappointing and scarcely in character with the building behind it, but the Piazza as a whole is noble in its effect,

the Palazzo Apostolico being especially fine in design.
The great fountain in the midst of the Piazza was erected
in 1604 from the design of Carlo Maderno and Giovanni
Fontana. The Piazza is at its best at sunset when the
level light turns all to gold and the crowded booths of the
rosary-sellers, heaped with trinkets, glitter and shine, and
the great bell of Leo x, weighing eleven tons, in Vanvitelli's
campanile rings out the Ave Maria. The Piazza della
Madonna, as one might expect, is the centre of life in Loreto,
and full as it is of constant movement, of a continuous
coming and going before the great church, of bands of
pilgrims from all over Italy and indeed Christendom, it
is incomparably the most interesting spectacle in the
Marches.

The Basilica della Santa Casa, as the great church is
called, is entered by three mighty doors of bronze in
the façade. Over the main door in the midst, a work of
Girolamo Lombardi and his sons, is a life-size statue
of the Madonna and Child. The door to the left is by
Vergelli of Camerino; that to the right is by Calcagni of
Recanati.

Within, the church is noble and spacious, and there
in the midst under the dome, quite surrounded by a marble
screen designed by Bramante and carved and executed by
most of the greater sixteenth-century masters, stands the
Santa Casa of Nazareth. On the western front of this
great screen are carved the Annunciation by Sansovino,
the Visitation and the Holy Family by Francesco Sangallo,
and two prophets, Jeremiah and Ezekiel, by Sansovino.
On the south wall we see the Nativity and Adoration of
the Shepherds by Sansovino, on the east the legend of the
Santa Casa and the death of the Blessed Virgin by Tribolo,
on the north the Nativity and Marriage of the Blessed
Virgin and figures of the seven Virtues by Sansovino and
others. The effect of the whole is undoubtedly feeble.
I do not know why, but for once the work of Sansovino
fails utterly to convince us, and the sentiment and charm

we expect in his work seem altogether to be wanting. The failure, for failure it is, of this great work to please us is not the fault of the architect. The design of Bramante is a marvellous and exquisite masterpiece worthy of antiquity. It is Andrea Sansovino who fails, and in spite of the fame of the sanctuary, the nobility of the architecture and splendour of his materials, his work has no life in it, and might seem indeed to be a translation without sincerity or conviction of other men's thoughts, the thoughts of Raphael and of Michelangelo.

Very different is one's emotion within the Holy House itself. No shrine in the world that I have ever seen is half so impressive as this little House of rude brick polished bright with kisses. Without, upon the marble of the platform about the Santa Casa, the Sacristan points out two deep grooves in the marble that in the course of centuries have been worn so deep by the knees of the waiting pilgrims. I do not wonder. Here is a sanctuary claiming a holiness and antiquity beyond any other in Europe which in its touching simplicity and charm can have no rival, unless indeed it be the Porziuncula at Assisi, but that has not the claims upon our reverence the House of Mary has, and it is twelve hundred years and more later in time than this. Here, so the peasants think, as S. Ignatius and S. Carlo Borromeo thought, is the House of Mary, and the maiden from the Abruzzi comes here and dreams of the girlhood of Her who was to be the Mother of God, and crouched there, with beating heart, sees Gabriel in all the splendour of his snowy wings kneeling before Our Lady, hears the words that redeemed the world, AVE MARIA GRATIA PLENA, DOMINUS TECUM BENEDICTA TU IN MULIERI-BUS. . . . Indeed, I think he who is less simple of heart than this child should not enter that little House, sacred at least to the childhood of the world and hallowed now if only by the faith, the love, and the lives of such as she. Those rude walls of bricks are, for her, those which sheltered Madonna from sun and rain and homelessness, which

harboured the Holy Dove and received the Archangel;
and was it not between them Our Lord as a little child
played as a child plays and prayed first at His Mother's
knee ? The place is so small and so humble there is no
room for doubt.

There over the altar remains, but loaded now with
priceless jewels and dresses in cloth of gold and silver
tissue, the statue of the Madonna and Child of which
S. Helena speaks. No one, I think, who has once looked
upon that amazing image but must confess it, perhaps,
the most astonishing idol in Europe. It smiles and smiles,
secretly as with some inner beatitude, with something
of the interior and inexhaustible delight one finds in a
Buddha. It is a poor comparison, but I can find nothing
else to which to liken it ;—an amazing thing. At the
other end of the sanctuary over the little window, as
S. Helena reported, there still hangs the painted Crucifix.
The walls are still in part covered with ruined frescoes as
she found them, but the place is so dark, only lighted by
the many tapers of the shrine, that it is almost impossible
to see anything clearly.

After seeing this wonderful shrine one has time to
examine the church, the roof of which is painted in grisaille
by Luca Signorelli, but has grievously suffered from
restoration. The church for the most part consists of
various chapels belonging to different nations and adorned
by them. It is perhaps unnecessary to add that England
is not represented there.

It is, however, in the Sacristies and the Treasury that
what remains to the church of its ancient splendour is to be
found. To the right of the central chapel, in the right
transept, is the Sagrestia di S. Marco, over the entrance to
which is a beautiful terra-cotta of S. Luke by Luca della
Robbia. Within, the sacristy is magnificently painted by
Melozzò da Forlì. This great master has painted the cupola
to resemble architecture much as Michelangelo later painted
in the Sixtine Chapel. Here in the cupola the painter has set

STATUE OF THE MADONNA
Santa Casa, Loreto

ight windows through which angels enter bearing emblems
f the Passion, one the Cord with which Christ was scourged
nd the bag of Money with which He was bought, another
he Chalice, another the Paschal Lamb, another the Cross,
nother the Column to which He was bound, another the
Pincers, another the Nails and Hammer, and the last a
branch of Olive. Beneath the windows are figures of David
nd the Prophets, and the whole is so grand and glorious
hat one can never look at it long enough. Beneath is a
delightful but somewhat spoiled fresco of the Entry of
Christ into Jerusalem, painted by Palmezzano after
designs by Melozzò da Forlì.

To the left of the transept chapel is the Sagrestia della
Cura, with a fine terra-cotta of S. Matthew by Luca della
Robbia. Within, the sacristy is decorated by Luca
Signorelli. Here, too, we have the cupola painted archi-
tecturally and divided into eight compartments on which
we see music-making angels, and beneath them the Four
Evangelists and the Four Doctors of the Church. The
angels are wonderfully lovely in their gracefulness and
beauty, and the four Evangelists and Doctors very impressive in their grandeur. Beneath, in the seven divisions
of the walls, we see the Twelve Apostles, two in each com-
partment save two, where our Lord appears rebuking S.
Peter and showing the marks of His wounds to S. Thomas.
This latter composition seems to have been broadly modelled
upon the bronze group of Verrocchio in the façade of
Or San Michele in Florence, and it is perhaps the finest of the
series. Better even than this, however, is the fresco over the
door, of the Conversion of S. Paul, in which the master's
work at Orvieto is prophesied. These frescoes were
painted here certainly before 1484, and everywhere are full
of Florentine impressions. The doorway and fountain
are by Benedetto da Maiano, the intarsia by Domenico
d'Assisi.

In the north transept is the Treasury, which is well worth
a visit, though the value of its contents is nothing like what

it was before the Napoleonic spoliation. The French eve
carried off the wonderful figure of the Madonna and Chil
in the Santa Casa, and did not hesitate to spoil the Treasury
which, however, even as it is, is worth a visit.

Really the only other thing worth seeing in Loreto, from
the mere sightseer's point of view, is the Palazzo Apostolico
which, as I have said, Bramante planned and began in 1510
Here is a small collection of pictures containing a Descen
from the Cross by Guercino, a Nativity by Annabil
Carracci, and twelve pieces by Lorenzo Lotto. The earlies
of these is the SS. Christopher, Sebastian and Roch (30
which the master painted while he was in Ancona. It use
to hang in the chapel to the right of the entrance of the
church. As an old man Lotto came to Loreto " resolved,
according to Vasari, " to finish his life in the service of the
Madonna, making his habitation in the Holy House. There
upon he began the execution of historical representations i
figures of one *braccia* high or less, around the choir and abov
the sedilia. In one of these he depicted the Birth o
Christ ; in another the Adoration of the Magi ; the Pre
sentation to Simon occupies the third ; and following this i
the Saviour baptized by John in the Jordan. The Woma
taken in Adultery and led before Christ is also among thes
pictures, which are executed in a very graceful manner
Two other stories which Lorenzo likewise painted in thi
place exhibit a large number of figures ; one of these re
presents David offering sacrifice ; the other exhibits the
Archangel Michael in combat with Lucifer, whom he ha
driven out of heaven."

All these works are now here in the Palazzo Apostolico
the David offering Sacrifice of which Vasari speaks bein
the Sacrifice of Melchisedek (50), to which belong th
SS. Lucy and Thecla and the two Prophets (25, 27, 24
28).

Vasari tells us that " no long time had elapsed after th
completion of these stories before Lorenzo died, as he had
lived, in the manner of an upright man, and good Christian

resigning his soul to the hands of God his Maker. The last years of his life were passed in the utmost peace and tranquillity of mind, nay, what is more, he was by them, as is to be hoped and believed, enabled to obtain the riches of life eternal, which might possibly not have been secured to him had he remained to the close of his days exclusively wrapt up in the affairs of the world. . . ."

Lorenzo Lotto, however, was not the only great artist who died on the threshold of the Holy House of Loreto. Perhaps that is not wonderful, but the reader will probably be surprised to hear that the other I have in my mind was an Englishman.

I have said that I had business in Loreto. That business was to discover, if I could, the grave of Richard Crashaw, who died in Loreto, a Canon of the Cathedral, in the year 1649. In this I was not successful. Crashaw, already unsettled in his religious convictions, was a fellow of Peterhouse, Cambridge, when the Civil War broke out; and when Peterhouse College was sacked by the rebels, in 1643, he refused to take the Solemn League and Covenant. Therefore, with five of his friends, he was expelled. He went to Oxford and later to London, and thence he made his way to Paris, where Cowley found him in 1646 in great distress. He was then a Catholic. Cowley introduced him to Queen Henrietta Maria, and she gave him introduction to Cardinal Palotta and others in Rome, whither he wished to go, and a purse of gold, as indeed became her, poor lady. Crashaw set out, was well received by the Cardinal and given some minor position about him. We read that " Mr. Crashaw infinitely commended his Cardinal but complained extremely of the wickedness of those of his retinue, of which he, having the Cardinal's ear, complained to him. Upon which the Italians fell so far out with him that the Cardinal, to secure his life, was forced to put him from his service, and procuring him some small employ at the Lady's of Loreto, whither he went on pilgrimage in summer-time, and, overheating himself, died in four weeks after he came

thither, and it was doubtful whether he was not poisoned."
So perished beside Our Lady's House perhaps the greatest
religious poet England ever had.

Requiem eternam dona ei Domine
Et lux perpetua luceat ei.

CHAPTER XII

RECANATI

NIGHT had already fallen and hidden the sea, when I left Loreto to walk in the summer moonlight up to Recanati some seven miles away in the hills. Over all that great world of mountain and valley, darkness had fallen like a transparent veil, the luminous darkness of summer, out of which there came to me as I went the soft noises of the night, the hoot of an owl, the bark of a fox, the curious and bitter song of the night *cecco* among the olives, the wind among the leaves. I shall not forget the beauty of that way. The road lay over the hills ; high in heaven, the moon, crescent still, hung like the immaculate Host in an invisible monstrance about which were set, for candles, innumerable stars. One by one as I went the little cities far away each on a hill-top shone out full of lights, glittered and was lost between the infinity of earth and sky. So to the north across the valley of the Musone, Osimo greeted me once more and Castelfidardo ; so, far away to the south, across the gulf of the Potenza, Potenza, Monteluppone, Macerata ; and words I had always known came back to me as I watched them shining there : " a city that is set on a hill cannot be hid."

Thus I went through the summer night, and one who went before me, invisible in the darkness, was humming a song, something like this—

> Sona vespro alla bonora
> L' angeli canta e Dio adora ;

Quanno l' angeli cantava
Gesù Cristo predicava ;
Predicava ad alta voce
Gesù Cristo è morto in croce ;
Morto in croce per la via
'Ndo ne vai Madre Maria ? . . .

Presently I came to the big gate, deserted and silent in
the midst of the night. Up and up I passed through the
paved, deserted streets between the tall houses, looking for
the inn ; missed it and had to return, back through the
silent street, to find it at last with the help of another
benighted like myself.

The first appearance of the Albergo della Pace was any
thing but promising. The entrance was at the bottom of a
dirty, dark court, lighted only by a small lamp burning
before an image of the Madonna ; but it was too late and
I too tired to trouble about appearances, and when the
door was opened and a room was shown me I accepted i
without demur and was soon in bed. And it happened here
as indeed everywhere through the Marches, that good
fortune waited upon me. I slept well and peacefully
When I awoke it was to find the room still in darkness, for
the window was closely shuttered. I jumped out of bed
and unhooked the iron fastening and thrust back the
creaking casement, to be almost blinded by the sudden
blaze of light. But when my eyes had grown accustomed to
the sun, what a sight met my gaze ! The whole world
seemed to be spread out at my feet. The inn, it appeared
was set upon the city wall ; fifty or sixty feet sheer below
me the road wound down towards Loreto, and before me on
their hill-tops rose half a hundred little cities, half lost in the
sunlight, in a great world of mountain and valley backed by
the far dim peaks of the central Apennine. It was a sight
almost to stop the heart, so great it was ; a landscape in
deed, if it were a landscape, and not rather something in a
dream, that could never be forgotten, and its gentle seren
nobility won me at once. How often and how long I sat
by that window in Recanati that I might never forget the

lines of the hills, the sunlight and the shadow over the olive gardens, the visionary glory of those far-away peaks ! And now when I would, if I could, express something of all that perfection, I can say nothing but the commonest words. It must be seen to be loved as I loved it, and so must Recanati : that tragic and hospitable little town of grey stone and rosy brick on the hill-top where Leopardi for so long ate his heart out in bitterness and despair.

Recanati is said, without much confidence however, to have arisen from the ruins of the Roman Ricina, some twelve miles away towards Macerata in the valley of the Potenza, probably in the Gothic wars. At any rate, Recanati itself was taken by the Lombards and occupied, even so late as 772, by Desiderius, their last king, before, with the rest of the Exarchate and the Pentapolis, it finally came into the hands of the Holy See by the act of Charlemagne. Nothing or almost nothing is known of the early history of the city, but its position upon these almost impregnable hills, along whose summits the city winds, doubtless enabled it to maintain a large measure of independence from outside interference, and as a free commune, for such it appears to have been, its chief enemy was neither Emperor nor Pope, but its neighbour, Osimo. The people of Recanati were, however, ardent Guelfs, and they faced the Ghibellines of Osimo with a certain success until Pope Innocent III imposed peace upon them. But the little city does not appear ever to have suffered the tyranny of a Signore. It was governed consistently under the suzerainty of the Popes by a close oligarchy of its own citizens, of whom two hundred formed the Council by right of birth, of whom ninety-seven, it is said, were nobles. The ninety-seven nobles provided the executive, but were always in a minority in the Council, and thus a sort of equilibrium was maintained which on the whole brought much good fortune to Recanati. Now and again we find the city in rebellion against the Holy See, but that is exceptional, and on the whole it may be said that Recanati

was in the main faithful to its overlord and fortunate and
happy under the Papal suzerainty. To-day it appears to
us as a little sun-baked, rain-washed city stretched upon a
great saddle of the hills, a city that we can love, lost in the
enormous quiet that surrounds it, full of simple people and
littered with beautiful things.

I have already spoken of the Albergo della Pace on the
city wall, certainly not the least delightful thing in Recanati
with its wonderful view towards Macerata over the Musone
valley, but a view almost as fine is to be had from the
northern loggia of the Municipio, which looks towards
Loreto and the sea, and gives you Castlefidardo, that famous
place, and Monte Cònero over Ancona.   The Municipio, too,
for all its modernity, for the fine old Palazzo Comunale has
been destroyed, contains more than one very precious thing :
a fine altarpiece of the Madonna and Child with S. Vito,
S. John Baptist, S. John Evangelist, and another Saint on
a gold ground with nine saints in the predella, a work by a
local master of considerable merit, Pietro da Recanati,
painted in 1422 ; and two works by Lorenzo Lotto, one an
early picture, a Transfiguration, the other an altarpiece in
six compartments, painted in 1508, which comes from
S. Domenico.

This church, which stands close to the Municipio in the
Corso, has been newly restored ; it contains another Lotto,
a rather feeble fresco of S. Vincent in glory.   The Dominicans came to Recanati in 1272, and eighteen years later
obtained from the Bishop of Umana, Fra Salvo, a Dominican himself, the parochial church of S. Gregorio, which they
demolished, and built in its stead the church we see.   The
main portal is very lovely and is attributed, like that of S.
Agostino and the Loggia of the Palazzo of Cardinal Venier,
to Giuliano da Maiano.   The church has, as I say, suffered
a good deal from restoration, but something of the old
building may be seen in the Via Porta S. Domenico.

But undoubtedly the most interesting work of art
to be found in Recanati is Lotto's picture of the Annuncia-

THE ANNUNCIATION. BY LORENZO LOTTO
Chiesa dei Mercanti, Recanati

tion in the little church of S. Maria sopra Mercanti. This is certainly one of the most interesting pictures in the Marches. In a great and high room, very different from the Santa Casa, and open under a lofty round arch to a garden full of trees and a pergola, Madonna, who has been kneeling in prayer at a prie-dieu upon which lies an open book of hours, has suddenly turned away with uplifted protesting hands in astonishment and even fear at the sudden entrance of the archangel S. Gabriel, whose streaming hair tells of the swiftness of his flight. So sudden, indeed, has been the advent of the angel that Madonna's little cat, asleep till then in some corner, scampers in terror across the room. Under the arch appears God the Father, a majestic figure, His two hands stretched forth like those of a swimmer; He seems indeed to have dived down from heaven. The room is furnished with almost Flemish realism and completeness; on the mantel over the hearth, before which clothes are hanging to dry, is a candlestick, with horn and books; above again, but in an impossible situation, is the leaded window; to the left is the curtained bed, and before the hearth on a stool stands veiled what looks like the Chalice, which, however, according to the legend as well as according to the vision of Catherine Emmerich, was the property of S. Veronica, not of the Blessed Virgin. This extraordinary and fascinating work is undated and unsigned.

There are three other churches in Recanati worth some notice, the Duomo of S. Flaviano which, though in the main a building of the seventeenth century, has some remains of an earlier church, and in the sacristy an extraordinary altarpiece of great interest, by Ludameo de Urbanis, and the churches of S. Agostino and S. Vito. S. Agostino, as I have said, is chiefly notable for its fine fifteenth-century façade attributed to Giuliano da Maiano, and the brick façade of S. Vito is perhaps the work of Vanvitelli, the author of the Campanile of Loreto.

These three churches can be seen on the way to what

the people of Recanati to-day certainly consider the most important sight in their city, I mean the Casa Leopardi, where Giacomo Leopardi the great poet was born in 1798. Of this great man the city is to-day full : his statue stands before the Palazzo Municipio, under the mighty campanile in the Piazza renamed after him, and as incomparably the greatest of her sons, Recanati cannot make enough of him. The house which contains his library and that of his father with many of his manuscripts is most courteously shown to visitors on presentation of a card.

Giacomo Leopardi, indeed, one of the great poets of the modern world, was the eldest son of Conte Monaldo Leopardi and of Adelaide of the Marchesi Antici, and was born upon 29th June 1798 in the Palace of the Leopardi, which, as I say, you may still see and visit in Recanati. His father had been educated by a Jesuit, and all his life remained an eager and devout Catholic and a bitter enemy of the new ideas then so violently offered to the world by the Revolution. He was, however, a man of culture, studious and upright, the author of several little works against the novelties he hated, and what is more, against those lukewarm defenders of all he loved, whom his passionate nature despised and distrusted even more than avowed enemies. He was too, as his library bears witness, a great lover of learning and literature, and his generosity was such that in 1812 he opened his collections *filiis, amicis, civibus.* But he was not a practical man, and in 1803 the management of his financial affairs was taken out of his hands. In this curious household, under the eye of his father, Giacomo the future poet was brought up with his brother Carlo and his sister Paolina, and taught at first by Giuseppe Torres, a Mexican and ex-Jesuit, who had been his father's tutor, but later by the priest Sebastiano Sanctini, whom he always loved. It can be well imagined, however, that if the youthful poet did not find much food for his intellectual and spiritual hunger in such company, this old palace in Recanati with its store of books was not the worst place in Italy in which to bring up a boy of a temperament like his. Already at ten years of age he had begun to think his own thoughts, to live his own life, to educate himself, and from his thirteenth year he spent all his time in his father's great library lost in the study of the Greek and Latin poets. No doubt he was allowed to carry his too early devotion to literature too far; his health suffered, and perhaps the physical deformity which presently declared itself was encouraged, if not caused, by the long hours spent indoors crouched over huge folios. At sixteen, it is said, he had read all the Latin and Greek classics, could write with accuracy English, French, Spanish, and Hebrew, and had already composed a commentary upon Plotinus. In 1817 he began a correspondence with Pietro Giordani, who counselled moderation in his studies, and as, about this time, he fell in love with his cousin Geltruda Cassi-Lazzari, a married woman, twenty-six years of age, then living in his father's house, the which turned him to poetry, it is possible that for a time Giordani's advice was taken.

But Giacomo Leopardi's life was foredoomed to tragedy. His physical deformity and debility induced in him a black pessimism such as is rare in a European ; this grew upon him, and though he found some happiness in the affection of his brother and sister, his father was uncongenial to him on account of his temperament and view of life, his mother by reason of her perhaps excessive parsimony, and he hated his home, Recanati, the Marches, everything he saw and experienced, the noise of the little city, its boisterous winds, its hot sun, its bitter rain. It would be a mistake to blame his parents or his upbringing, it was his health which was at fault, which denied him an active life, the love of woman, a sane outlook upon the world. As his life dragged on he only acquired more learning, not a wider or more tolerant outlook. Sometimes he seemed to have found a temporary relief from his gloomy thoughts in escapes from his home, but as he was entirely dependent upon his family, and his health would not allow him to follow a profession, he was always obliged to return. We hear of him now in Florence, now in Rome, now in Bologna, meeting all the most eager men of his day, befriended by Niebuhr and Bunsen, but always unfortunate in his humiliating love affairs, and unable to bear the strain of a life of activity even of the mildest sort. He dreamed of an Italy rejuvenated and free, but his love for his fatherland was spoilt by hatred and bitter regret, and this again was the result of disease, of the misery of physical distress. In Naples, however, in 1833 he seemed for a time to recover a certain lightness of heart that had, since his early youth, been almost a stranger to him; but this did not last, and three years later he succumbed to the dropsy which for long had threatened him, dying upon 14th June 1837 at the early age of thirty-nine.

It is easy to feel a sort of disgust at the misery of Leopardi; it is easy, but it is unjust. His miserable health excuses him and explains the enormous difference we find between his outlook and that of Shelley or Byron. It is when we compare him with Keats that he seems smallest. Keats was a man fundamentally sick all his life, and yet his love, enthusiasm, and enjoyment of nature are not a whit less noble or characteristic of him than of Shelley or Byron. But Nature, the material world, its sublime order and beauty are not only nothing to Leopardi, but are regarded almost as a personal grievance, a sham and a mockery, hiding the devilish truth. Nor does he feel the splendour of history or the greatness of the achievement and destiny of man, he is immersed and rendered mad by his bodily suffering, his wounded self-esteem, his disappointed affections, and thus, as a man, means infinitely less to us than how many of those who, without his genius and with much more than his physical distress, have yet contrived to face life bravely and to smile at fortune.

It is as a poet and only as a poet that Leopardi really wins our admiration. He is a great artist and nothing else, a

Greek in this, born out of due time, and worthy of that title for the best of all reasons, his sheer perfection as an artist. Perhaps no other poet of the modern world can boast just that astonishing faultlessness and inevitableness which we find everywhere in his work and which make it indestructible and immortal.

So that though it is of him one thinks most in Recanati, it is not upon his wretched life one cares to dwell, but, here in the Piazza before that old palace he found so dreary, of that song he alone knew how to utter which we have seen utterly refuted, but whose perfect beauty can never pass away :—

> O patria mia, vedo le mura e gli archi
> E le colonne e i simulacri e l' erme
> Torri degli avi nostri
> Ma la gloria non vedo. . . .

CHAPTER XIII

FERMO AND MONTE GIORGIO

THE sun was shining after the rain which for two days had involved Recanati in its misery, when I stood under the great tower in the Piazza Leopardi waiting for the public automobile that would carry me in less than an hour from this lofty hill city to the railway and the sea at Porto Recanati.

And here let me say that these new motor services which are everywhere in Italy, and not least in the Marches, replacing the old *diligenza*, are in every way to be recommended to the traveller afoot, and especially in such a country as this, where going from north to south one is faced at every ten miles or so by a profound valley running from east to west, the negotiation of which is always a matter of hours, and where every city one desires to see is set isolated, high on a hill-top, the ascent to which is always tantalizing in its winding about and about and never less than a morning's walk. In these circumstances the new automobile service, swift in its passage, easy in its gait and altogether democratic, is the one modern thing in Italy that one can altogether commend or praise. It has already brought many almost inaccessible places within reach of the ordinary traveller, and is every year opening up new districts which, till its appearance, were impossible for most of us to hope to reach.

I was intent on Fermo. Now, to reach Fermo from Recanati, two ways are open to the traveller : the laborious and picturesque route by road through Macerata, Pausula

THE PIAZZA FERMO

and Monte S. Giusto, or the way by rail from Porto Recanati
to Porto S. Giorgio. I chose the latter because the automobile service rendered it the more convenient, and I made
up my mind to see Macerata on my way homeward, after I
had had a glimpse of Ascoli, the most southern town of the
Marches.

Porto S. Giorgio, where I found myself early in the
afternoon of the day I left Recanati, is the ancient Castellum
or Castrum Firmanum, the port or emporium of the Roman
Firmum (Fermo), though no one seeing it to-day would
think it so old. It stood, and it still stands of course, on
the coast road which united the Via Salaria and Via
Flaminia, and was the market of the almost inaccessible
Fermo on its hill-top.

How difficult Fermo must always have been to reach
he learns best who tramps the steep five miles of good road
which joins it with Porto S. Giorgio, the railway, and the
sea. Steep as it is, however, and laborious, that road has
many compensations for the traveller afoot, for it is one
of the loveliest in this part of Italy, and with the exception
maybe of Camerino, no other city in the Marches is so
well worth reaching as Fermo at the end of it.

The little walled city with its curious acropolis so
wonderfully lifted up above its neighbours is the queen of
all this country of profound valley and restless abrupt
upland, noble, lovely and graceful, a worthy sister of Siena
and Perugia, a place hard to reach if you will, but far
harder to leave, so strangely does it capture all who come
to it.

For when climbing through the vines and olives on a
summer afternoon you first catch sight of it under the sky
crowned by its cathedral, bastioned and very strong,
you are caught at once, and can never quite rid yourself of
its curious fascination or forget its amazing beauty, its
wonderful outlook over mountain and sea, to the hills of
Dalmatia they say, and certainly westward to the great
still peaks of the central Apennine. All one's days there

are days of quietness, of contemplation and remembrance. For Fermo is very old, has faced and outfaced every revolution which has shaken Italy since first Rome began to build that mighty Empire out of which all of us are come and to which we owe everything that is fundamental in our civilization.

It is true we know nothing of Fermo before the Roman conquest of Picenum, but its situation alone would assure us that it was a strong city long before that event, which came to pass at the beginning of the First Punic War. When Hannibal so nearly overthrew the Roman power Fermo, we read, was steadfast in most trying circumstances. That it was even then a strong fortress seems certain, and it is as that it appears in the Social War when Pompey took refuge there after his defeat by Afranius, whom, however, he was able to defy from this stronghold and later to defeat in his turn under these walls. In the Civil War it gave itself to Cæsar, and then was reinforced by Augustus, and seems to have continued a place of importance all through the long years of the Empire. With the fall of the Empire it again appears as a fortress to be contested for time and time again by Belisarius and Totila ; and when at last it came with the Exarchate and the Pentapolis into the hands of the Pope, it is still a place of consequence, the See of a Bishop, as it is to-day, and the capital of a province, the Marca di Fermo, for it was the strongest place in all this country, as the old rhyme has it—

> Quando Fermo vuol fermare
> Tutta la Marca fa tremare.

In the hurly-burly of the Middle Age here in the Marches that strength was its principal characteristic. On account of it, it was always the object of desire on the part of any captain or noble or adventurer, who hoped to cut a lordship for himself out of the March hereabout. So it fell to various tyrants, but was never for long in the hands of a single family : Gentile da Mogliano, Rioraldo da Monte

Verde, Ludovico Migliorati, Visconti d'Oleggio, Oliverotto Euffreducci, Alessandro Sforza, such are the names of some who set their hearts as high as Fermo and held it for a time only to lose it at last. In the middle of the fifteenth century, however, the people of Fermo, weary of the price they had to pay for the fame of their city, deliberately destroyed that mighty acropolis, which, dismantled still, rises so suddenly out of the midst of the city, and upon which the Cathedral stands. No vestige of the Rocca which once threatened the Marches from that high place remains to us, and to-day where of old men-at-arms marched and counter-marched, sentinels of the citadel, children play and men and maidens make love in a great shady garden about the old church.

In Fermo, however, the Cathedral is not the first church one visits, for at the gate, far beneath, stands the beautiful Gothic sanctuary of S. Francesco, where are, too, some Roman remains and the tomb and the name of one who recalls the mediæval city very forcibly to our minds. It is the tomb of one of the Euffreducci, though not of that Oliverotto whom Machiavelli chose for his model " of those who have raised themselves to power by their atrocities." In the achievement of this man we obtain a very good idea of the sort of thing the people of Fermo more than once suffered in those turbulent years.

" Oliverotto," we read, " was left an orphan in his infancy and was brought up by his maternal uncle Giovanni Fogliani, who sent him to study the art of war under Paolo Vitelli, one of the greatest of the mercenary captains of that day. Under this teacher of the art he became a celebrated leader, and his master's close friend and ally. Paolo Vitelli, however, having been hung by the government of Florence for treason, Oliverotto for a short time joined his fortunes with Vitellozzo Vitelli, and then took service with Cesare Borgia, under whom he was eminently successful and increased his military experience and power. It was in January 1502 that, having thus earned the reputa-

tion of being one of the most successful soldiers of his day
he returned to visit his native city. Before doing so he
wrote to his uncle Fogliani announcing his intention, and
telling him that as he had toiled only for the sake of honour,
and as he should wish that the citizens might see that he
had not laboured in vain, he was desirous of making his
entry creditably, accompanied by an hundred horsemen
of his friends and followers, and begging his uncle to
dispose the citizens to receive him with that retinue.
All this Fogliani did, and received his nephew in his palace,
where he was entertained with every sort of distinction.

" Oliverotto spent two or three days in feeling his ground
and maturing his plans ; and then at one of the festivals
given in his honour, to which all the leading citizens of
Fermo were invited, his soldiers suddenly burst into the
banqueting hall and slew Fogliani, his son, and several
others of the principal citizens. No sooner was the deed
done than, mounting his horse, he put himself at the head
of his men and rode off to the Palazzo Pubblico, where he
obliged the magistrates, who were terror-struck at what
had happened, to proclaim him Lord of Fermo. And
having put to death all those whose discontent might have
been dangerous to him, he strengthened himself in the
government by means of new civil and military dispositions
so that for the space of a year, during which he held power
he was not only safe in the city of Fermo, but was formidable to all his neighbours. And it would have been
exceedingly difficult to oust him from his position, had he
not suffered himself to be ensnared by Cesare, who put
him to death a year later, together with others at that
famous Sinigaglia banquet."

Machiavelli proceeds to moralize the tale, as we can well
imagine, by an appeal to common sense. For us it will be
more interesting to note that other Euffreducci, Ludovico
whose tomb in this church of S. Francesco recalls the more
famous Oliverotto. Ludovico Euffreducci was the nephew
of Oliverotto, and at the time Cesare killed that captain was

still but a boy. His mother had saved him from the fury
of the citizens after the fall of his uncle by fleeing to Perugia,
for she was a Baglioni. There, in that great hill city of
Umbria, he was educated and soon became as great a soldier
as his uncle. He returned to Fermo in 1514 as the first
citizen of a free state, but in his absence his kinsmen, the
Baglioni, attacked Fermo and sacked it. This was too
much for most of the people of Fermo. The heads of the
Brancadoro family, the chief rivals of the Euffreducci,
easily persuaded the populace that Ludovico was privy to
the outrage. A feud arose, the city was divided into two
parties, and eventually both Ludovico and Bartolommeo
Brancadoro were summoned to Rome to explain matters
to Pope Leo x. On the way thither, however, Ludovico
waylaid his enemy and killed him. In consequence the
magistrates of Fermo declared him an outlaw, and in reply
he gathered together a band of ruffians and ravaged the
country. But it was already too late in the day for this sort
of thing to be successful. The Papacy was firmly established
in the control of its state, and Pope Leo x had little difficulty
in ousting the outlaws, though Ludovico died fighting to the
last. His end is curious and characteristic. The captain
of the Pope's troops was the Bishop of Chiusi. He came
upon Ludovico, we read, " fallen from his horse and dying.
With a dying sinner unshriven and unabsolved at his feet,
the fighting Bishop felt that his work as a soldier was done
with and that the priest must appear. Quickly dismounting
he knelt by the side of the dying man, heard his confession,
absolved him and received his last breath."

One realizes such stories as these, common enough in most
of these hill towns, better, I think, in Fermo than elsewhere.
For the whole city is still full of mediæval buildings, steep
alley ways, and courts, and narrow, climbing *vicoli*, and all
lies in the shadow of the great acropolis upon which stands
the Cathedral.

One comes into Fermo up that beautiful climbing
country road which continually offers you finer and ever

13

finer views of that great hill country in the midst of which
Fermo stands so high, through the vineyards from Porta
S. Francesco to another gateway as large almost as a
fortress, to find oneself in the beautiful long Piazza which is
the true centre of the town.   Out of this Piazza, uphill and
downhill, innumerable little streets pass between the tall
houses, and in the chief of these by-ways the inn, the Albergo
Vittoria, is to be found.   It has little to boast of.

It was a Sforza, perhaps the great Francesco, then lord
of the March, who built this noble Piazza to which the
arcades which surround it were added in the sixteenth
century, when the great gate was built and the statue of
the Pope erected on high before the Palazzo del Governo
here, with its beautiful steps, to mark the passing of Fermo
in 1550 under the direct control of the Holy See.   Here, too,
are the Archbishop's Palace and the University and
Biblioteca.

From this Piazza by the steep by-ways one may climb
up to that lofty acropolis upon which of old the Fortezza
stood, but which is now all a garden about the noble and
ancient Cathedral.

This grand old church dates back to the eleventh century,
when the atrium, part of which still remains, was built.
The façade and the campanile, however, are of the fourteenth century, and, within, the church has been altogether
modernized.   A fourteenth-century monument, however,
remains, in the atrium, the tomb of Giovanni Visconti, the
nephew of the great Archbishop of Milan, who ruled in
Fermo from 1360 to 1366.   Close by is the sixteenth-century
sarcophagus of the condottiere Mateucci.   The crypt is
interesting : it dates from the tenth or eleventh century,
and contains a sarcophagus older still and a marble column
with the figure of a bishop of the same date as the building
itself.

The main street of Fermo, the Corso, leaves the Piazza
Maggiore beside the Palazzo del Governo and passes under
the acropolis upon the north.   Close to the Albergo, in the

Corso, is the church of the Carmine, where is a fine altar-piece by Rondinelli [?] which shines very nobly and quietly in the rather blatant mediocre building. There we see the Madonna enthroned with her little Son between four saints, S. Jerome, S. Vito, S. Catherine of Alexandria and S. Francis.

Farther on stands the little old church of S. Pietro. Here once there was a triptych by Lorenzo da San Severino, painted in 1481, of the Madonna and Child with S. John Baptist and the Magdalen. It is now in the Biblioteca, where too is a charming Madonna and Child from the hand of Antoniazzo Romano, that Umbrian master who owed so much to Melozzo da Forlì and later to Fiorenzo di Lorenzo of Perugia.

There are other pictures to be seen in the various churches of the city, and some in private hands. In the church of S. Spirito, for instance, there is a Holy Family ascribed to Rubens, but certainly not from his hand. In S. Agostino, the south entrance of which has some remnants of a fine majolica frieze, is a Holy Trinity falsely ascribed to Titian, and in the Spina Chapel in the same church, a work perhaps by Tintoretto. In S. Pietro are a fine Francescuccio Ghisi and a work by Andrea da Bologna.

In the Casa Bernetti there is an early work by Girolamo Savoldo, the pupil of Francesco Bonsignori who was so strongly influenced by Lotto, a S. Jerome in the desert.

But, after all, Fermo is to be loved not for the works of art or architecture or painting which it has to show, but for itself, for its own beauty and nobility, its wonderful command of the glorious world in which it stands up like a great tower or bastion looking so proudly across the mountains and the sea. No one, certainly, who has ever spent a few days within its walls can leave it without a real regret. For to live within its gates is to be made a partaker of the sky, to breathe an air so large and noble that even the greatest work of art, did it possess it, would be at last unregarded while we turned to Nature herself, here for once wholly satisfying and able, without leaving us a single resentment, to absorb us into herself, to overwhelm us with her largeness, her majesty, her sweetness. Those lines of hills that lead our eyes up to the great mountains, those mysterious sweet valleys, those silver gardens of olives against the darkness of the cypresses yonder, the spaciousness of the sky where God dwells, the largeness of the earth He has surely especially blessed : where in the world shall we possess them with such completeness as here, or where shall we be made at one with them so profoundly and without an afterthought ? Not in Perugia, where all day long one looks upon Assisi and thinks of S. Francis, not from the great rampart of Siena, whose bitter *contado* is crowded with so many splendid and melancholy things, nor in Spoleto, nor in Orvieto. Only a little village near to my heart on Mont' Amiata in southern Tuscany gives you at once and freely so real a possession of the world as a garden—the garden where God walked in the cool of the day. But there at last, upon the farthest horizon, you may see Soracte, and your thoughts are disturbed by the apparition of Rome. Here there is nothing but the absolute. Fermo, aloft on her height, is alone with the mountains, the valleys, and the sky, for which we are homesick, and to which one day we shall return.

It is so hard to leave Fermo without a heavy heart, that almost any excuse is good enough to delay departure ; and when the excuse is the necessity of an excursion to a famous Franciscan convent it is not to be denied.

Monte Giorgio, easily visible due west from the acropolis of Fermo, lies some thirteen miles away, across the profound valley of the Tenna, and there, if it be pictures you seek, you will find a splendid Ghisi, the master's finest work.

I know not rightly how to speak of this place which I love so much, nor how to persuade him who is secure in Fermo and set down at an inn more or less furnished with

modern comforts, to visit a place so humble, so poor and
so holy. For holy it is. Figure to yourself a little white
village shining on the hills under the stainless sky above
a thousand valleys beautiful with vineyards and olive
gardens, and surrounded by hills greater than its own,
crowned by villages scarcely less fair. Such is Monte
Giorgio, whose heart is the convent of S. Francis, which
should be one of the most famous Franciscan shrines in
Italy, for it was there that the *Fioretti* were written by
the Ugolino da Monte Giorgio, who, as he looked out of the
window of his cell, could see shining across this blessed
country all the little holy places of the March, humble
Franciscan dwellings which figure in his beautiful book :
Massa, Fallerone, Penna S. Giovanni, Fermo, Monte-
rubbiano.

The convent, as we see it to-day, is fair enough and holy
still and full of manuscripts, and there and in the olive
garden about the place one may, better than anywhere
else in the world, turn the pages of that matchless volume
in which all the simplicity and charm of the Middle Age
which produced S. Francis lies hid, as in no other book
that was ever written, for the *Divine Comedy* is too passionate and terrible, too much concerned with the great of this
world and with the next, while the *Imitation* is, after all,
the meditation of a monk penned for Religious. But the
Fioretti is for all, for ever—for all who may find in their
hearts, even in middle life, even in old age, that something of the little child, without which no one can enter the
kingdom of heaven.

That precious volume, whose pages one turns again and
again and with a new emotion in such a place as this, was
originally written in silver Latin, and there we read :
"Provincia Marchiæ Anconitanæ quasi quibusdam fuit stellis
notabilibus decorata, sanctis scilicet fratribus Minoribus qui
sursum et deorsum, coram Deo scilicet et proximo, radiosis
virtutibus relucebant, quorum memoria vere in benedictione
divina est." Or, as we have it : "The Province of the

March of Ancona was in olden time adorned, even as the sky with stars, with brothers that were patterns of holy life ; the which like shining lights of heaven have illumined and adorned the Order of Saint Francis, and the world with ensamples and with doctrine." Frate Ugolino goes on to tell us of these brothers, among the rest of Brother Lucido Antico, "whose glorious tongue, taught by the Holy Spirit, brought forth marvellous fruit in preaching " ; of Brother Bentivoglia of Sanseverino " who was lifted up in the air for a great space, whilst he was at prayer in the wood" ; of Brother Peter of Monticello " who was borne by angels to the feet of the Crucifix of the church, in front of which he was at prayer " ; of Brother Conrad who in the house at Forana saw the Blessed Virgin, who for a moment "laid in his arms her little blessed Son " ; of the conversion, the life, miracles and death of the holy Brother John of Penna ; of Brother Peaceful who saw the soul of Brother Humble going up to heaven ; of Brother Jacopo of Massa who " saw in a dream all the Friars Minor in the world in the likeness of a tree, and learned the virtue, the merits and the vices of each" ; and, lastly, of Brother John of Fermo who saw Jesu Christ, and on All Souls' Day, as he said Mass, beheld many delivered from Purgatory ; who alone of all men in a vision " understood all the order of the Holy Trinity," and a little later saw Christ Himself in the house of Moliano as he was saying Mass. For it seems that " having come at length to the act of consecration, and having said one-half of the words over the Host, to wit, ' *Hoc est*,' he could by no means proceed further, but only repeated the same words, to wit, ' *Hoc est enim*.' And the reason wherefore he could proceed no further was this, that he felt and saw the presence of Christ with a great company of angels, whose majesty he was not able to endure ; and he saw Christ entered not into the Host, or that the Host was not changed into the body of Christ until he should utter the other half of the words, to wit, ' *Corpus Meum*.' Wherefore, as he abode in this anxiety

THE ROAD TO FERMO

THE TRONTO, ASCOLI

and could proceed no further, the guardian and the other brothers, and likewise many lay folk that were in the church for to hear Mass, drew near unto the altar ; and were astonished to behold and see what things Brother John did ; and many of them were weeping out of devotion. At the last, after long space, to wit, when so it pleased God, Brother John uttered the words, ' *enim Corpus Meum* ' in a loud voice ; and straightway the form of the bread vanished, and in the Host appeared Jesu Christ the Blessed One, incarnate and glorified, and showed forth to him the humility and love which made Him to become incarnate of the Virgin Mary, and which makes Him every day to come into the hands of the priest when he consecrates the Host ; for which cause he was the more lifted up in sweetness of contemplation. Wherefore when he had elevated the Host and the consecrated chalice, he was rapt out of himself ; and his soul being lifted up above all bodily feeling, his body fell backwards ; and if he had not been supported by the guardian who stood beside him, he would have fallen on his back upon the ground. Whereat the brothers, running up to him, and the lay folk, men and women, that were in the church, he was carried into the sacristy as one dead, for his body was cold and the fingers of his hands were so tightly clenched that scarce could they at all be opened or moved. And in this manner he lay as one half dead or rapt away even until tierce ; and it was summer time. And because I, who was there present, desired much to know what God had wrought in him so soon as he had returned to himself again, I went to him and prayed him for the love of God to tell me all ; wherefore seeing that he trusted much in me, he told all unto me in order. . . ."

Of such is the kingdom of heaven.

CHAPTER XIV

ASCOLI

FROM Fermo one summer afternoon I made my way down to Porto S. Giorgio and came first to the village of Torre di Palma, where I found, in the parish church, a noble ancona by Crivelli. Towards evening I passed through Cupramarittima, famous for its Temple to Juno. In the Palazzo Pubblico there was just light enough to see a spoilt picture, again by Crivelli perhaps, of the Madonna and Child, with S. Sebastian and S. Catherine. Cupra is not a very charming place, and I did not wait to examine the mosaic pavements and Roman remains I heard of, but went on to Grottammare, which consists of an upper and a lower town, the latter a quite modern suburb for sea-bathers. The upper town, however, is well worth a visit, for the ruined castle on the steep offers one a great view over land and sea, and then Grottammare was the birthplace of that learned Pope who was so great a builder that during his pontificate of five years he transformed the city of Rome, and left it much as our fathers saw it before the advent of the Piedmontese. Pope Sixtus v was a peasant, Francesco Peretti by name, born in Grottammare in 1521. As a child he herded the swine and peddled onions up and down the coast, then he entered the Franciscan Order, acquired a wide and even profound knowledge of theology, became devoted to archæological studies and the art of building, and as Pope completed the dome of S. Peter's, restored the Roman Aqueducts, rebuilt the City, put down the brigands that infested the

great roads and reclaimed a good part of the Campagna by
encouraging agriculture.

He was the man—Pope Sixtus, that Fifth, that swineherd's son.
He knew the right thing, did it and thanked God when 'twas done.

I slept at Grottammare, and in the morning went down
the road across the low shore, the mountains standing
here a little back from the sea, to Benedetto del Tronto, a
curious and charming little walled town with a suburb on
the beach, and there I took the train for the famous frontier
town of Ascoli, the most southern point of all my journey.
That way, as I found on another journey, should be followed
afoot or by carriage, for it is, especially towards Ascoli,
very glorious, with views of the far-away mountains of the
central Apennine, and even, on a fortunate day, gives you a
glimpse of the Gran Sasso.

As for Ascoli, who can ever praise it enough or fail to
regret the day he left it ? That little city of many towers
on the banks of the Tronto is as lovely a place, as interesting and as charming a city, as is to be found in all the
Marches, whose southern frontier it has guarded so long.
It is a Roman town too, so Roman that it stands to-day
in the very shoes, as it were, of the Roman city, its Palazzo
Pubblico and its cathedral being indeed founded upon the
Roman ruins of similar buildings, and every approach to it,
and there are many, being indeed across a Roman bridge.

For Ascoli is as old as anything has need to be in
Europe, and in all the years it has not changed its name ;
Asculum Picenum, Cæsar called it,[1] and Ascoli Piceno it
remains to this day, and as in his day so down to our own
time it has been a place of great strength, almost inaccessible by reason of the rugged and tremendous nature
of country in which it stoops like an eagle ready to pounce
upon an enemy.   At first that enemy was Rome, for Ascoli
is older than the Roman occupation, indeed it led the
Piceni to oppose the great mistress of Italy, till in 268 B.C.

[1] *De Bello Civili*, i. 15.

it was taken by P. Sempronius Sophus and the Piceni wer
broken. But not without difficulty was Ascoli to submit
In the midst of the Social War her people rose up an
massacred the Roman pro-consul Quintus Servilius, hi
legate Fonteius and all the Roman colonists, and whe
Pompeius Strabo came with an army to punish the rebelliou
city which had raised the whole province against th
Roman name, they defeated him and held their walls fo
two years against the Romans, till, in despair, Judacilius o
Ascoli, who had conducted the great defence, put an end t
his life, and Pompeius entered and slew all the magistrate
and principal citizens and exiled the inhabitants, leavin
Ascoli desolate, if not utterly destroyed. It quietly re
covered, however, and outgrew its former greatness.

Some part, though not a great one, it played in the Civi
War of Cæsar. He, knowing its strength, hastened t
occupy it as he came down the long roads from Rimini an
the Rubicon. It was held by Pompey's friend, Lentulu
Spinther, with ten cohorts, but he and his men fled o
Cæsar's approach, and the city flung wide its gates to th
deliverer.

It seems it was Augustus who gave it colonial rank, an
according to Pliny, it was in his day the most illustriou
colony in Picenum. Nor did its greatness fail in all th
years of the Empire, but rather increased, and was able i
the last years of the Gothic war to face Totila though not t
withstand him. He took the city and ravaged it, but i
recovered, and long after we hear of it as still one of th
chief cities of the old Roman province. Later it appears a
one of the great cities of the Maritime Pentapolis ; but th
Lombard Dukes of Spoleto seized it, till, with the advent c
Charlemagne, it passed to the Holy See. The Pope governe
his state by means of his archbishops, and this was never
very efficient or stable means of government. Early in th
eleventh century we find Ascoli governed by its counts an
bishops. Then, in 1185, it threw off this yoke and declare
itself a free commune. It had belonged to the Lombar

League, but now declared itself on the side of the Emperor, so that in 1192 Innocent III excommunicated it. This seems to have been effectual, for Ascoli acknowledged the Pope as its overlord, but nevertheless welcomed the Emperor Henry VI with so great an enthusiasm that it is astonishing to find it Guelf again in 1242, when Frederick II sacked it. The truth would seem to be that to maintain its independence it was ready to side with either party as circumstances seemed to dictate, and therefore, after the death of Manfred, Ascoli returned to her allegiance to the Pope.

Frederick II, when he had broken Ascoli, had given her leave to build a fortress at the mouth of the Tronto valley by the sea. This created a new enemy for the city ; Fermo was jealous and enraged, and a long series of wars now began between her and Ascoli. In this struggle the city lost her liberty, though not to Fermo. Weakened by the long war, it was at the mercy of those professional soldiers, condottieri and freebooters who were especially rife in the Papal Marches. First Ascoli fell to Galeotto Malatesta, whom she called to her aid against Fermo (1350–56), then to the lord of Ancona, Francesco Sforza ; but with the departure of the latter on more important business she was able to buy her liberty, or at least the right to call herself a republic, from Sixtus IV for an annual payment of 3000 scudi. But if the foreigner was disposed of, civil discord was not. The jealousy of the great families was as dangerous to the liberty of a city as invasion. Riots were common in Ascoli as elsewhere, and in 1535, during one of them, the Palazzo Pubblico was burned to the ground. In 1555, after Pope Paul III had rebuilt the great fortress of Porta Maggiore, the governor was murdered and the city lost its privileges. Some of these it obtained again from Gregory XIII, and thenceforth it seems to have lived contented under the Papal sway till in 1860 it entered the newly made kingdom of Italy.

Ascoli to-day, as we see it, is one of the most charming of those country towns which are the delight of Italy.

Almost surrounded by the Tronto and its tributary the Castellano, which meet on the north-east of the city just below the Ponte Tufillo, it is everywhere, save on the west, where the Porta Romana gives access to the city, approached by bridges—the Ponte Solestà and the Ponte Tufillo on the north, the Ponte Maggiore and the Ponte di Cecco on the east, the Ponte Cartara on the south. Two of these, the Ponte Solestà and the Ponto di Cecco, are Roman works. The former is a magnificent structure of a single arch, built in the first years of the Empire ; the latter, which gets its name from the popular legend that Cecco d'Ascoli, the poet and astrologer, a friend of Dante's, built it in a single night with the assistance of the devil, is, in fact, a work of the last years of the Roman Republic. It consists of two arches of unequal span, upon the greater of which stands the gate. Over this bridge ran the Via Salaria.

Most travellers, however, do not to-day approach Ascoli by either of these bridges, but by the Ponte Maggiore, a magnificent viaduct consisting of three arches a hundred feet high, built in 1373. This is the modern approach from the railway, but he who approaches the city from Amàndola or the mountains enters by the old Roman gate, Porta Gemina, near which remains a part of the Roman walls of the city. Without, again, is the sixteenth-century Porta Romana.

Coming in by the Porta Maggiore the traveller sees to his left, at the head of the Roman Ponte di Cecco, only less lofty than the viaduct he has just crossed, the Fortezza Malatesta, built by Galeotto Malatesta of Rimini in 1348 to hold the city against the people of Fermo. Two centuries later, Pope Paul III, by the hand of Antonio Sangallo, refortified it towards the city and proposed to dominate Ascoli thence. Sangallo, according to Vasari, brought this fortress " to such a state in the course of a few days, that it could be held by the guard ; whereas the Ascolani, as well as other people, having supposed that it could not be put

orward to that extent under a lapse of years, stood con-
ounded on seeing the garrison so instantly appointed and
nstalled ; the people, indeed, remained looking at each
other in utter astonishment, and could with difficulty
credit what their eyes beheld." To-day, however, the
Fortezza has lost much of its grandeur owing to the new
buildings which in the last years have sprung up about it.

Close by the Fortezza, to the south of the Public Gardens,
stands the church of S. Vittore, where there is a fine altarpiece by Cola d'Amatrice of the Madonna and Child,
enthroned with four saints. To the left of the picture we
see towered Ascoli in its landscape, and above, in heaven,
the battle of S. Michael and his angels, with the dragon or
perhaps angels warding off a pestilence from the city.

From the Porta Maggiore the Via Larga, now called
the Corso Vittorio Emanuele, leads straight into the Piazza
dell' Arringo, so named since the time of the mediæval
commune, when the parliaments, or " arenghi," were held
here, which is the centre of the old life of the city, as is at
once obvious, for it is surrounded by the Cathedral, the Baptistery, the Bishop's Palace and the Palazzo del Comune.

The Cathedral, first dedicated in honour of the Assumption and known as S. Maria Maggiore, but later in honour
of S. Emidius, the first bishop of Ascoli martyred early in
the fourth century, stands upon the ruins, it is said, I know
not with how much truth, of a Temple of Hercules, and
certainly of a church that goes back to the time of Constantine. A few fragments of this building would seem
to remain beside the northern portal called Lamusa. The
octagonal cupola is as old as the eighth or ninth century,
and the basilica as a whole is built on the ancient plan ;
but the church was rebuilt in 1482 in the form of a Latin
cross, when the three Gothic naves we see were constructed.
The façade is later still, dating from the sixteenth century,
and the Ascolani affirm that it is due to Cola d'Amatrice,
their one artist of distinction. Within, the church is
disappointing, having been entirely painted in modern

times, but we are reminded of the ancient dedication of the church by the picture of the Assumption in the lunette of the great arch, where we see the Blessed Virgin caught up from Ascoli from a group of local saints, among them S. Emidius. In the tribune is a noble work, a great polyptych by Carlo Crivelli in fifteen compartments, painted in 1473. This is the sole work from the hand of this master which remains in Ascoli of all those which of old were her boast. Not less than four of the eight pictures of this master in the National Gallery come from the Marches, two of them, the Annunciation (739) and the great Altarpiece in thirteen compartments (788) from Ascoli, the one from the Annunziata and the other from S. Domenico. Happily, however, this glorious altarpiece in the Duomo remains in Ascoli. In the midst we see the Blessed Virgin enthroned with Our Lord in her lap, to the left stand S. John Baptist and S. Peter, to the right S. Emidius and S. Paul. Above, in the midst, we see the Pietà, and at the sides S. Jerome, S. Catherine, S. George and S. Ursula. In the predella, in eleven little compartments, are Christ and His Apostles, but not S. Peter, who appears above. The light is bad in the church and it is in consequence difficult to see this majestic work in all its beauty.

Before leaving the church the fifteenth-century choirstalls should be examined and the crypt visited. The latter is borne by pillars of various dates ; but, on the whole, apart from modern restoration, is a work of the tenth century. Here is the shrine of S. Emidius.

Beside the Duomo stands the Baptistery, which, without, is still largely a building of the twelfth century, but, within, goes back to much earlier times. It consists of two parts, a lower square building surmounted by an octagon, the upper part of which is arcaded without. Within, we have an irregular octagonal building, possibly a Roman work. In the midst stands a vast font for immersion, within which is a smaller font of the thirteenth century.

The Bishop's Palace, with a poor façade attributed to

ALTARPIECE BY PIETRO ALEMANNI

Pinacoteca, Ascoli

Cola d'Amatrice, contains nothing of much interest, and
the long Palazzo Comunale, a building of the seventeenth
century, would not call for notice, but that within it are
to be found the Museum and Picture Gallery of Ascoli,
together with the library and the municipal archives.
None of these are of much account for the traveller (al-
hough some documents in the Archivio would lead one
to conclude that the Buonaparte family was of Ascolan
origin), but the Pinacoteca, which contains some works by
Pietro Alemanni, Cola d'Amatrice and other masters of the
school of Crivelli, and a spoilt picture by Titian, should
not be missed. Titian's work is of the master's latest time
and comes from the church of S. Francesco. It was painted
in or about 1561, and represents S. Francis receiving the
Stigmata, while the donor, Desiderio Guidi, kneels in adoration.

Here, too, are many works by Cola d'Amatrice, the
disciple of Crivelli, an altarpiece of the Madonna and S.
John from the Annunziata, a Via Crucis and other pieces
from S. Francesco, a polyptych of the Madonna and Child,
with S. Bartholomew, S. Mark, and S. Mary Magdalen, and
S. Lucy, and the Pietà from the village of Piagge, the Last
Supper from the church of Corpus Domini and the Beato
Giacomo della Marca from the Cappuccini. Other pictures
are by another imitator of Crivelli, Pietro Alemanni, and
of these especially notable are a Pietà, with S. Sebastian
and another saint, part of an altarpiece, and a Madonna
and Child enthroned with four saints. A splendid piece
of Opus Anglicanum should also be noted. Its curious
history includes its theft, its purchase by the late Pierpont
Morgan and its return by the millionaire to Ascoli.

A little to the south of the Piazza dell' Arringo, in the
Via di Tornasacco, stands the interesting church of S.
Gregorio, a building originally of the eighth century,
standing in the midst of a pagan temple of the time of the
Republic, remains of which are still visible.

From the Piazza dell' Arringo one passes through the

Via Venti Settembre into the Piazza Montanara, so called because the peasants from the mountains used to sell their stuff there. Here is the church of S. Maria della Carità, with a façade by Cola d'Amatrice. Thence one goes northward into the busy Piazza del Popolo, where the great market is now held every Saturday, a very picturesque sight here, as elsewhere. The Piazza, which in the main as we see it is of the sixteenth century, is surrounded by arcades : to the west stands the Palazzo del Popolo, to the north the great church of S. Francesco.

The Palazzo, though imposing, is not very interesting, the best thing about it being the old and massive tower, but S. Francesco is the finest church in the city and dates back to early Franciscan times.

That S. Francis himself came to Ascoli we learn from the first Life of Thomas of Celano. " At the time when (as has been said) the venerable Father Francis preached to the birds as he went round about the cities and fortresses scattering seeds of blessing everywhere, he came to the city of Ascoli. Here, when, according to his wont he was fervently uttering the Word of God, almost all the people, changed by the right hand of the Highest, were filled with such grace and devotion that in their eagerness to see and hear him they trod on one another. And at that time thirty men, clerks and lay-people, received from him the habit of holy religion. Such was the faith of men and women, such their devotion of mind towards God's saint that he who could but touch his garment called himself happy." This was probably in 1215, and S. Francis had not long been dead when the people of Ascoli, who had received him with so much enthusiasm, determined to build a church in his honour. This seems to have been completed in 1262. What we see is in part the sober Gothic church then built, in part a later work of the sixteenth century, when the statue of Julius II was erected over the Gothic doorway.

To the east of the Piazza del Popolo, in the Via della

Prefettura stands the imposing palace of the Prefecture of the sixteenth century. To the west not far away opens the Piazza Bonfino, where is the fine and very ancient church of SS. Vincenzo ed Anastasio. This church consists of two parts, the central nave with the apse and the Campanile dating from the eleventh or, as some say, the ninth century, and the two aisles and the façade whose compartments were originally filled with frescoes, dating from 1389. In the fine doorway of the façade are three little sculptures in relief of the Virgin and Child, with SS. Vincenzo and Anastasio, which seem to date from the eleventh century. The church has been closed for repairs, and little remains within it of much interest except the crypt, which has a remarkable vault.

We shall find the sister to this church in S. Maria *inter vineas* to the north of the city on the height above the Tronto, best reached from the Piazza del Popolo by the Via d'Ancaria. This church, which has a beautiful campanile, originally consisted of three naves, but only the central one remains, the others having fallen into the river. Within is a fine tabernacle of the fifteenth century.

But Ascoli is full of interesting churches, as is the country round about her. To the south, just within the walls on the Colle dell' Annunziata, whence there is a fine view of the city, is the ex-convent and church of the Annunziata. This was originally a hospital, but came into the hands of the Augustinian nuns in the thirteenth century, and in the fifteenth to the Osservanti, who held it till 1861. It is now a school of agriculture. Here in the refectory is a very lovely fresco by Cola d'Amatrice, the only one left in Ascoli of all those he painted, of Christ bearing His Cross ; unhappily it has been badly restored in modern times. The church, which is still used, though generally closed, was built by the Osservanti in the fifteenth century, but within it has been spoilt in the seventeenth. Here of old hung three works by Crivelli, the Annunciation of the National Gallery, the Beato Giacomo della Marca

14

of the Vatican, and another polyptych, of whose fate I am
ignorant.

Above the Annunziata stands the Fortezza Pia, built by
Pius IV to hold the city in 1564.   It is now little more than
a picturesque ruin.

Not far outside the Porta Solestà is another interesting
monument, the church of S. Emidio alle Grotte marking
the cave where S. Emidio, the first bishop and evangelist
of Ascoli, is said to have dwelt in hiding, and where his
body was for a time hidden after his martyrdom.   The place
is curious, though the little church we see is largely of the
eighteenth century.

But when all these churches and others beside have
been seen, there still remains Ascoli to be enjoyed.   It
is a little city, and few there be who find it at the head
of its long valley far from the great roads and the main
line of railways beside the sea, yet how well it repays one
for seeking it out !   And in its beautiful piazzas and
curious by-ways how many pleasures await the traveller
who is wise enough to love best the humble and meek !

CHAPTER XV

TO AMÀNDOLA, MONTEFORTINO, MONTE SAN MARTINO, SARNANO AND URBISAGLIA

IT was already past noon upon a fair summer's day when I set out from Ascoli to cross the mountains and to make my way by the pass of Amàndola in the shadow of the Monte Sibillini under the great peaks of Monte Vettore, Monte Torrone, Monte Argentella, Monte Sibilla, Monte Priore, Monte Rotondo of the central Apennines, to the city of Macerata uplifted between the valleys of the Chienti and the Potenza.

It is a road that once traversed can never be forgotten. Something of the awe and strength that lie behind all beautiful things, and that are for the most part hidden from us when we look upon the beauty Italy offers us in so great a profusion, are there laid bare before the wayfarer. The barren and tremendous Apennine rises up before you upon that road as nowhere else, I think, in Italy, till at evening the whole world is overwhelmed and lost in its awful shadow and silence, and all you know and love, that is brotherly to you and a part of this dear transitory life, is forgotten amid the stones and precipices that draw so near upon that road, in the barren height and depth of the cruel mountains whose life is our death.

A man might follow that way alone easily enough without mishap, but he would not be happy. In the silence and the shadow of those tremendous peaks he would be in danger, though from no material foe, for the road is good all the way, and between it and the great peaks which

threaten him a great gulf is fixed. But, after all, a
companion is better than a coach on any journey, and
remembering this I determined not to adventure into
these solitudes alone. Therefore in Ascoli I sought ou
the diligenza.

My search was long, and when at last I found the office
a mere stable, whence the rough *vettura*, little more than a
broken-down wagonette, closed in on all sides by curtains
was to set out for Amàndola by the mountain road, I was
only just in time to secure the last place, outside, as i
happened to my great content, beside the driver.

We were to start at noon ; but when at noon I arrived a
the office with my wallet there was no sign of departure
and it was only when a good hour had passed, and my
fellow-travellers one by one had straggled in from *caffè* and
market that the *vettura* was drawn out from its noisom
shelter loaded with all sorts of bundles and luggage, th
flea-bitten, wiry horses harnessed, their shoes blackened a
they waited to start, and we were off at last more than a
hour late.

Of that journey, which brought me long after nightfall t
the wonderful inn of Amàndola, I cannot speak with all th
eloquence it deserves. We left Ascoli by the Roman gat
and followed the Tronto up stream so far as Taverna Picci
nini. There we turned to the north, and presently bega
to climb into the tremendous pass, the highest part of whic
is, I suppose, some two thousand feet above the sea. Thi
bald statement of feet, however, gives no idea of the amazin
splendour and beauty of that wonderful road. It might b
eight thousand feet rather than two, its greatness presse
so upon you, and the awful prospect it affords into the ver
heart of the most barren mountains in Europe is so intimat
and appalling. Its extraordinary steepness, too, is a facto
in the impression it makes upon you. For a good half o
the way up the diligenza is dragged by oxen harnessed unde
the yoke before the horses. Then, indeed, the valleys ope
one after the other in vista after vista of olive garden an

vineyard, then of wood and copse, and at last of stone and heath, till all that is human falls away from you; the mountains rise up in their naked majesty and threaten and beckon you into their unbreakable silence, their appalling solitude, their everlasting barrenness, while between their awful precipices little white clouds, shaped like the wings of birds, sail at evening from the Mediterranean to the Adriatic.

The day upon which I came this way offered me all that strangely beautiful but terrifying world in its greatest majesty, but if the day be obscure the traveller will see but little of all that I saw, all will be lost in the clouds, that barren world of stone will be hidden from him, and only the thin keen air and the great silence will make him aware of the adventure whose significance has passed him by. But if the day be fair, nothing that may happen to him thereafter will ever quite erase from his mind the vision of elemental things which it has vouchsafed him ; in the glory of the sunset over all that mighty desolation, the hand of God seems to rest upon those riven mountains.

One human scene remains in my mind, anchoring those vast uplifted heights, floating in space, to the world I know and love. About the roots of these mountains, in the lower valleys where there are a few stricken trees and poor plots of corn, men live and build there a habitation. One of their huts or cottages I discerned not far from the road in the shadow and shelter of a great rock, past which a torrent foamed after we had passed Casale. And there at the door a man stood waiting, gazing down the road, shading his eyes. Presently I knew what it was he expected. For up the road to meet us toiled two oxen drawing a great wain, and upon the wain was set a bed, and over the bed was spread a beautiful bright yellow quilt, as it might be an altar frontal at Easter, and on the quilt were spread four pillows, and behind came a woman, all in bridal array, with her companions. It was a bride going to her husband with her *corredo*. She was coming from the lowlands, and she passed in silence, looking back again and again towards the valleys she was leaving.

It was already night when, after a brief halt at Comunanza, a wretched but beautifully situated village of the lower hills, the diligenza came up to the gate of Amàndola and stopped in a bleak Piazza at the foot of the little hill town, of which I could discern nothing but a gaunt and shadowy tower. There was no sign of an inn, but presently I was led by the hand over the cobbles, for it was very dark, to a little door that opened on a vast kitchen reeking with a most savoury smell of cooking. The place was full of light and warmth, and crowded with all kinds of people, peasants and a priest or two, but especially I noticed an amazingly ugly old woman, who presently came up to me and demanded my business. Then when she knew I desired a bed she too took me by the hand and led me up a foul and broken stairway to the first floor of her house, where, to my astonishment, I saw that all was fair and clean, as was the room and bed she offered me. And here let me say at once that my days in Amàndola were all days of delight and happiness. It is never well in Italy to judge by appearances, and in Amàndola, as I soon found, least of all. Nowhere have I received greater kindness; nowhere have I found so nice a courtesy. Nothing I required was denied me; everything was done for my comfort and pleasure. I slept soft and I lived well, I fared sumptuously every day. The kitchen became my sitting-room, though I was given one of my own, and there I found the best company in the world, among the shepherds and peasants and priests of the mountains. They brought me fruit out of their little store, the children danced and sang songs for me, the shepherds blew me mountain airs on their pipes and told me tales of the snow, of witches and the evil eye, and of the adventures of Our Lady fleeing with our little Lord from Herod and the Pharisees, which befell, it seems, but yesterday, as is indeed most true. And so I, who had feared to stay a single night

AMÀNDOLA

in Amàndola, remained for my own delight a whole
seven days, not one of which I reckoned ill-spent or
unrepaid, though Amàndola itself is little more than a
village.

Figure to yourself a little place of rosy brick piled up on
a great precipitous hillside, on the crest or saddle of which
it is spread out eastward, threaded by rude and stony
streets between gaunt houses. A wretched place enough,
but filled with a people so hospitable and charming that
when I think of the Marches Amàndola appears in my mind
as the heart and rose of a country which for friendliness and
charm is second to none in Italy.

The origin of this gaunt little town is curious. It seems
that it was founded in 1248 by the people of the three
neighbouring *Castelli*, Leone, Agello, Marabbione, who
withdrew themselves from the government of their lords to
form themselves into a Commune within a single line of walls
or *mandorla*, whence it is said comes the name Amàndola.
The Commune flourished exceedingly, and in less than a
century boasted of 14,000 inhabitants, but its success
aroused jealousies, and we find it fighting for its life with
the people of Ascoli, Montefortino, Sarnano and Monte San
Martino. In spite of these wars and the universal faction
fights that weakened every city in Italy, Amàndola flourished,
chiefly by reason of its wool, all through the fourteenth and
fifteenth centuries ; but in the latter part of the seventeenth century it began to decay, and to-day it is as poor
and tumble-down a place as one can find even in the
Marches.

Its artistic possessions are few. The convent, the
church and the campanile of S. Francesco are buildings
of the fourteenth century, said to occupy the site of a
chapel or hermitage founded by S. Francis himself. In
the campanile are the remains of fine frescoes, perhaps of
the school of Gentile da Fabriano, and the doorway of the
church is a fine fifteenth-century work. The church of
S. Trinità, too, is worth a visit, as is that of S. Agostino,

which has a good campanile and a notable doorway of the
fifteenth century ; the former said to be the work of Pietro
Lombardi. The walls of the town on the great hillside are
largely still of the thirteenth century.

There are two things just outside Amàndola to the
south-east which should not be missed. I mean the
fortified wall built in 1496 and the neighbouring bridge
over the Tenna constructed in 1425. From the hill beyond,
a very fine view of Amàndola may be had, with this lofty
bridge in the foreground.

From Amàndola I made an excursion to Montefortino,
a little *castello* very loftily and beautifully situated some
five miles to the south. Apart from its own beauty,
Montefortino is chiefly noteworthy for the pictures that
are to be found in its Municipio. Here is a fine tondo
of the dead Christ by Perugino, and a panel of a saint
by Antoniazzo Romano, as well as a picture of the Madonna
and Child, with Tobias and two archangels painted in 1497
by Pier Francesco Fiorentino, the imitator of Neri di Bicci,
and a Madonna adoring her little Son by Neri di Bicci's
pupil, Botticini. In the church of S. Agostino is a
picture, once attributed to Perugino, of the Adoration of
the Magi, and a S. Antony painted on wood that has
much charm. Other works will be found in the Santuario
dell' Ambro and in the Madonna del Fonte outside the
castello, where there are fine frescoes.

Another excursion that should be made from Amàndola
brings one across many hills to the north-east, to Monte
San Martino, another of those picturesque hill towns
which are so wearying to reach, though always worth the
trouble and fatigue of the long climb at the end of which
they shine. Here in the Municipio is a Crucifixion by
Girolamo di Giovanni da Camerino. Another work, a
polyptych, painted by the same master in 1473, is in the
parish church of S. Maria del Pozzo. This represents
in the midst the Madonna and Child enthroned with four
angels ; above in two tondi we see the Annunciation. On

ALTARPIECE BY GIROLAMO DI GIOVANNI DA CAMERINO
Parish Church, Monte S. Martino

either side stand S. Thomas holding the girdle of the
Blessed Virgin and an open book, and S. Ciprian vested as
a Bishop holding his crozier. Above in the midst we see
the Crucifixion with the Madonna and S. John, and on
either side S. Michael and S. Martin, beneath two little
half figures of S. Peter and S. Paul—a very notable
work.

I left Amàndola one morning in the public automobile
for Sarnano on my way to Macerata. The road thither,
delightful though it be, has not the splendour of the way
between Amàndola and Ascoli, but it gives you Sarnano,
which is worth any trouble to see.

Sarnano, unlike almost every other city in the Marches,
is not set on a great hill. The automobile passes quite
through this picturesque little place with its great tower
and piazza and rosy churches. Here in the Collegiata,
in a niche, Lorenzo da Sanseverino, the pupil of Girolamo
di Giovanni da Camerino, has painted in fresco the Madonna
and Child with saints. This noble work is signed and dated
1483. A work, perhaps by Girolamo himself, is to be seen
in S. Maria del Rosario, where is a Crucifixion with the
Annunciation behind it, as it were the beginning and the
end, the alpha and omega of the Redemption of the
world. A more curious master has perhaps been at work
in S. Maria in Piazza : Niccolò da Foligno, to whom is
attributed the picture of S. John Baptist with three other
Saints.

After leaving Sarnano for the road to Macerata, he is
wise who turns a little out of his way to climb up to the
hill town of S. Ginèsio. It is true there is not much to
see but the delicious countryside, with its olive gardens
and vineyards climbing up to the beautiful little city,
which every one who has ever seen it must always
love.

Some eight or ten miles farther along the road to
Macerata stands Urbisaglia, that Roman place an utter
desolation in Dante's day. The road then crosses the

Fiastra torrent, down whose valley it has come all the way from S. Ginèsio, and goes down at once into the great valley of the Chienti, across which it passes by the great Ponte to climb swiftly and steeply up into the noble city of Macerata.

CHAPTER XVI

MACERATA, HELVIA RICINA, FORANO, MONTECASSIANO, POLLENZA, PAÙSULA, MONTE SAN GIUSTO

MACERATA, on its great isolated hill piled up upon lesser hills that are covered with gardens of olives, with vineyards and terraces, where the corn waves purple and gold in the July sun, is among the noblest of the hill cities of the Marches. There is nothing in all this wide and various country, everywhere broken by great hills and valleys, more gentle and more delicious than the country out of which Macerata rises like an acropolis, itself the gentlest, happiest, busiest place in all the old Papal States, a city at one with itself, rejoicing at every sunrise. This air of contentment, of peace if you will, strikes you at once in the Piazza where the automobile deposits you, and is only increased by the lightness and cleanliness of the Albergo Centrale with its aspect of a convent almost, and of the gaiety and civilization of the Trattoria Fanfulla, where it is a pleasure to take breakfast or to dine. In all the Marches there is no place where a stranger may feel more at home or will receive a warmer welcome than in Macerata. And this I put down largely to the effect upon the place of its university, an effect wholly happy and to be commended. In Ascoli or Fermo or Recanati one could live well enough for a few weeks without home-sickness; in Macerata I think one might take up one's habitation and never regret all one had left behind in Florence and Siena. For to the good living this little hill town provides for its guests must be added a charming society, cultured, sympathetic, and perfectly ready to admit with a smile its limitations, its country air, and, if I may say so, its innocence. Every day one spends in Macerata is a delight, there is indeed nothing to be excused or passed over; it offers itself to you without pretension and without any false humility, with a perfect understanding of its charming provincial beauty, which it most delightfully makes the best of, you feel, really for your pleasure, and with no thought of boastfulness.

Macerata stands, or rather lies, on a great hill between the profound valleys of the Potenza to the north and the Chienti to the south. It is a walled city from whose gates sudden and lovely glimpses may be had over the surrounding country, especially from the Porta del Duomo to the eastward, and indeed all along the Viale Leopardi on the north, the Viale Puccinotti on the west, and the Viale delle Mura di Mezzogiorno, without the walls. But no one who thus walks about it and sees and understands the splendour of its situation but is surprised to learn of the comparative modernity of a place which might seem to have been formed by nature for dominion. Nevertheless, Macerata does not date further back certainly than the year 1000. A few years after that date we hear vaguely of three villages upon this hill—Mons Sancti Juliana, a stronghold probably grouped round a religious house on the summit, a village on the north-east, and the Castellum de Macerata on the south-west. The village on the north-east would seem to have been the most important of these. It was governed and held by the Bishop of Fermo, while the Castellum was in the territory of Camerino. It was not till 1138 that the village or stronghold on the summit was united with the Castellum, and not till 1236 that all three villages came under the dominion of the Bishop of Fermo. About a century later, in 1320, Pope John XXII raised these three villages to the dignity of a city, under the name of Macerata, and the old Pieve of S. Giuliano became the Cathedral. Since 1252 there had existed here a Collegio degli Avvocati della Curia Generale, and in 1290 was opened a Studio di Legge, and these in 1543 by a bull of Paul III were erected into the University, which still exists. Macerata had in the thirteenth century declared itself first Ghibelline and then Guelf. Its main interest was ever its own independence, but this it was not always successful in maintaining. For two short periods it fell into the power of the Mulucci family, and three times came into the power of the Varani of Camerino. It also came for a few years in the earlier part of the fifteenth century into the power of Francesco Sforza, when he was Lord of Ancona, but in 1445 it returned into the direct government of the Holy See. It seems to have been during Sforza's brief rule that the walls we see were built about the city. These did not include, however, one of the three original villages, the stronghold of S. Giuliano on the north-east. In consequence of this, in 1460 a new cathedral was built within the walled city. But neither of the churches which may claim to be and to have been the seat of the Bishop is to-day of any greater antiquity than the fifteenth century. The oldest monument left to us in Macerata is the little church of S. Maria della Porta, half-way down the Corso, parts of which date from very ancient times, certainly from the tenth century, and even the façade is in part a late Romanesque work, with a doorway of the fourteenth century. Perhaps the only other monument that may claim to date even from the fourteenth century is the Fonte Maggiore without the Porta del Duomo, two hundred yards away to the north of it. This was the most important fountain Macerata could boast of, and its position goes to show how late the Poggio del Monte di S. Giuliano, and indeed the whole S. Giuliano quarter, remained the most important part of the city.

But apart from its ways and by-ways and houses, which are often as truly mediæval as anyone would desire, Macerata, in so far as it is old at all, is of the fifteenth century, of the time of Sforza and the return of the Papacy to power here. To this age belong the church of the Madonna della Miseri-

cordia, with its beautiful picture by some pupil of Perugino
of the Madonna with S. Giuliano, S. Andrew, S. Sebastian
and S. Roch, the Residenza del Podestà near the picturesque Piazza del Mercato, the Porta del Convitto, and the
Loggia dei Mercanti, the noble Palazzo della Prefettura.
Unhappily the Duomo is a work of the eighteenth century,
built on the site of the fifteenth-century church, of which
only the campanile remains. It contains nothing of any
interest. The church of S. Giovanni, old in its title alone,
a building of the eighteenth century like the Cathedral, is,
however, happier in this that it possesses a fine picture of
the Crucifixion, perhaps by Cola d'Amatrice.

If one wants pictures in Macerata, however, one must not
look for them in the churches ; for they have all been
carried away to the Pinacoteca in the Biblioteca Comunale,
the best library, it is said, in all the Marches. There,
among other lovely things, is a fine Crivelli, a picture of the
Madonna and Child painted in 1470, two works by that
rare master, Alegretto Nuzi of Fabriano ; a noble triptych
painted in 1369, and a Madonna and Child with S. Giuliano
and Antony, which comes from the parish church of Monte
Cassiano ; two panels with four saints, perhaps by Lorenzo
Salmibeni, Nuzi's follower, and a very lovely Crucifixion
painted on a gold ground with the Blessed Virgin and S.
John.

When all is said, however, Macerata is itself more interesting and charming than any of its monuments or works
of art, and one can, as I have already said, live there more
happily and comfortably than in any other city of the
Marches. And this is doubly fortunate, for it not only
encourages the traveller to remain in a place so variously
charming, but allows him without an afterthought to
make it his headquarters for many an excursion into the
country round about, which otherwise he would be inclined
to forego. And the excursions which can be made from
the city are not few.

First, there is the journey, little more than a morning's

THE MADONNA AND CHILD. BY CARLO CRIVELLI
Biblioteca, Macerata

walk there and back again, to Helvia Ricina, on the other side of the valley of the Potenza. This was the old Roman municipal town from which, as it is said, both Macerata and Recanati sprung. Pliny is the only author who speaks of it, but we learn from an inscription that it received a colony under Severus. Its chief interest lies for us in the fact that its ruins are still visible. They include some great arches of the theatre and other buildings, among the most notable Roman remains of the kind in all this great province.

Macerata would not be worthy of its place in so Franciscan a province as the Marches if it had nothing to offer us in the way of a Franciscan sanctuary. This we shall find in the Convento di Forano, about as far to the north of Helvia Ricina as those ruins are from Macerata.

This convent, or rather its predecessor, for it has been rebuilt, was opened in the time of S. Francis ; it is mentioned in the *Fioretti*, and is holy ground therefore. In that fifth gospel we read : " In the days of the holy Brother Peter, there lived also the holy Brother Conrad of Offida ; while they dwelt together in the same house of Forano, in the territory of Ancona, the said Brother Conrad went one day into the wood to meditate on God, and Brother Peter followed him by stealth, for to see what might befall him ; and Brother Conrad began to pray, most devoutly beseeching the Virgin Mary with great piety to beg of her blessed Son this grace, that he might feel a little of that sweetness that Saint Simon felt on the day of the Purification, when he held in his arms the blessed Saviour Jesu. And when he had made his prayer the Virgin Mary of her pity heard him ; and, behold ! there appeared unto him the Queen of heaven with her blessed Son in her arms, with a great light exceeding bright, and coming near unto Brother Conrad she laid in his arms her little Son ; who, taking Him with great devotion, embracing and kissing Him, and pressing Him to his breast, was melted altogether, and dissolved in the love divine and consolation unspeakable.

And in like manner Brother Peter, who from his hiding-place saw all that befell, felt in his soul exceeding sweetness and consolation. And when the Virgin Mary had departed from Brother Conrad, Brother Peter gat him back in haste to the house that he might not be seen of him ; but thereafter when Brother Peter said unto him, ' O what heavenly great consolation hast thou had this day ! ' quoth Brother Conrad, ' What is this that thou sayest, Brother Peter ? and what dost thou know of that which I have had ? ' ' I know, full well, I know,' said Brother Peter, ' how the Virgin Mary with her blessed Son hath visited thee.' Then Brother Conrad, who being truly humble desired to keep secret the favours of God, besought him that he would tell it unto no one ; and from that time forth so great was the love between these twain that they seemed to have but one heart and soul in all things."

This was not the only vision which Brother Conrad was vouchsafed at Forano. For again in the forty-fourth chapter of the *Fioretti* we read how the Mother of Christ S. John the Evangelist and S. Francis appeared to Brother Conrad, and told him which of them suffered the greater grief for the Passion of Christ.

" At the time when there dwelt together in the territory of Ancona, in the house of Forano, Brother Conrad and the aforesaid Brother Peter, the which were two shining stars in the Province of the March, and like denizens of the heaven ; for between them was there such love as seemed to spring from one and the self-same heart, and self-same soul, they bound themselves together each to each by this agreement that every consolation that the mercy of God might vouchsafe them, they would reveal the one to the other in love. This fact being established between them, it befell on a day that Brother Peter being at prayer and most devoutly meditating on the Passion of Christ and how the most blessed Mother of Christ and John the Evangelist, the most beloved disciple, and Saint Francis were depicted at the foot of the Cross through grief of

soul being crucified with Christ, there came to him a long-
ing to know which of those three had the greater grief for
the Passion of Christ—His Mother that had borne Him, or
the Disciple that had slept upon His breast, or Saint Francis
that had with Christ been crucified ; and as he continued
in such pious thoughts there appeared unto Him the Virgin
Mary with Saint John the Evangelist and Saint Francis, clad
in the noblest robes of beatific glory ; but Saint Francis
appeared clad in more beautiful vesture than Saint John.
And Peter, being sore adread at this vision, Saint John
confronted him, and said : ' Fear not, dear brother, seeing
that we are come to console thee in thy doubt. Know
then that the Mother of Christ and I, above all other
creatures, sorrowed for the Passion of Christ ; but next
after us Saint Francis felt greater grief than all others, wherefore dost thou behold him in so great glory.' And Brother
Peter asked him : ' Most holy Apostle of Christ, wherefore
doth the vesture of Saint Francis appear more beautiful
than thine ? ' Replied Saint John : ' The reason thereof is
because, when he was in the world, he wore on his back
viler raiment than I.' And said these words, Saint John
gave unto Brother Peter a glorious robe that he was
carrying in his hand, and said unto him : ' Take this
robe which I have brought for to give it thee,' and when
Saint John sought to array him in this robe, Brother Peter
fell to the ground, sore amazed, and began to cry out :
' Brother Conrad, Brother Conrad, most dear, quick, help
me ; come and see things wonderful,' and at these holy
words that holy vision vanished from his sight. Then
Brother Conrad coming, he told him everything in order ;
and they gave thanks unto God.''

These wondrous things befell at Forano here in the
Marches, and they make the little church here a holy
place. It is true that it has been largely rebuilt, but there
still remains to the right of the door by which one enters
that part of the ancient church where is the door by which,
as it is said, S. Francis himself has passed. The friars

15

have recovered their convent, stolen away from them ; it is full of the humble beauty and peace of such places. Not far away is a pretty chapel dedicated in honour of S. Mary of the Angels.

Another delightful excursion from Macerata takes one again through Helvia Ricina, and thence, by a by-way to the right, up to Montecassiano. This is a curiously picturesque little town, whose chief boast is the possession of a very late work of the Robbia school in the first chapel on the right in the parish church. It is an altarpiece representing the Madonna and Child enthroned under a canopy upheld by two angels. On either side kneel two Franciscans, and below stand S. Roch, his wound tended by an angel and S. Sebastian. At Madonna's feet are three cherubs, and at the foot of the throne two *putti*. Above, in the lunette, God the Father appears between two angels. The frame, which is all of terra-cotta and is niched for saints, is everywhere covered with little figures, while the predella displays scenes from the life of Our Lady. The church itself is old, and is worth more than a glance in passing, while the Palazzetto del Comune is a building of the thirteenth century.

There is a road out of Macerata to the south-west that in some six miles or so brings one to the hill town of Pollenza. Here, too, one finds a place of much picturesque beauty, and in the church of S. Francesco, beside a fine Romanesque door, there is a picture of S. Antony of Padua, painted in 1496 by Lorenzo da Sanseverino.

Two other places, at least, should be visited from Macerata, Paùsula and Monte San Giusto. Paùsula, once known as Mont' Olmo, is a large town, again picturesquely grouped about a hill-top. It is said to occupy the site of the old Roman town of the same name which Pliny alone mentions. It has more than one fine building, but its chief interest for the traveller lies in the church of S. Francesco, a baroque building now, but still in possession of its pictures. Among these is a fine triptych by Lorenzo da Sanseverino of the

Madonna and Child, with S. John Baptist and the Magdalen, painted in 1481 ; a Sienese picture, perhaps by Sassetta, of S. Francis ; and a Madonna and Child by Baroccio over the high altar. In S. Agostino, too, there is a Madonna and Child by Crivelli, and another by Andrea da Bologna (1372).

Beyond Paùsula, by a rough and hilly road across the Cremone valley, we come to the little walled town of Monte San Giusto, and there in the church of S. Maria is a Crucifixion by Lotto, painted in 1531. Here, again, one is astonished to find great stone-built palaces. Monte San Giusto might seem too far away from any great road and too remote from any great city to have played a part in the life of the province, but the local histories soon disillusion us, and show us even this far hill-top entangled in alliances and engaged in war, riven in twain by faction, boastful, passionate, and full of a life so furious, it seems, that our own time, with all its haste, appears lanquid enough beside it. Lying there to-day in the shadow of the vines, listening to the *cicale*, it is hard to believe it.

CHAPTER XVII

TOLENTINO

IT is little more than fourteen miles by road or rail up the valley of the Chienti to the famous city of Tolentino, the birthplace of the humanist Filelfo. The only notable thing passed on the way is the restored Castello della Rancia. Famous for its antiquity, its great S. Nicholas, and the treaty signed there between Pope Pius VI and Napoleon Buonaparte, Tolentino is a quiet and beautiful little town, set really in the valley, and in this different from most of these March cities, which are generally only to be reached by a winding road after a long climb.

Of the antiquity of Tolentino there can be no doubt. Pliny speaks of it as Tolentinum, and its municipal rank is attested by the Liber Coloniarum and by inscriptions, but we know almost nothing about it, save that it was set then, as it is to-day, upon the high road from Rome to Ancona, which ran through Helvia Ricina, and is known to-day as the Strada della Marca or Strada Lauretana. Of its fate in the fall of the Empire and the Dark Age I know nothing, but in the Middle Age it appears, as indeed do all these cities, as part of the Papal dominion, and it has always been Tolentino's boast that it was never subject to any other sovereign than the Pope. It is true that in the fourteenth century the great family of Accoramboni usurped or attempted to usurp its lordship, and tried to involve Tolentino in a quarrel, with the Holy See. The truth would seem to be that the cities under the Papal dominion enjoyed a far greater measure of real freedom than those subject to a mere Signore, and that the difference between being actually independent and being subject to the Pope was a negligible one. Says an historian of Tolentino : " The Accoramboni were never lords in Tolentino. It is false to assert it. *We were always free under the Church. The people of Tolentino would never endure tyranny.* The men of Camerino—yes ; but we were made of different stuff." And this feeling, which we may be sure was based on substantial fact, was really universal throughout the Romagna and the Marches. When the Piedmontesi came in, in 1860, " the people of Ravenna," we read, "were forced to the polling booth at the point of the bayonet." And thus the new liberty was recommended to those who had enjoyed the reality for ages !

Tolentino, it may be thought, as the birthplace of a great saint, may have been more Papal than her neighbours, but in fact this is not so. The great figure of S. Nicholas is not in any sense of the word political ; its appeal is altogether human and universal.

S. Nicholas, called of Tolentino, for it was there he spent the most considerable part of his life, was born at S. Angelo in Pontano, in the territory of Fermo, about 1245, of poor but honest parents who, for long without children, made pilgrimage to the shrine of S. Nicholas of Bari, and receiving in answer to their prayer a son, called him Nicholas, since that saint was obviously his patron. The usual stories are told of his unnaturally devout childhood, when he would spend whole hours together at prayer and befriend and visit the poor and afflicted. He certainly seems early to have had a genius for the love of his fellow-creatures, and his parents, who had from the first devoted him to the service of God, encouraged him in all he did. His intelligence and modesty attracted the notice of many about his native village, so much so, that while he was yet a student he was given a canonry in the church of S.

Salvatore. While in enjoyment of this preferment he heard a sermon preached by an Augustinian hermit on the vanity of this world, and immediately he knew his own mind ; he resolved to quit his present way of life and to enter the Order to which the preacher belonged. He therefore sought the convent of the Order in Tolentino, and there entered upon his novitiate, as it happened, under the direction of the man who had revealed him to himself ; before his eighteenth birthday he had made his profession. From the convent of Tolentino we may trace his progress through the Marches, to the Augustinian convents of Recanati, Macerata, and Cìngoli, not to mention others. At Cìngoli he was ordained priest by the Bishop of Osimo. From that moment, it is difficult to say exactly why, he became famous. It might seem that in S. Nicholas of Tolentino we have an example of that rare sweetness of character which is perhaps in greater or lesser degree the portion of all the saints, but which in him was so over-whelming that men and women followed him, flocked to his Masses, or sought him in the confessional for no other reason. As a preacher, no doubt, he was amazingly successful, but rather by reason of some inward sweetness and charm than of the victorious eloquence of his mere words. For thirty years he lived in Tolentino in the Augustinian convent there, a star in the March, something which men could not explain or dismiss from their minds, an influence so compelling and so sweet that little children ran to him as he passed by, old men caught at his hands, women knelt to kiss his robe, and even those in the flower of their age gladly heard his voice, as though it had been some sweet far-away music. By the very beauty of his nature he drew thousands from the half-brutal worldliness in which they lived, and seems indeed to have brought to them something of the strange incomprehensible beauty of his own vision. It is not wonderful that he was able to work cures which seemed miraculous, and which indeed were so, and that this expenditure of spiritual energy afflicted him with more than one painful illness. He died on 10th September 1306 in Tolentino, and was buried in the convent church there in a chapel in which he was used to say Mass. After his canonization in 1446 by Pope Eugenius IV the day of his death became his Feast Day, and the church where he lay buried was rededicated in his honour as S. Niccolò.

This church, by far the most interesting monument in Tolentino, has been spoilt, but it still retains a fine fifteenth-century western doorway, over which is a curious figure, perhaps of S. Michael, perhaps of S. George, perhaps of Niccolò Mauruzzi of Tolentino, the celebrated condottiere, who presented this doorway to the church. The champion, whoever he is, is trampling on the devil or some enemy in the form of a dragon. The chapel of S. Niccolò, where the great saint lies, is to the north of the high altar. Close by is a chamber finely decorated in fresco with the story of his life, perhaps by Lorenzo da Sanseverino, but as seems far more likely by Allegretto Nuzi or some follower of his in or about 1350. The beautiful Gothic chapel is entirely covered with these notable works. On the roof are the Four Evangelists and the Four Doctors of the Church, together with figures of Hope, Prudence, Faith, Temperance, Charity and Fortitude, Justice, and In-justice to fill the eighth space, very noble and lovely amid all sorts of decorative work Cosmatesque in character, and little medallions of saints. The walls are covered with frescoes in two series. Above, we have the life and miracles of Christ ; beneath, the life and miracles of S. Niccolò, His imitator. There we see the parents of S. Niccolò at the shrine of S. Nicholas of Bari ; the saint announces to them that they will have a son. Then we are shown the young S. Niccolò at his studies ; hearing the Augustinian preacher ; and received into that Order. Then we see one of his visions, in which an angel appears to him and offers him a crown. There follow the funeral of the saint, and certain miracles worked by him after death : the raising of a dead woman, the healing of a blind girl, the liberation of a prisoner, the saving of a crew from shipwreck, the deliverance of one who has been hanged, and a group of those healed and saved by him. A Crucifixion divides these stories from the scenes of the life of Our Lord, where we see the Annunciation, the Visitation, the Nativity, the Adoration of the Shepherds, the Presentation in the Temple, the Massacre of the Innocents, Christ in the Temple, the Marriage in Cana, the Entry into Jerusalem, the Garden of Gethsemane, Christ in Hades, the Resurrection, the Pentecost, and the Assumption of the Blessed Virgin. The beauty and interest of these little-known works cannot be disputed. They are either from the hand of Allegretto Nuzi or by some close follower of whom we know nothing. Nothing else of much interest remains within the church of S. Niccolò, but the cloisters dating from the thirteenth century with their clustered columns should be visited.

Two other churches in Tolentino should not be missed. These are S. Francesco and S. Catervo. In S. Francesco, close to S. Niccolò, there are a few fading fourteenth-century frescoes, and another of the end of the fifteenth century, of the Madonna and S. Amicone di Rambone healing the sick. The church which dates from the thirteenth century is of some interest. In S. Catervo, near the railway station, is the early Christian sarcophagus of S. Catervo and some frescoes of the school of Pintoricchio.

I have said that Tolentino is famous for three things. The last of these is the famous or rather infamous treaty which Napoleon forced upon Pope Pius vi, by which was forfeited the greater part of the Papal dominions. A contemporary writer, unfriendly to the Pope, recounting the events of that time, tells us that " the year 1796 concluded in Italy with a series of Napoleonic successes so brilliant and rapid and numerous that the military history of the universe cannot perhaps furnish a more memorable epoch. . . . In the beginning of 1797, Buonaparte, from his headquarters at Bologna, declared that his armistice with the Pope was broken. Immediately after the promulgation of this species of manifesto the French army invaded the Ecclesiastical state, seized Imola, Forlì, Cesena (the Pope's birthplace), and in the outset Pius suffered the loss of four or five hundred men killed, a thousand prisoners, four pieces of artillery, etc. . . . In a few days the French made themselves masters of Romagna, the Duchy of Urbino, and the Marquisate of Ancona ; and on the thirtieth of Pluviose (Feb. 18) Buonaparte met the Papal envoys at Tolentino. ' If you do not,' said he, ' give unreserved consent to all my propositions to-morrow, I will march against Rome.' On the morrow, Feb. 19, 1797, Cardinal Mattei told them, ' We consent to the whole.' Immediately they began to draw up the articles ; they dined ; after dinner the treaty was concluded ; they signed it ; they supped, embraced each other, and separated. The next day Buonaparte, with the officers of his staff, was on his way to Austria. . . ." By that treaty the Pope lost the whole of Romagna, and was compelled to admit a French garrison into Ancona.

Tolentino itself is, apart from its charming Piazza and the churches I have already spoken of, without much interest for the curious traveller, but it is a very good place from which to make three excursions into the hills to Belforte, Caldarola, and Serrapetrona, all of which may be taken in a single day by carriage between Tolentino and Sanseverino.

Belforte, in the Chienti valley to the south of Tolentino, is a little town on the great high road to Rome, the Strada Lauretana, and there in S. Eustachio is a splendid polyptych by one of the rarer masters of the Umbrian school, Giovanni Boccatis, whose lovely altarpiece in Perugia, with its delicious singing angels, one can never forget. Boccatis was probably the pupil of Lorenzo Salimbeni (Lorenzo da Sanseverino the Elder), but he came later under the influence of two very great masters, Piero della Francesca and Fra Lippo Lippi. He is known to have been active from 1435 to 1480, and this work here at Belforte, dated 1468, is his masterpiece. It is a great polyptych, quite complete in all its parts save for two little panels in the predella. In the midst we see the Blessed Virgin, the Child lying in her lap, surrounded by choirs of angels, and tended by two angiolini, one of whom kisses His feet. On either side are two saints. Above is the Crucifixion, and on either side two saints ; above again we see God the Father surrounded by the cherubim. The whole frame is panelled with figures of saints, and in the predella are various scenes from the life of S. Francis and other saints.

From Belforte it is not more than three miles to Caldarola, one of the loveliest of villages, set high amid gardens and vineyards, with cypresses towering over it, and with wonderful views over all this noble country. There in the church of the Madonna del Monte is a fine work, dated 1491, by Lorenzo de Sanseverino of the Madonna and Child with eight saints and worshippers. This is worth any trouble to see, even though Caldarola were not, as it is, one of the most beautiful of those villages, which are every year becoming rarer in Italy, and which I sometimes fear—they slip away so fast—my little son will never see.

From Caldarola one goes down to Pievefavera, and then crosses the Chienti, and climbs up through Borgiano to Serrapetrona. This is another wonderful village, and in the parish church is another polyptych of the Madonna and Child, with saints, by Lorenzo da Sanseverino, according to Mr. F. Mason Perkins and Mr. Berenson, who have done all or nearly all that has yet been done by way of annotation upon the pictures to be found in the Marches.

An easy, winding mountain road brings one at evening into the city of Sanseverino, in the valley of the Potenza.

CHAPTER XVIII

SANSEVERINO

SANSEVERINO, in the narrow valley of the Potenza, under the steep hill upon which its Castello still stands, wins you at once by its beauty, its smiling aspect, its air of the Middle Age, of whose works it is full, and of which it might well stand as an example in its picturesque and daring loveliness. The days one spends there wandering from the beautiful long Piazza so happily arcaded on the south, from church to church up to the old Castello, entered by that prodigious gateway, Porta S. Francesco, on the hill, are all days of delight and happiness. There can be no one who has ever wandered through these long valleys, or climbed these great hills, but has rejoiced to enter Sanseverino and regretted to depart, though it be for a city so marvellous as Camerino, or so hospitable and delicious as Matelica. For Sanseverino, in some wonderful way known only to itself, renews one's youth and one's first careless delight in Italy—in these beautiful hill cities always so surprising to an Englishman, who is wont to build his towns and villages anywhere rather than upon a hill; but, then, how much that is left to us in England is as old as Sanseverino ?

The Roman town of Septempedanus was a famous place mentioned by all the geographers, a municipium, according to Pliny, set upon that branch of the Via Flaminia which left the high road at Nocera, crossed the Apennines, and descended the valley of the Potenza as far as Helvia Ricina on its way of Ancona. Its importance, too, is witnessed by the fact that it very early became an episcopal city, and obtained its present name, as it is said, from one of its bishops. In 545 it was destroyed by Totila, at whose approach the inhabitants left the city, which then, as now, lay in the narrow valley beside the river. They fled to the hill called Montenero, where they built a church to their Bishop, S. Severino, dead a few years before, and there they established themselves, rescuing S. Severino's body from the smoking ruins of Septempedanus, and placing it under the high altar of the church in the walled town or fortress called the Castello, which they built on the hill-top. In course of time, for purposes of trade, the people of the Castello issued forth, and began in the plain to build a borgo on the site of their old city, and it is this borgo which to-day makes the chief part of the city of Sanseverino.

It is generally supposed that all through the seventh and eighth centuries Sanseverino was under the domination of the Lombards, till with the advent of Charlemagne the city came to the Church. It is certain that in the eleventh century the Bishop of Camerino gave a certain Marchese Guarniero the investiture of the Castello, that later, in the time of Barbarossa, a certain Marcoaldo ceded it to his relation Atto. From this Atto, the local historians assert, was derived the family of the Smeducci, which for more than two hundred and forty years, sometimes as vicars of the Church, sometimes as rebels and absolute lords, ruled Sanseverino. But in spite of the interdicts of the Church and the rebellion of the Sanseverinati, when these lords were, more than once, turned out of the city, they always returned to rule, till in 1426 Pope Martin v sent against Antonio Smeducci a force of two thousand men under Giacomo Caldora and Pietro della Colonna. After fifteen days of siege the Papal force entered the town on the 19th June, crying *Viva la Chiesa! Morte al Tiranno!* and proceeded to sack the place. Antonio Smeducci, with his wife and sons, took refuge in the Tower of the Castello, and were there taken and sent as prisoners to the Rocca of

Ascoli, and thence to Narni, where they were condemned by the Pope to perpetual exile. And as the local historians tell us, " when the evil rule of the Smeducci was over, Sanseverino returned to her free estate under the high protection of the Church, governing herself with the municipal statute that was re-established in 1427."

But, like every free city, Sanseverino soon became a prey to faction, and perhaps also to the overbearing tyranny of the Papal Legates. Among these, Astorgio, Bishop of Ancona, who established himself in Sanseverino soon after the expulsion of the Smeducci, is said to have been the worst. And it was on account of the conduct of this man that Sanseverino in 1433 gave herself to Francesco Sforza, on condition that he maintained all the privileges the Commune had so hardly won. On the same terms, Alessandro Sforza, Francesco's brother, was accepted as protector, if not as lord. But in 1445 Sanseverino returned under the immediate dominion of the Church, and there, in July 1449, Nicholas v, with ten Cardinals, took up his abode for a few days, as did Pius ii in 1464 on his way to his death-bed at Ancona.

In the first years of the sixteenth century, Sanseverino was attacked by the Lord of Camerino, Giulio Cesare Varano, but she beat him off. Then in 1517 it was the Duke of Urbino Francesco Maria della Rovere whom she managed to bribe to go away, as did many other cities of the Marches, including Fabriano, Ancona and Recanati. Corinaldo was saved by a well-timed sally, but Jesi was sacked by the Duke's Spanish troops. The price Sanseverino paid to be let alone was one thousand ducats, ten barrels of powder and a piece of black velvet. This, however, was almost the last of the grave dangers that threatened the peace of the little city, which henceforth lived uneventfully enough until the appearance of Napoleon, and the prophecy, fulfilled in 1860, of the Italian kingdom.

To-day Sanseverino appears to the traveller, as I have already said, as one of the most charming of the smaller

cities of the March. Her beautiful oval Piazza catches you
at once when you first come into it, and little by little, as
you make your way through the town, in and out of the
churches and up to the old tower on the hill, you are
fascinated by her old-time loveliness, her wealth of beauty,
her architecture and pictures, in which, in contrast with
Tolentino, she is so rich.

The Piazza is for the most part quiet enough, but if you
happen there on a market day, or, better still, on the day
of the fair in September, you will be overwhelmed by the
gay and noisy crowd that fills it, the acrobats and jugglers,
the noise of the drums beaten before the booths, the
amazing conglomeration of goods for sale—laces, stays,
razors, spades, fruit, live ducks and chickens, and I know
not what else. An arcade runs round the Piazza on both
sides of it, but it is finer upon the south under the hills on
which stand the old Duomo and the Castello.

The new Duomo of S. Agostino, once dedicated in honour
of S. Maria Maddalena, is just beyond the Piazza. In the
thirteenth century it was in the hands of the Augustinians,
and was largely rebuilt in 1473, and within was entirely
renewed in 1776 and again in 1827. Over the second altar
on the right is a curious picture, painted in 1508, or perhaps
in 1538, representing, above, the Madonna di Loreto enthroned, and beneath, S. Peter, S. John Baptist, S. Martin
on horseback, and S. Augustine. It was painted by the
brothers Antonio and Giovanni Gentile di Lorenzo da
Sanseverino. The inscription is as follows : FACIEBAT ·
APELLES · ANTONIUS · ET · JOANNES · GENTILIS · MAGISTRI ·
LAURENTIJ · SEPTEMPEDANI · PINGEBANT. *Chi · vuol · bias-
mare · l'opra · manifesta · facciane · un' · altra · Lui · può ·
dana · qta. Sapienti · pauca · MD (XXX) VIII.*"

But interesting as this work is, two far better pictures
are to be seen in the sacristy, one of them a very noble
masterpiece. This is the beautiful work of Pintoricchio,
and it probably dates from about 1496. It represents in a
beautiful landscape—a valley with far-away mountains and

MATER PACIS. BY PINTORICCHIO
Duomo, Sanseverino

curious rocks beneath woods—Madonna seated with her little Son standing on a rich cushion on her knee, as He blesses the donor, a priest, said to be Liberato Bartelli, protonotary Apostolic and Canon of S. Maria in Trastevere, who kneels humbly, his hands pointed in prayer. In Our Lord's left hand is a crystal ball surmounted by a little cross ; and on either side of Madonna is an angel. Above, in the lunette, appears God the Father, surrounded by the cherubim. This very noble work is called the Madonna of Peace, Madonna Pacis, and its effect upon one is just that ; it is as though all the softness of Umbria had suddenly crept, on some summer afternoon, into this harder and more violent country of narrow, broken valleys, and precipitous mountains, and had left here for ever this much of its own beatitude.

Close by hangs another Umbrian work, but very different in spirit from that of Pintoricchio. It is a work by Bernardino di Mariotto, and was painted in 1509. It represents the Madonna del Soccorso, surrounded by little angels, and saving a child from pestilence. Here, too, is conserved a fine statue of S. Severino in silver, made by Lotti, the Roman goldsmith, in 1659.

Some way beyond the new Duomo, on the left on the hillside, is the church of S. Lorenzo Vecchio or, as its true title runs, Chiesa Abaziale di S. Lorenzo in Doliolo. This is the oldest church that is to be found in the city of Sanseverino. It was founded upon the ruins of an early Christian basilica, which itself stood upon some earlier Roman building. It was, when I saw it last, entirely in the hands of the masons, and what it will be like when they have done with it I cannot say. Its great treasure had been carefully transferred to the clergy house close by, and was most courteously shown me by the parish priest. This was a fine altarpiece of the Nativity, by Lorenzo da Sanseverino. When I had looked at this lovely picture and praised it, my smiling host led me back into the church and down into the crypt, where I found many fragmentary frescoes

by Lorenzo Salimbeni, Lorenzo da Sanseverino the Elder,
that is.

Lorenzo Salimbeni, according to the inscription upon the
triptych, which we shall find presently in the gallery, must
have been about twenty-six years old in 1400. Sixteen
years later, in company with his brother, Jacopo, he painted
the great series of frescoes in S. Giovanni Battista in Urbino.
These are the only works of his of which we know the dates.
He seems to have been a native of Sanseverino, and a
second painter, known as Lorenzo da Sanseverino, probably
a nephew of Lorenzo Salimbeni, appears seventy years later.
Four dated works from his hand are at Paùsula, dated 1481 ;
at Sarnano, dated 1483 ; at Caldarola, dated 1491 ; and the
last at Pollenza, dated 1496, giving us some idea of the
period at which he was at work.   These men, no doubt, had
a school at Sanseverino, and it is the work of pupils of the
latter we see in the curious picture of the Madonna di Loreto
in the new Duomo.

The church of S. Domenico, near the railway station in
the lower town, dates as to its foundation from the tenth
century.   It was at one time known as S. Maria del Mercato,
and near to it the Smeducci built a fortress.   It possesses
to-day a picture by Francesco Ghisi of Fabriano, which
represents the Madonna della Neve and two panels of S.
Eustace and S. Taziana, by some disciple of Bernardino di
Mariotto.   A work by that master himself stands over the
high altar.   It represents the Blessed Virgin on high,
enthroned with the cherubim, with her little Son in her
arms, S. Dominic, S. Sano, S. Catherine of Siena, S. Severino
and the little S. John Baptist below, under a fine Renaissance
arch, through which we see a landscape and the sea.

But the greater part of the pictures that once glorified the
churches of Sanseverino are now in the Pinacoteca in the
Palazzo Pubblico.   There we find a fine altarpiece with
eight saints in niches on a gold ground, with, above, six
half figures of saints (5) ; a small panel of the Virgin and
Child, a Sienese work (15) ; two Pietà on canvas by Ber-

nardino di Mariotto (6 and 7) ; two panels, eight pictures
in all, of the lives of S. Cosma and S. Damiano (16 and 17) ;
a Madonna and Child on a gold ground by Francescuccio
Ghisi of Fabriano (22) ; a Pietà by Coda da Rimini (2) ;
a great polyptych painted on a gold ground with the
Madonna and Child and angels in the midst, two saints on
either side, and above four half figures of saints and a
Pietà, and beneath, in the predella, the Last Supper with
twelve small figures of saints (8), perhaps by Crivelli. Next
to it is a triptych of the Marriage of S. Catherine, with two
saints (4), by Lorenzo Salimbeni, and close by an Annunciation, by Bernardino di Mariotto (1). We then come
to what is, after the Crivelli, the most striking picture in
the Gallery, a polyptych of the Blessed Virgin and Child
with four saints. Above is God the Father holding a crown
for the Virgin, surrounded by Cherubs, with Daniel and
Jeremiah on either side and the Annunciation in little.
Beneath, in raised *gesso*, is Our Lord with S. Peter and S.
Paul and ten apostles (18). This noble and learned work
comes from the old Cathedral and is from the hand of
Niccolò da Foligno and is dated 1468. Close by is a charming work by Lorenzo da Sanseverino, a Madonna and Child,
with S. John Baptist, and a Bishop from S. Domenico (3),
and a picture by Giovanni di Paolo the Sienese, of the
Assumption. Altogether the gallery is amazingly interesting for a little town like Sanseverino.

Such are the chief, though by no means the only sights
of the lower town or borgo. To reach the Castello one
should go up out of the Piazza past the church of S. Pacifico
and climb quite round the hills to the west, entering the
city proper by the noble great gateway of S. Francesco,
through which one sees the lofty and famous tower, and to
the right, within, the Duomo Vecchio.

The great tower was built, as it is said, by the Smeducci
in the thirteenth century. It rises from the old Piazza, on
one side of which stands the ancient Palazzo Comunale and,
in front of it, the Duomo Vecchio of S. Severino. This

16

church, which in its foundations dates from the sixth
century, and as we see it from the eleventh, remained the
Cathedral of Sanseverino until 1827, when the Bishop
translated his *cathedra* to the church of S. Agostino in the
borgo, and this church came into the hands of the Friars
Minor, who held it till 1860. Within, the church is very
interesting, and the fifteenth-century choir-stalls are delightful. In the last chapel on the left are some remains of
frescoes by Salimbeni, representing the life of S. Joseph, a
rare subject at the time these works were painted.

The only other church of much interest up here on the
hill is that of S. Chiara, where, in the choir, are some fine
stalls of 1511.

When the traveller has seen these things he has seen
perhaps the finer sights of Sanseverino, but no one should
forget that the city remains—remains to be loved and for
our delight. Anyone can follow a guide-book, if he can
find one, from church to church and picture to picture,
but let not such an one deceive himself ; when he has seen
everything that is there set down there must always remain
the city itself with its by-ways, shrines and, above all, its
people and the life and happiness of the place. These, in
such a book as this, I have not the space nor perhaps the
skill to speak of, as they should be spoken of. They remain
when all is said, not merely what is best worth seeing in
Sanseverino, but are rightly understood Sanseverino itself.
For all that we look for and search out with so much in
dustry is dead, after all, but these are living, and by our
pleasure in them, ourselves may judge ourselves.

Before leaving Sanseverino for Camerino, far away on its
hill-top, there are two places it is easier to visit from this
little town than from elsewhere, though even from San
severino they are hard to reach; I mean Cìngoli and Apiro.
A long drive of some fifteen miles brings you to the lofty
hill city of Cìngoli, whither one goes chiefly for the sake of
Lorenzo da Sanseverino, and a little for Lotto's sake also.
In the church of S. Esuperanzio, in the left transept, is a

noble great polyptych, an early work by the Sanseverino master which one should not pass by ; while in S. Domenico there is a fine altarpiece, painted in 1539 by Lotto, of the Madonna and Child enthroned with six saints, and in the predella fifteen small scenes from the life of Christ and the life of the Blessed Virgin.

It is a bitter, hard way, but beautiful withal, between Cìngoli and Apiro, but one's labour is amply repaid by the fine Nuzi there, dated 1366, a picture of the Madonna and Child, with Saints, in S. Francesco.

These two hill cities are as difficult to reach as any in the Marches, but, after all, it is the greatest part of one's pleasure in Italy to be upon the road, and when the road is as fine as that between Cìngoli and Sanseverino, even though there were nothing to be seen at the end of it, it would be a delight to traverse it. And for myself, I know not any other happiness so satisfying as that to be found afoot upon such a road.

CHAPTER XIX

CAMERINO

FROM Sanseverino the traveller sets out always with reluctance for Camerino, not knowing what awaits him on that lonely hill-top, and full of regret for the little town in the valley of the Potenza which contains so much beauty and charm. It is but a short journey of some seven miles from Sanseverino to Castel Raimondo, with its ruined Rocca, where one must leave the railway and proceed up the long hill to Camerino afoot, or sit for an hour or more in a stuffy train. But Camerino is worth all the labour it costs to reach her. Of all the March cities she is the most characteristic, with the most to offer us, at any rate in the way of natural beauty. For even in a country which can boast of such a place as Fermo or Macerata she is easily queen—a noble, dark, mediæval city set on the top of a mighty hill nearly two thousand feet over the sea, commanding a view of unsurpassed splendour and beauty, towering over her world. There is no town in Umbria or Tuscany, not even Perugia or Siena, which has so wonderful a position, so lovely a command of a world of mountain and valley, noble in gesture and expression and certainly blessed. It is true that Perugia looks over a world famous and holy beyond any other in Italy; it is true that Siena all day long looks on Mont' Amiata, the most beautiful mountain in Tuscany, as lovely and as characteristic indeed as Fuji, but neither the one nor the other possess such landscapes as Camerino has in abundance, each and all of which might seem to be a picture by Perugino, full of the largeness and

the spaciousness of that master, who alone among the
painters of Umbria and Tuscany understood the evening
earth, the mystery of sunshine, the opening wonder of
the morning, the beauty of the garden of the world.

Therefore, though for no other cause, yet for this Camerino
should never be passed by. For though she has pictures and
churches in some abundance it is not for these you seek her
out, but for her own sake and that of the world she offers
you at once, and freely, at her gate. She is the queen of
all hill cities, not for the reasons which go to make up the
claims of Siena or Perugia to that title, but by natural right,
because of the beauty that lies at her feet, which is hers
and hers alone to give you, and which she gives you at once
nobly and freely without an afterthought. No one who
has ever looked out from the road beyond Porta Giulia at
evening will ever forget what he has seen. It is as though
all those dreams of landscape, which were all that Perugino
really cared about, had suddenly been translated into a
reality more beautiful and more wonderful than anything
of which he had been able to conceive, and suddenly at a
corner of the way, in the quietest and longest hour of afternoon, God Himself and none other had spread out this His
treasure for your delight and opened your eyes that you
might enjoy it and praise Him for ever and ever.

But it is a long way to Camerino and seems longer than
it is in the horrible tram which, shrieking and groaning,
carries you through a whole hour from Castel Raimondo,
winding about and about the beautiful city up to Camerino
at last. And even then, when you have arrived and
forgotten the wretchedness of the journey and passed
through the city to the inn, you do not realize what
Camerino is. It seems a place a little broken down, a
little too big for its population, melancholy and dark and
full of the moaning wind that fills these narrow streets so
often with a rather bitter music. Its emptiness is emphasized, I think, chiefly by its innumerable churches, so
many of which have passed into the brutal service of the

world. The tramway station, for instance, is a church, the cinema theatre is a church, the museo is a church, and yet no one seems to be sorry or to miss them at all. The city is full of half-discarded and neglected sanctuaries, in which the cold and the wind are at home, and that seem not to be loved by anyone or to be anyone's care. But this may very well be nothing but appearance. The whole city looks a little desolate, as though it were always at the mercy of the wind, and winter were more at home there than summer ; a grey town of melancholy streets and wide, windy piazzas, full of old churches which have nothing to say, of palaces which seem to have been closed for ever, of little gaiety, but full of friendly people for all that—a noble city that has been passed over by the modern world and is crumbling away there like a neglected altar on its bleak hill-top in the midst of the most wonderful landscape in Italy.

Set thus on its great hill, an outpost of the central Apennines, guarding the sources of the Chienti in the pass between Umbria and Picenum, Camerinum, as the Romans called the city, would seem at first sight not to be much more ancient than the Roman Civil Wars, when it appears for the first time in history as a place of some consequence. But, indeed, although we have no mention of the city before that time, the people of the Camertes, as early as 308 B.C., were recognized as one of the most considerable nations in central Italy ; so important indeed did they appear to the Romans that the Roman deputies sent forth in 305 B.C. to explore the Ciminian forest, having advanced, as Livy tell us, " usque ad Camertes," took much trouble to establish friendly relations with them. What exactly " usque ad Camertes " meant we do not know, but it seems not unlikely that it referred to the people then settled about Chiusi, and with a city thereabout as their capital. In 268 B.C. we hear of the conquest of the Camertes by Appius Claudius, and it might seem that it was then they retreated across the Apennines and established this city of Camerino. Thenceforth they lived at peace with the Romans as their allies. We know little or nothing of Camerino in Roman times or of its fate in the fall of the Empire ; but in the eighth century it was a part of the Lombard Duchy of Spoleto. It came to the Holy See as part of the donation of Pepin which Charlemagne confirmed, and its happiest years were spent under the government of the Church. Its strong Guelf sympathies led to its destruction by Manfred in 1259, and during the exile of the Popes in Avignon it fell under the despotism of the Varani, who were among the worst of those tyrants the March suffered in such abundance. Nothing, however, to be found in the story of any of the other cities of the March can match the doings of the Varani in Camerino. At last the people, assisted by the Papal Governour of the March, Vitelleschi, determined to make an end of the whole stock. To this end, and aided by the counsel of Arcangelo di Fiordimonte, one of the confidants of the Varani, who wished, like the rest, to re-establish freedom in Camerino under the Church, the four brothers Varani then living were invited to meet Vitelleschi in Sanseverino, and it was arranged that they should be murdered in the Castello there. The plot, however, had to be given up on account of the advent of the Emperor Sigismund. In August 1433, however, everything was again ready. Vitelleschi came to Sanseverino and the four were invited to meet him. One of them, Giovanni, perhaps suspecting foul play, roundly refused to leave Camerino; two others sent excuses by their sons ; only one of the brothers, Pier Gentile, went. The young men were spared, but Pier Gentile was taken prisoner to Recanati and there beheaded. When the two young men got back to Camerino they found their fathers disputing with Giovanni over the affair. There was much jealousy between the brothers, which had been fostered by Arcangelo di Fiordimonte, and at a sign from their fathers, as Giovanni left the room, they cut him down in his rage. This murder was at once seized upon by the people as an excuse for rough justice, and in the following year Bernardo, the father of one of the young men, was murdered in Tolentino, and then suddenly, on the morning of a feast-day, the whole family being at Mass in the church of S. Venanzio in Camerino was massacred, only one tiny child, Giulio Cesare, escaping in the arms of his Aunt Tora, who hid him in a truss of hay and carried him secretly to Foligno, her native city, for she was of the Trinci, the tyrants of that place. She had scarcely arrived, however, when the people rose and the Trinci were destroyed; but she fled away to Fabriano, eventually, after a third flight, hiding her treasure in a nunnery. There, however, he was discovered by a soldier of fortune such as at that time were so plentiful in the March, and stolen away, to return to Camerino as despot at the age of twelve, and to live to become a soldier of some distinction, but to be slaughtered at last when he was sixty-seven years old by the order of Cesare Borgia, who had a few months before taken Camerino.

In Rome the news of Cesare's success was not received more joyfully than it was in Camerino. " Two hours before sunset," we read, " news was brought to the Pope that Duke Valentino had gained possession of Camerino by capitulation. Therefore many bombs were let off from the Castle of S. Angelo. In the evening there was a great illumination, and rockets were let off, and a great festival was made in the Piazza di S. Pietro. On the Sunday evening the great bell of the Chapter was rung, and with great triumph still bigger fires were made than on the previous evening. The victory was in this wise. A truce having been made with the Lord of Camerino by the Duke Valentino, the latter rushed into the city when he was least expected."

It is a most extraordinary thing, but perhaps only helps us to understand, or at any rate to realize, the confusion that was the Renaissance and the violent contrasts that were its chief characteristic—it is an extraordinary

thing, I say, to find that though all or almost all the men
of the Varani family were mere bravos and blackguards,
the women were often of an extraordinary sweetness and
culture, and even saintly. There is, for instance, Camilla,
daughter of this Giulio Cesare, who has left us a record of
her religious experiences, a sort of *Apologia pro Vita Sua*,
in which she can write as follows : " Being one day in
prayer and having clearly felt that He was in my soul, I
heard Him say, when He chose to leave me, ' If you wish
to see Me, look upon Me,' and it was as when a person
leaves another and turns his back to him and goes his way.
So exactly He did to my soul. When I began to see Him,
He was distant from me more than six paces off, in a room
at the end of which is a small door like the door of a
chamber. I continued to see Him until He bent His head
by reason of His tallness and passed in at that door.[1] And
I saw neither Him, nor the hall, nor the doors any more.
He was robed to the ground ; and the dress was bordered
at its extremity with a border, having letters of gold on it
a full finger large, which I could not read because they were
too far off from me ; and He walked away quickly and did
not stop. He was girded very tightly at the girdle, with
a band of massive gold two fingers wide. He was taller
than all other the tallest men. Falling from His shoulders
His hair appeared all golden and reaching almost to the
girdle. The hair was rather wavy, but I could not see all
the top of His head, so as to perceive whether He wore a
crown, or diadem, or garland of flowers and roses. This He
did not choose me to see. I suppose that He wore on His
head something so beautiful that I was unworthy to see
it. . . ."

The last of the Varani did not perish when Giulio Cesare
fell under the knife of Cesare Borgia, but though Sigis-

---

[1] This took place in the great hall of the ancient palace of the
Varani, built by Venanzie Varani, at the end of which, as Lilli the
historian of Camerino tells us, " there is to this day a communica-
tion with other rooms by that little door."

mondo Varani had the backing of the Duke of Urbino, the
Varani reign was really over, and the city passed into
the hands of Duke Guidobaldo II of Urbino, who had
married Giulia Varani before she was twelve years old, in
1534. It is true that Pope Paul III coveted the city for
his grandson, Ottavio Farnese, and went to almost every
length to acquire it for him, even appointing him lord in
1545. But the people of Camerino would have nothing
to do with him, and in 1546 the Pope revoked his gift.
Thus the city came back into the hands of the Church.

Wandering about Camerino recalling these things to
mind, one is touched by the melancholy of this city from
which everything except the beauty of the world in which
it stands seems to have fallen away. How empty are
all these churches of which there are so many; all the
pictures have gone, and the fragments only remain and these
not in the places for which they were painted, but gathered
into another empty and desecrated church, now a museum.
Only in S. Venanzio and the Cappuccini some few things
remain.

In S. Venanzio there is a curious picture by some unknown master, dated 1518, where we see S. Anne and the
Blessed Virgin with Our Lord in her arms on her knees, and
S. Joachim and S. Joseph on either side. All this is seen
under a fine Renaissance arch, through which a landscape
appears and the curious and rich yellow of the robes lend
it a certain startling brightness. In the Duomo of S.
Savino—S. Savino was the first bishop of Camerino in the
third century—there remains a fine tomb of the thirteenth
century, a very noble thing. And then, in the Cappuccini,
there is an altarpiece of late Robbia ware, in which we see
Our Lady seated with Our Lord in her arms, and on either
side S. Francis and S. Agnese, a charming piece of work.

It is well, I always think, that something has been left
to the Cappuccini, for it was very much owing to the protection Matteo di Basso received in Camerino that that
reform of the Franciscan Order got itself established.

Matteo di Basso was a Franciscan Observant who gave his followers a long pointed hood (cappuccio) which he believed to be that worn by S. Francis. The Order was originally one for hermit friars devoted to the contemplative life, but they remained under the Observants until 1617, when they were established as a separate Order. Even to-day, however, there is a large number of friars among them not in priests' orders. They were humble people who went bearded, whose very chalices were to be of nothing more precious than pewter and whose churches were to be as simple as possible. They existed solely upon alms, and lived a hard life, rising at midnight for Matins and keeping two Lents in the year. To the asylum Camerino offered them in 1528 they owe very much.

The churches of Camerino are, as I say, empty now of all their riches, and some fragments of these have been collected in the Museo, which is to be found in the desecrated church of the Annunziata. These treasures very largely consist of works by Girolamo di Giovanni da Camerino, by whom there is one picture and some spoiled frescoes. This master is generally thought to have been the son of Giovanni Boccatis, by whom nothing remains in Camerino. He was working in the middle of the fifteenth century, and came, of course, very strongly under the influence of his reputed father, and learned much from Umbrian and Venetian masters, chiefly perhaps Crivelli. The noblest of his works here is an Annunciation with a Pietà above (8), a very notable and lovely thing, in which Girolamo has solved a problem that baffled Titian, for here the donors look on without offence. Beside this we have two frescoes by the same master, a Madonna and Child with two Saints, painted in 1449 (2), a Madonna and Child with six saints and donor (3), and two fragments of frescoes, an angel (89) and a Madonna enthroned (98), a fresco by Bernardino di Mariotto of the Baptism of Our Lord, a frescoed niche in which we see Christ standing in Jordan, while S. John baptizes Him and four angels bear witness, in the lovely landscape of Umbria, and above, God the Father in heaven amid the Cherubim speeds the Dove and claims Our Lord as His Beloved Son (1).   Beside these well-attested works are a few others : a Crucifixion with the Blessed Virgin, S. John Baptist and donor on a gold ground (5), a lovely Madonna and Child with two angels on a gold ground by some imitator of Gentile da Fabriano (6), a S. Bernardino of Siena preaching (7) and a Madonna and Child with S. Venanzio on the other side (9).

That is all, and when one has seen these one has seen really all that Camerino has to show us in the way of works of art.   But she is not to be despised on that account. Let a man who feels disheartened at her poverty after the long labour of reaching her go down to Porta Giulia and look out towards the mountains and the valleys that are hers.   No other view in the Marches is nobler or more wonderful than this, nor can any words describe it.   Wave after wave, the hills break upon the valleys dim with mist, and far away against the pale gold of the evening sky clouds whiter than any snow, shaped like the wings of angels, sail as in a picture by Perugino over the hills.   From the church, not too near, a bell rings Ave Maria, and up into the city a little procession wends slowly, slowly through the summer twilight, the tapers burning, singing a hymn at the close of the day to Her whom all of us remember at evening.

> Ave maris stella,
> Dei Mater alma,
> Atque semper Virgo,
> Felix cœli porta.
>
> .   .   .   .
>
> Monstra te esse matrem,
> Sumat per te preces,
> Qui pro nobis natus,
> Tulit esse tuus. . . .
>
> .   .   .   .

That landscape calls us all the time we are in Camerino, and we shall do well to hear the call, for there are many

BORGO S. GIORGIO.   CAMERINO

PALAZZO MUNICIPALE, MATELICA

places in the contado of the melancholy city which are smiling and gay enough, and some of them hold treasures.

There is Pioraco, for instance, and its wonderful gorge and walls, a delicious village, which no one should miss. It lies north-west from Camerino and is best reached by road from Castel Raimando. And there, though we miss him in Camerino, we shall find Boccatis, for the little church of S. Maria del Seppio possesses two of his works, a fine Madonna and Child with angels and a S. Sebastian, painted in 1466.

And then, in quite another direction to the south-east of Camerino, a walk from the city is Varano, with its castle of the blackguard great family who only produced tyrants and saints.

And the best and yet the longest and most difficult excursion to make from Camerino takes you by public automobile miles and miles away to the south into that mysterious country which calls one so persistently from the walls of Camerino—to Visso. It is a long way, and though Visso is a very remarkable walled town, lying high in a bare valley among bare hills and guarded by a great towered fortezza set on a hill-top to the south, yet, after all, it only has one work of art for all the journey, and that is a chapel in the Collegiata, frescoed by Lo Spagna, that delightful Umbrian who littered the way between Foligno and Spoleto with his loveliest work. Something less even than this we find at Visso, but something not to be lightly missed, since there is added to it all the beauty of the little city itself and the splendour of the long road under the mountains to and from Camerino.

CHAPTER XX

MATELICA

THE curious poverty of Camerino, that noble city, in works of art, cannot but strike every traveller; happily, not far away at the foot of that prodigious hill upon which Camerino stands, there is a little city in the valley of the Esina which is as rich in paintings as Camerino is poor; its name is Matelica.

I am not sure that my happiest hours in the Marches have not been spent in this delightful, interesting, and unrenowned place, and if that is so I owe it chiefly to the charming company and hospitality of the Reverend Arciprete Bigiaretti, whose enthusiasm and love for the little town for which he has done so much it is a delight to witness and to share. To see Matelica in his company, to wander from church to church, from altar to altar, from shrine to shrine, is to learn to love what he loves, and to realize more keenly than ever what a crime it is to tear pictures and altarpieces away from the sanctuaries for which they were painted. Happily, Matelica has suffered very little in this way, her wealth of pictures being for the most part *in situ*, but the better these are known the more all who love her must be afraid lest presently the little Museo shall wonderfully expand into one of those horrible art prisons, where all art dies, which are the tombs of pictures and which are so plentiful up and down Italy. Not that Father Bigiaretti has any theories of this kind, or if he has he did not confide them to me, but that his enthusiasm, simple and natural in its eagerness and expression, leads one to love what he has loved and to wish with all one's heart that here in Matelica, at any rate, things may be left as they are, to delight, to charm and to console us all. But Father Bigiaretti, a Father indeed to all Matelica and, of course, since they are in his parish, though only for a few days, to every traveller who comes to his little city, is not only a generous host, a charming companion and a devout lover of all that is lovely in a lovely place, but a collector too, especially of majolica, of which he has certainly the most various private collection in the Marches. No one who comes to Matelica should miss seeing this collection, if only that thereby he may by chance discreetly become acquainted with one of the kindest and most unassuming of men.

I write in a tongue foreign to Father Bigiaretti, and, happily for my peace, he will never see these words, but one learns at least this in one's wanderings, to value a kind heart and the rare hospitality that an Italian offers to strangers. I came as a stranger into Matelica, I took lunch at the inn, the Aquila d'Oro, a not very brilliant hostelry, and after lunch, in the very hour of the siesta, I demanded of all and sundry the way to the Museo, expecting to see everything there was to see in an hour or two. The Museo was closed and I was directed by the barber, who had courteously accompanied me, to apply to Father Bigiaretti, the director. I did as I was bid. I found Father Bigiaretti, like any other decent and sane person at that hour of a summer day, taking his siesta. But do you think he sent me away ? Not at all. Cheerfully and without complaint he brought his siesta to an end and issued out of his cool house into the appalling heat because a stranger wanted to see his beautiful city. Without a thought he devoted the whole of his leisure to showing me not only the Museo, but everything he thought I should care for in Matelica, and this not for the sake of this my book, of which he was quite unaware, but because I was a stranger. I say that such kindness

is rare anywhere, perhaps it is less rare in Italy than in
any other country of Europe. Nevertheless, I have not
enjoyed it too often, even in Italy, and I cannot in justice
to Matelica refrain from recording it here, and recalling
certain words spoken long ago : *Hospes eram, et collegistis me.*

And now as to Matelica. I have said no one who travels
through the Marches should miss it, and, indeed, there is no
excuse for passing it by, since it stands upon the line of
railway which runs from Macerata through Tolentino,
Sanseverino, Castel-Raimondo (the station for Camerino)
and Fabriano. It is but a few minutes in the train from
Castel-Raimondo, and may be seen comfortably, though not,
of course, quite satisfactorily, in one day from Camerino.
It is a little gay town, as gay as Camerino is melancholy,
set about a fine open Piazza, where is a double loggia, a
fountain of 1590, the great Palazzo del Municipio and the
church of S. Soffragio. This charming Piazza is the centre
of Matelica ; all the churches, which are the great feature
of Matelica, are to be sought from it, the Museo and the
Duomo being but a few steps away.

Coming into Matelica from the railway, the first church
one passes is that of S. Teresa, where, in the sacristy, are two
panels by Lorenzo da Sanseverino. These two panels hang
very high upon the walls of the sacristy, but two Carmelite
brothers most courteously brought me a ladder so that I
was able to see them more or less at my ease. I suppose
they were hung so high to make theft more difficult ; they
are certainly lovely enough to tempt anyone to make off
with them. They represent in one panel S. Sebastian and
S. Catherine, with the Prophet Daniel above in the sky, and
on the other S. Benedict, wearing spectacles, and S. John
Baptist, with the Prophet Hezekiah above. These two
exquisite works greet you as you enter Matelica and
prophesy of all the lovely things that little city keeps hid
in its dear sanctuaries.

From S. Teresa the Corso runs into the Piazza. Just
before coming into the wideness of that noble square in

street on the left stands the Palazzo Piersanti, and here
is the Museo. A great eighteenth-century coach stands in
the atrium, and then there are the pictures. Among these
the following should be noted. First there are a small panel
of the Coronation of the Blessed Virgin, by Bernardino di
Mariotto, and a Madonna and Child, the Madonna reading,
by Brescianino, the sixteenth-century Sienese. Between
these two pictures is a noble Crucifix painted in 1452 by
Antonio da Fabriano. One then comes to a fine triptych by
Lorenzo da Sanseverino, representing the Crucifixion and
painted on gold, the central panel of which is very fine :
note the broken legs of the two thieves. In the predella
there are three scenes from a seventeenth-century hand.
Close by is another picture of the Crucifixion, with eight
predella scenes of the life of S. Helena and the Invention of
the Cross. In the frame are the heads of the twelve Apostles.
Then comes a fifteenth-century triptych of the Madonna and
Child, with the Cardinal Brancaccio, S. Saba, S. Michele,
S. Giovanni and another. Above is the Annunciation.
From this one passes to a beautiful small panel of the
Crucifixion by Niccolô da Foligno, and lastly to a noble work
by Vittore Crivelli of the Madonna and Child, enthroned with
S. Biagio, S. Sebastiano, S. Rocco and S. Bernardino, a work
now broken up into separate panels. The gallery is notable
for the beauty of the pictures it possesses and is alone worth
the trouble—if trouble it be—of a journey to Matelica,
quite apart from the other noble things the little city
possesses.

Close by the Museo in the same street is the church of S.
Agostino, with an interesting doorway and an old desecrated
Augustinian convent, with remains of frescoes in the charm-
ing cloister.

In the Piazza to which one now turns stands the church
of S. Soffragio, where is a fine seventeenth-century picture
of the Crucifixion. Another work, apparently by the same
master, representing S. Onofrio in the Desert, is to be found
in the Municipio close by. Opposite this too modern build-

17

ing stands the delightful fifteenth-century Loggiata with the old clock tower beside it. The whole Piazza is gay and charming, and, on a market day, full of stalls and a gaily dressed multitude, it makes as animated and happy a scene as one could wish.

Down beyond the Piazza to the right stands the Franciscan church of S. Francis, a beautiful and spacious building. Here again are some notable pictures. Over the fourth altar on the left is a work by Simone and Giovanni da Caldarola, painted in 1519, representing the Stoning of S. Stephen. Over the next altar is another work, from the same hands, of the Adoration of the Magi, with a ring of singing angels above in the sky. In the first chapel on the right is a copy of a picture by Lotto of the Crucifixion, by Duranti de' Nobili di Caldarola, painted in 1560. This picture is on the left. On the right is a fine altarpiece of the Madonna and Child, enthroned with S. Francis and S. Catherine, by Palmezzano, signed and painted in 1501, with three predella scenes and eight saints at the side, a very splendid work. Over the second altar on this side of the church is a work, perhaps by Sassoferrato, representing the Madonna and Child. In the next chapel, on the right wall, is a fine triptych, where we see the Madonna and Child with S. Anthony holding a book and a cross, and S. Francis with two angels holding a linen cloth under his feet. There are six saints in little at the sides, and beneath four predella scenes from the life of S. Anthony, with two donors at the sides. This is a work of the fifteenth century and very interesting indeed to the Franciscan student on account of its curious representation of S. Francis, preserving for us a legend in which angels spread a cloth beneath his feet, wounded with the sacred wounds of Christ.

Upon the opposite side of the same chapel is a fine piece of needlework representing the Crucifixion. Where this tapestry hangs, of old there hung the picture, now in the National Gallery, of the Madonna and Child, enthroned with S. Jerome and S. Sebastian (724), by Carlo Crivelli, and signed:

CAROLUS CRIVELLUS VENETUS MILES PINXIT. It was known, from the swallow we see there, as the Madonna della Rondina. In the predella are S. Catherine, S. Jerome in the Wilderness, the Nativity of Our Lord, the Martyrdom of S. Sebastian and S. George and the Dragon. It was purchased by the National Gallery in 1862 from the Conte Luigi de Sanctis of Matelica.

In the fourth chapel on this side of the church is a picture on the right wall of the Madonna and Child, enthroned with S. Andrew and S. Giovanni Evangelista, and in the midst the child Baptist. Before the throne kneel S. Anthony and S. Francis by Eusebio da Perugia, a rare pupil of Perugino, painted in 1512. Upon the left side of the chapel hangs a curious and significant work by a certain Ramazzano, painted in 1573, of the Immaculate Conception.

On leaving the beautiful and quiet church of S. Francesco, one passes outside the Porta to the Ospedale, where, in the chapel, is an exquisite fresco by Lorenzo da Sanseverino of the Madonna and Child between four, now three, angels, a very lovely thing.

Here, too, outside the gate of the city, is the church of S. Trinità, where there is a fresco by Lorenzo da Sanseverino of the Madonna and Child with two saints.

Close by the church of S. Francesco stands the little chapel of the Confraternità di S. Angelo, where is one of those curious pictures in which one sees the Blessed Virgin seated on the knees of her mother S. Anne, who here holds the Child. On either side stand S. Sebastian and S. Roch, while above is a Pietà with S. Michael and S. Domenic.

In the church of S. Giovanni Decollato there is a Madonna and Child by Eusebio di San Giorgio.

I have left the Duomo till the last, because it is the least interesting church in Matelica. Even here, however, over the second altar on the left, there is a curiously fascinating picture of the Madonna and Child, a miracle picture famous through the country round Matelica. In the sacristy, too, there is a fine Byzantine Crucifix.

When all these fair things have been seen then most of us, I suppose, will hurry away for Camerino or Fabriano. In truth, that is just the moment to begin to see them all over again, and to wander haphazard about Matelica and to enjoy it. A city has indeed a soul, which in the hurry and worry of sightseeing is hidden from us, that we never guess at even in our hearts till we come upon it by chance in some fortunate hour intent on nothing, or some other business. The soul of a city, the *genius loci*, least of all of such a quiet and retiring place as Matelica, cannot be taken by surprise, it can only be had for love between two heart-beats or after a whole lifetime of service and intimacy. Even so, how often it escapes the assiduous and him who possesses no patience, but would see all in a moment and pry into secrets that belong to the ages, betwixt his hurried meals at the inn. For such an one they have built the railway, which, though better, or at least quieter, men use it now and again, for the most part is utterly avoided by them that go afoot—and these are the real travellers—or by carriage, and these must be rich, or by automobile, and these too often lack understanding and are without mercy. He is a fool who despises even the meanest way of travel, I mean the railway, but he is a greater fool who never ventures to leave it. Let not such an one linger in Matelica. Let him hurry away : it is not for him. After all, we are in the Marches ; at their best the trains are all too slow for such an one. His mind is a whirlwind and he has lost the command of his own heart. What are the flowers by the wayside to him, and what are the works of Lorenzo da Sanseverino, Crivelli, Palmezzano and the rest of the pictures which hide shyly in these little churches but flowers ? Just because these beautiful things have not been collected here into a museum for those who come by railway, they are living still by their wayside, filling the little churches with their beauty and their pageants shining in the love of the lowly and meek, who kneel shyly and silently before them, offering up their petitions and watching with a new wonder every morning the priest make Christ out of bread and wine—things they know, of which we are ignorant, things they find precious, for they are poor, and more precious still because they are the instruments of a Sacrament and a Sacrifice which has given a new meaning to life, which has involved even the hills in its mystery and lifted up for ever the souls of men. But if such things in our misery and pride are hidden from us, are too great for us, and too good to be true, let us tread softly by these peasants as they kneel with free hearts and bowed heads before Him who has made all that was so worthless most precious, in Whose honour and for Whose glory every picture in Matelica was painted, not that it might rest for your sake or for mine in some melancholy museum, but that it might speak to the simple of heart of Him of Whom all beautiful things serve to remind them.

Here, in Matelica, how the children linger in the churches, so that, though they be but peasants, they are acquainted with all that the highest culture can give as a reward after long years—sweetness and light ; so that from their earliest years they are used to the ways of a great court, the greatest court in the world, the sanctuary of the King of kings, with its beautiful ceremonies, precious robes and elaborate ritual. It is not the bursting and the falling of the leaf, the sudden advent of the flowers, the robing and unrobing of Nature that for them alone mark the seasons, but the wonderful procession of the ecclesiastical year also, the purple of Advent ushering in the snow and fire of Christmas, the purple of Lent serving but to make more lovely the lilies of Easter, the roses of Whitsuntide, the green of the fullness of the year. But because of this, which even in the humblest village, and assuredly in Matelica, the smallest and poorest children may follow and love, there is about them a graciousness which one misses altogether in the north, that four hundred years ago was ours also, and is visible, for instance, in every gesture of Chaucer's pilgrims, but that we have missed and shall perhaps never have again.

And because Matelica is a little place, and yet most industrious and tidy withal, it suggests to one, wandering there day after day, such thoughts as these till one wonders whether, after all, we have been the gainers by that great sacrifice of sweetness and light which was asked of us, and paid by us, now nearly four hundred years ago, the wounds of which still throb and will not be healed.

CHAPTER XXI

FABRIANO, SASSOFERRATO, GENGA, ARCEVIA, CAGLI AND THE FURLO PASS

ONE goes on from Matelica down the valley of the Esino, through Cerreto and Albacina, till, a little beyond the latter place, which stands off the high road on a great hill, the road turns south and west into a wider valley, at the head of which stands Fabriano. No greater contrast can be found in all the Marches, I think, than that which I found between the city of Matelica, which I had just left, and the city of Fabriano, into which I came one August afternoon.

If it can possibly be avoided no one should ever sleep in Fabriano. To begin with, the Alberghi are dirty and noisome, and the curiously untidy town, without beginning, middle or end to it, is noisy and utterly unattractive. It chiefly consists of a large and filthy borgo, from which one enters the city proper by a vast gateway, really a long archway covered within with more than one layer of ruined frescoes. The Piazza within this gate is, it is true, rather charming with its loggias, its fountain in three stories, Palazzo Pubblico and Palazzo Episcopale; but it is more than a little gloomy as well, and nothing to boast of in any case, on the frontiers of Umbria and the Marches. This, however, must be said that even in Fabriano the people are courteous.

Fabriano is still mainly engaged, as it was in the fifteenth century, in the manufacture of paper; but one comes to it for the sake of Allegretti Nuzi, whose work is plentiful there and nowhere else in the world. This solemn and delightful painter was the master of the great Gentile da Fabriano. Born early in the fourteenth century, Allegretto's name appears on the register of painters at Florence in 1346, and he appears to have died in Fabriano between September 1373 and September 1374. His earliest dated work (1365) is, however, not in Fabriano at all, but in the Museo Cristiano of the Vatican. It is a triptych that comes from the Ospizio of the Camadolesi in Rome, while another of his works I have already spoken of at Apiro. Here, in Fabriano, there are many of his beautiful panels, forgotten till yesterday, which, in their solemn hierarchical beauty and richness, are among the loveliest things left to us in the Marches.

In the gallery of the Palazzo del Municipio, however, there are other things beside pictures by Nuzi. The first picture we come upon there—none of them is numbered—is a large altarpiece of the Madonna and Child sailing over a city, perhaps Fabriano, with S. Peter and the Baptist below. This is signed: OPUS PHILIPPI VERONEN ANNO SALUT. 1514. Close to it are two fifteenth-century panels of S. Sebastian and S. Lucia. Then we come to our first Nuzi, a panel of S. Anthony, adored by worshippers. Next to this hangs a picture of the Madonna and Child, with S. John Evangelist and S. John Baptist, perhaps by Antonio da Fabriano. Above this is a triptych of the Madonna and Child, between S. John and S. Catherine. Then comes another Nuzi, a picture of three Saints, very rich, solemn and lovely; S. Augustine, S. Anthony of Padua and S. Stephen. Beside it hangs a fifteenth-century picture of the Death of the Virgin.

Next to this is a lovely Giottesque Crucifixion, and beside it a Byzantine Crucifix. A work by Simone da Caldarola, dated 1570, follows—a Nativity of Our Lord. A fifteenth-century picture of the Madonna and Child sailing over the world, appealed to by S. Peter, a Bishop, S. Francis and perhaps Blessed Columba of Rieti in a fine landscape is a curious and notable work, as is the next picture, perhaps by some disciple of Signorelli, a Madonna and Child, with S. Francis and S. Anthony, S. Clare and S. Agnese, and music-making angels.

The second room of the gallery is full of spoiled pictures and rubbish. The third room, however, has a wonderful early figure of the Dead Christ in gesso, more than life-size, a similar Pietà, coloured, and a Crucifixion ; also a great fresco of the Madonna and Child, with three saints and two angels.

From the Municipio one climbs up out of the Piazza to the Cathedral. Here, in the third chapel on the right, is a curious miracle-picture of the Madonna. In the sacristy are remains of a fresco of the Crucifixion, with a very charming group of the Maries and a fine figure of S. Joseph of Arimathea in armour. The Magdalen at the foot of the Cross is passionately looking upward with hands spread before her, a fine piece of work.

One passes out of the Cathedral into a charming but ruined double cloister, and then into the Episcopio where, in a room upstairs, are several works by Nuzi ; a beautiful polyptych of the Madonna and Child, with four saints, another polyptych spoiled of its gold, in which we see the Madonna and Child, with SS. John Evangelist, Mary Magdalen, Bartholomew and another ; and two panels where, on a gold ground, we see S. John Baptist and S. Venanzio, and S. Anthony and S. John Evangelist. Here, too, is a very charming altarpiece on canvas on wood of the Madonna and Child, painted on a gold ground, with four saints, among them S. Andrew, on the right ; and in the predella an exquisite Pietà. Close by is a Madonna and Child in glory, with S. John Baptist and S. Augustine, painted in 1545. In the predella are the Baptism of Christ, the Visitation and a miracle of S. Augustine. This picture comes, I think, from the church of S. Agostino, where there are some fragments of frescoes by Nuzi. Better frescoes by the same master are to be seen in the sacristy of S.

Lucia. Three works by Nuzi are also to be found in the Fornari Collection in Fabriano, a Madonna and Child, a Pietà and a Madonna and Child enthroned, dated 1372, as well as a noble work by Gentile da Fabriano, the only work in the city by that master.

One is delighted to get away from Fabriano to the open road. This, which is not the great high road to Fossato, but a by-way leading over the mountains, at first through the wooded valley of the Bono, then over the great pass by Bastia and so down the Marena valley, brings one at last to Sassoferrato. All the way one is held by the beauty of the lines of the dark hills in the west, the central range of the Apennines, and indeed the road is everywhere so fair that every mile of it should be taken on foot or by carriage and the railway ignored. And beside all this there remains one thing to cheer one on the way; I mean the early Bernardino di Mariotto altarpiece, painted in 1498, of the Madonna and Child, in the parish church of Bastia, just off the road on a hill to the west. So one goes on to Sassoferrato.

Sassoferrato, the Roman Sentinum, was celebrated in ancient times as the scene of a great battle fought in the third Samnite War, 295 B.C., when the Samnites and their Gallic allies were defeated by Quintus Fabius the Consul. This victory was one of the most notable and decisive in the history of the Roman Republic. Sentinum, however, only attained municipal rank, and though a place of very great strength, played no great part in the wars of the decline and fall of the Empire, for it was far from the main route of travel, the Via Flaminia, which first crossed the Apennines at Scheggia, fourteen miles due west of Sentinum.

Sassoferrato does not exactly stand upon the site of the Roman city, but nevertheless is certainly its successor. It consists of two parts—the Castello on the hill, very strongly defended by two streams, the larger of which is the Sentino, and the Borgo upon that torrent. In the Castello, in 1605, the famous painter, Giovanni Battista Salvi, known as Il

Sassoferrato, was born. An early work from his hand
would seem to remain in the church of S. Pietro in the
Castello. This has not much interest, but in the church of
S. Chiara we shall find something more to our taste in the
frescoes there by some painter of the school of Fabriano :
delightful things. In the Borgo the only church of much
interest is that of S. Mona, which possesses an altarpiece
by Agebile, a local sixteenth-century master. Not far
away, however, in the ancient church of S. Croce, there is a
fine picture of the Virgin and Child between S. Joachim,
S. Benedict, S. Stephen, and S. Clare, with the Crucifixion
above between S. Peter and S. Paul and two other saints ;
in the pinnacles are God the Father and the four Evangelists,
and below are six predella scenes, by some follower of Gentile da Fabriano. In the parish church of Coldellanoce, near
Sassoferráto, we shall find, too, a notable triptych by Matteo
da Gualdo of the Madonna and Child with S. Sebastian and
S. Lawrence.

Nor should a visit to the beautiful village of La Genga be
omitted. Here in the parish church is a standard by
Antonio da Fabriano and a panel picture of the Madonna
and Child by Stefano Folchetti.

A longer excursion on a more difficult road will take us to
Arcevia, where in the church of S. Medardo is a noble
polyptych by that great master, Luca Signorelli, signed
LUCAS SIGNORELLUS PINGEBAT MDVII. It is in its original
frame, and represents the Madonna and Child and Saints,
and on the predella we see five little scenes : the Annunciation, the Nativity, the Adoration of the Magi, the Flight
into Egypt, and the Massacre of the Innocents. In the
Chapel of the Blessed Sacrament in the same church is
another work by the master, though not wholly carried out
by him. It represents the Baptism of Our Lord, and in the
predella we have five scenes from the life of S. John : the
Birth, the Preaching in the Wilderness, the Denunciation of
Herodias, the Feast of Herod, and the Beheading of the
Saint. In the church of S. Maria del Soccorso is a rather

mannered altarpiece of the Annunciation by one of the Robbia school, perhaps Fra Mattia.

From Sassoferrato one fine morning I went on by train to Cagli, for, in spite of the height of these high valleys, it was too hot to march.

Now Cagli is the most delightful of all these little towns between Fabriano and Urbino, a shady, cool, quiet little place, full of interesting buildings and beautiful pictures, and possessing a most excellent inn, which you may not care for at first sight, but in which you soon learn to feel thoroughly at home. I shall not easily forget my arrival in Cagli. I had waited for the evening to set out on account of the heat, so that when I arrived at Cagli, which is some distance from the station, it was quite dark. There was little or nothing near the house in the dark street where the *posta* put me down to indicate that here was an inn, and it was with some misgiving that I made my way up a dark staircase to the first floor. There, however, all my fears forsook me, for I was greeted by one of the most beautiful women it has ever been my good fortune to meet, and, what is rarer than physical beauty in Italy, she had one of the softest and most delicious voices I have ever heard anywhere. It was a great pleasure all the time I was in Cagli to be greeted every morning by this beautiful creature, and 'twixt sleeping and waking, while the sun came in little daggers through the closed shutters, to hear her say "acqua, Signore." I don't think I had ever realized before what a language of liquid music Italian is, nor how true the old saying that "the devil tempted Eve in Italian." This beautiful lady really managed the whole business of the inn, and with so glorious a dignity and so consummate a tact that even the Italian commercial traveller, about as horned a beast as flourishes in the peninsular, forgot his vulgarity when she was by, mended his flamboyant manners, and tried to look like a man. Beauty herself never had a more wonderful power over the Beast ; and, indeed, the power of this young woman was an effect of sheer beauty in which, yes, even in hers, which was provocative enough, there was something of holiness. I remember years ago remarking something of the same effect upon an unruly and strident crowd in the Costanzi theatre in Rome, on the first night of the production of D'Annunzio's *Francesca da Rimini*. The scene was really indescribable, but one may say that during the first half of the first act, in spite of the fact that Eleanora Duse was on the stage, not a syllable could be heard across the footlights. Then a quite minor character began to speak some lines ; it was a long speech, and little by little the theatre, till now mere pandemonium, grew quiet, till there was a complete silence, and the wonderful lines came to us in all their perfection. When the actor had finished, suddenly the house, hostile to frenzy till then, literally rose up with a roar. *Bello ! bello ! bello !* the crowd shouted, and from that moment, conquered by the sheer beauty of D'Annunzio's lines, the whole theatre listened attentively to the rest of the play, long drawn out though it was. I wonder if beautiful verses or a beautiful woman would have the power in England they both certainly have here in Italy ? I very much doubt it.

I wandered about Cagli day after day, till the heat drove me away up to Urbino ; but those days in the little city at the foot of the Furlo were among the most delightful I spent in the Marches.

To begin with, Cagli, as I have said, is in itself a charming place with a long history, and many signs of it remaining within and without her gates. The Roman town was Cale, and it was situated upon the Flaminian Way, which still runs through the modern town, approaching it by a very notable bridge, partly Roman still, over the Burano and the Bosso, from the north. Cale was set about halfway between the two most serious passes upon the Via Flaminia, that of Scheggia to the south, and that we call the Furlo, held in Roman times by the fortress of Petra Pertusa, to the north. Every Roman army that went northward across the Apennines to the conquest of the world must have marched through Cale, which, indeed, situated as it was between the two passes, must have been as famous as any place on the road. It is not, however, with any of those famous legions on their way up to the Wall or to the Danube we think of as we look down the white road out of the gates of Cagli northward towards Rimini and southward towards Rome, but of an adventure as tremendous and daring as any of those Rome undertook in the days of her glory. I mean the great march of Narses the eunuch, when he came thundering down out of Ravenna to find Totila, to crush him and to expel the Goths from Italy. The mighty eunuch, the general of Justinian, had come up out of Illyricum for this business with an imperial army, in which Ardoin, king of the Lombards, rode at the head of some two thousand of his people. He had come through Venetia round the head of the Adriatic close to the sea, for a formidable Frankish host held the great roads, crossing with what anxiety we may guess the mouths of the Piave, the Brenta, the Adige, and the Po, by means of his ships, and having thus turned the flank of the Frankish armies, he triumphantly marched into Ravenna. There he remained for nine days, as it were another Cæsar about to cross the Rubicon.

While he waited in Ravenna, an insulting challenge reached him from the barbarian Usdrilas, who held Rimini. "After your boasted preparations, which have kept all Italy in a ferment, and after striking terror into our hearts by knitting your brows and looking more awful than mortal man, you have crept into Ravenna and are skulking there afraid of the very name of the Goths. Come out with all that mongrel host of barbarians to whom you want to deliver Italy, and let us behold you, for the eyes of the Goths hunger for the sight of you."[1] And Narses laughed at the insolence of the barbarian, and presently he set forward with the army he had made, upon the great road through Classis for Rimini, till he came to

[1] Hodgkin's free translation of Procopius, *op. cit.* iv. 28.

the bridge over the Marecchia there, which Augustus
had built, and which was held by the enemy. In the
fight which followed—little more than a skirmish—the
barbarian Usdrilas came by his end, and Narses, ignoring
Rimini, marched on, his great object before him, Totila
and his army, which he meant before all things else to
seek out and to destroy. So he went down the Flaminian
Way to Fano, presently left it for a by-way upon the left,
rejoining the great highway at Cagli, as we may think,
some miles beyond the fortress of Petra Pertusa, which he
disregarded, as he had done that of Rimini. He marched
on till he came to the very crest of the Apennines, over
which he passed, and camped upon their western side
under the great heights, at a place then called Ad Ensem
and to-day Scheggia.

Meanwhile Totila had come to meet him from Rome,
and had managed to reach Tadinum, the modern Gualdo
Tadino, where he found Narses, unexpectedly, for he must
have thought the way over the mountains securely barred
by the fortress of Petra Pertusa, upon the great road before
him.

Narses sent an embassy to Totila, to offer " not peace
but pardon " ; this the barbarian refused ; and asked
when he would fight, Totila answered, " In eight days from
this day." But Narses, knowing what manner of man his
enemy was, made all ready for the morrow, and at once
occupied the great hill upon his left, which overlooked
both camps. In this he was right, for no sooner had he
seized this advantage than Totila attempted to do the
same, but without any success.

Then on the morrow Totila, having, meanwhile, been
reinforced with two thousand men, rode forth before the
two armies and " exhibited in a narrow space the strength
and agility of a warrior. His armour was enchased with
gold ; his purple banner floated with the wind ; he cast
his lance into the air ; cast himself backwards ; recovered his seat and managed a fiery steed in all the

paces and evolutions of the equestrian school." [1]   No doubt
Narses the eunuch smiled.   The barbarians were all the
same, and they remain unaltered.   Totila's theatrical
antics are but the prototype to those amazing cavalry
charges, excellently stage-managed, that may be seen
almost any autumn during the German manœuvres, a
new Totila at their head.

When Totila had finished his display the two armies
faced one another, the Imperialists with Narses and John
upon the left, the Lombards in the centre, and Valerian
upon the right with John the Glutton ; the Goths in what
order of battle we do not know.   At length at noon the
battle was joined.   The Gothic charge failed, Narses drew
his straight line of troops into a crescent, and the short
battle ended in the utter rout of the Goths, Totila flying
from the field.   In that flight, one Asbad, a Gepid, struck
at him, and fatally wounded him.   He was borne by his
companions to the village of Caprae, more than twelve
miles away, and there he died.   Thus in the year 552 ended
Totila the Goth, and with him the Gothic cause in Italy.

Nothing, however, could be less warlike than Cagli
to-day.   The city, very small as it is, is now quite charming, the people friendly, and remarkably handsome.   It is
a city of pictures, offering, too, to the traveller some magnificent landscapes, beyond its gates, of the gracious hills which
surround it on all sides.   One comes to it, I suppose, chiefly
for the sake of Giovanni Santi, the father of Raphael, who
has left there more than one delightful and innocent fresco,
and one remains for its own.

There is nothing at all to see in the Duomo, just out of
the Piazza, where stands the fine Palazzo Pubblico and
Fountain ; but if one turns down on the right past the
Duomo, one comes almost at once to S. Domenico, where
there is much to delight anyone who has eyes to see.

Between the first and second altars on the right is a fresco
of the Annunciation by Timoteo Viti, the master of Raphael.

[1] Gibbon's free translation, cf. Procopius, iv. 31.

Opposite this is a fine fresco by Santi, of the Pietà, with
S. Jerome and another. Over the second altar on this side
of the church is another fresco by the same master of the
Virgin and Child enthroned between S. Peter, S. Francis,
S. Dominic and a Bishop, with two angels. Before the Blessed
Virgin a candle is burning. Above is the Resurrection, and
under the arch Christ in benediction, with music-making
angels. On the front of the arch is the Annunciation.

One lingers over these lovely things half a morning before
one can tear oneself away. Then, after returning to the
Duomo, he is wise who follows the street parallel with the
Corso (I forget its name) to the south of the Duomo to find
the little church of S. Angelo on the left. Here there is a
strange picture by Timoteo Viti, in which we see Christ
appearing to S. Mary Magdalen, while to the left S. Michael,
with his scales in one hand, his sword in the other, slays
the dragon, and to the right S. Anthony Abbot, with his
pig, stands as though listening for some voice. Far away
we see Calvary, and a lovely landscape fills the background,
in which we see the angel telling S. Mary Magdalen that
Christ is risen.

A little farther on in the same street as S. Angelo is the
church of S. Francesco. Here beside the first altar on the
right, over a charming relief with two angels and an inscription, is a fresco, in which we see a miracle of S. Anthony
of Padua : a very interesting work by Guido of Gubbio.
On the left of this altar is another similar fresco from the
same fifteenth-century hand.

On either side of the high altar is a picture high up :
to the right S. Chiara and S. Agnese, to the left the Blessed
Virgin, Our Lord, and S. Catherine (?), both with lovely
landscapes under arches. A similar work on the entrance
wall of the church, to the right over the gallery, shows
us S. Anthony and S. Bonaventura. The sacristy of
S. Francesco is a fine vaulted chamber, once covered
with frescoes, now under the whitewash. That the whole
church was once covered with frescoes seems likely ; some

small but very lovely fragments near the west door of the Madonna and Child and S. Joseph and S. Agnes would suggest it.

It was still very hot, and therefore very early one summer morning when I set out from Cagli. Before me stretched the great white road, Via Flaminia, and above me presently rose the Furlo, its white brows just kissed by the sun in the dawn I could not see. It was not long before I was in the midst of a fantastic fairyland of strange and horrid cliffs, threatening crags, changing lights, and tremendous gateways. I cannot hope to describe the enormous grandeur of those gates, eyries for eagles, as indeed they are. Presently I came to the remarkable tunnel or gallery which Rome hewed through the living rock to make a way for her armies, and which she knew as Petra Pertusa ; it held the pass, as Narses knew for one. This work was achieved under Vespasian according to the inscription cut in the rock, and was constructed in A.D. 75 : IMP. CÆSAR. AUG. VESPASIANUS. PONT. MAX. TRIB. POT. VII. IMP. XVII. P.P. COS. VII. CENSOR. FACIUND. CURAVIT.

Procopius in the sixth century, who evidently knew it well, thus most accurately describes it. " This fortress was not built by the hands of man, but was called into being by the nature of the place, for the road is here through an extremely rocky country. On the right of this road runs a river, fordable by no man on account of the swiftness of its current. On the left, near at hand, a cliff rises, abrupt and so lofty that if there should chance to be any men on its summit they seem to those at its base only like very little birds. At this point, long ago, there was no possibility of advance to the traveller, the rock and river between them barring all further progress. Here, then, the men of old hewed out a passage through the rock, and thus made a doorway into the country beyond. A few fortifications above and around the gate turned it into a natural fortress of great size, and they called its name Petra."

Nothing in Italy is more amazing than this great Roman

thing, which seems indeed almost awful in its achievement, and curiously enough ends as suddenly and dramatically as it begins. One goes down towards Fossombrone through a smiling and delicious country of oak woods out of all that loneliness and silence, through which—yes, even through the impassable rock—Rome near two thousand years ago forged a Way.

I did not go on down into Fossombrone, but turned north-ward at Calmazzo, up, instead of down, the valley of the Metauro, for I was for Urbino, into which noble and lofty place, the last city of my journey, I came weary and very footsore long after dark.

CHAPTER XXII

URBINO

OF Urbino, who can speak as he should or conjure up in words, for the pleasure of him who has not seen it, that dark and gaunt city crouched upon its double hill, never venturing to tower up into the sky, but stooping there gazing over the tangled valleys to S. Marino, to S. Leo, to Pesaro, to the great peaks of the Apennines and to the sea? Bleak and rain-sodden, battered by the wind, burnt by the sun, Urbino seems the last place in Italy to have nourished a court renowned for its grace and courtesy. One can see there easily enough Count Guido Vecchio da Montefeltro, the terrific Ghibelline, who at the end of his life followed S. Francis, and forsook him at the Pope's request, so that Dante found him in Hell for giving fraudulent counsel. But who can picture the Duchess Leonora tripping along those steep, stony, narrow ways, or the fine courtier Baldassare Castiglione in a place that is all a fortress black and burnt with war and lean with long watching? Yet Urbino has known them all, and has besides produced the sweetest and the most temperate of all Italian masters, Raphael Sanzio.

For, astonishing though it may seem, civilization, the ritual of life—life itself being, as some of those great candid minds of the Renaissance were not slow to observe, a kind of religious service—was very punctually and strictly observed at Urbino in the sixteenth century. Here on the hills, in this rain-swept, sun-baked place, the Renaissance, in all its liberty, beauty and splendour, was played out in its

THE DUCAL PALACE URBINO

curious medley of contrasts, almost like a play. The most learned and refined of all the courts of Italy, the court of Urbino gathered to itself all the wit and genius of this imperishable Latin people, filled itself with the finest scholars and the noblest gentlemen of Italy, while its Duke and Duchess lived a life that reads almost like a fairy tale, till suddenly Cesare Borgia blasted the place like a lightning flash and nothing was ever really quite the same again. It might seem that that terrible figure, so full of reality, had in that one stroke withered the princely race so that it fell, weary at last and with only a dying man's reluctance, into the arms of the Church, too ready perhaps to claim what could not be denied. It is difficult to realize in the city we see the life of the ducal court in all its unreal existence of pleasure or business, but Urbino in the sunset looks still as though Cesare had but just passed by.

It is with Count Guido Montefeltro, in the middle of the thirteenth century, that the family, so illustrious in the history of Umbria and Italy, first comes to our notice. A Ghibelline, he went to Pisa with the rest from Tuscany and Romagna to greet the young Conradino who had come into Italy to dispute the crown of Naples with Charles of Anjou. Later, he appears again as captain-general of the Ghibellines, forcing all Romagna to be subject to him. Forlì was the capital of his conquest, and it was there he endured a siege by Giovanni di Appia, general to Pope Martin IV, extricating himself by one of those stratagems which, as Villani says, "established his reputation as a sagacious man, more cunning than any Italian of his time, masterly alike in war and diplomacy." However, Forlì was eventually surrendered, and Guido made his peace with the Pope. Not for long. As general of the Pisans against the Guelfs of Florence and Lucca, he was again censured by the Pope, and in 1295 we find him again in the dust and again forgiven. Meantime the Franciscan enthusiasm, almost a religion in itself, swept over Italy. Thousands forsook all and embraced a life of poverty and devotion. Among them was Count Guido. From the dreams of S. Francis he had learned a kind of introspection, so that he came at last to doubt the sufficiency of the Pope's pardon. Throwing away his county and his coronet, breaking his sword, which had never been rendered to his enemy, he went to Assisi, and, putting on the coarse habit of the Franciscans, sought forgiveness of God and peace for his own soul in the tiny cells of what had suddenly become a holy city. Pope Celestin, utterly unfitted for the crown of gold and iron and thorns which the Popes wore so resolutely, so uneasily, during those restless years, soon abdicated, making way for Boniface VIII. The new Pope, however, was soon at war with the Colonna, that mighty family which all through the Middle Age was alternately expelled from and returning to Rome. A general was a necessity. Remembering the experience and the victories of Count Guido, he sent for him, " silencing his religious scruples by a preliminary absolution for the sin of reverting to worldly schemes." Count Guido, that strange friar of Montefeltro, but lately the most " cunning and sagacious " general in Italy, counselled " deceitful promises as the surest means of conquest." So we find him in Dante's *Divine Comedy* a miserable soul without hope, to whom the whole of the twenty-seventh canto of the *Inferno* is devoted. Count Guido died in 1298, on 29th September, and is generally supposed to have been buried at Assisi. Thus the great family of Montefeltro dawned on Italy—a race of soldiers and leaders of men who, from their eyrie in the Apennines, swooped down on Italy at the head of innumerable legions, Florentine, Pisan, or Papal, as the case might be.

The next century seems to have been devoted by the House of Montefeltro to fighting their neighbours the Brancaleoni, the Malatesta, and the Ceccandi. Eventually Urbino would appear to have expelled the family; but in 1376 it was recalled in the person of Antonio, the great grandson of Guido il Vecchio. It was he who, " emancipating himself from the spell that had bound his race to a falling cause, gave to his posterity an example of loyalty to his overlord the Pope." He appears to have been a somewhat liberal ruler, bent on reform, which may well be, since he was a returned exile. At any rate, both Cagli and Gubbio welcomed his rule, and after a struggle of nearly ten years he won Cantiano from the Gabrielli. He died in 1404. He had three children—Guidantonio, who succeeded him, Anna and Battista.

It was Guidantonio who in 1420 received the Golden Rose from the Pope, becoming later captain-general of the Florentines in their war against Lucca. Apparently through no fault of his own he was defeated. Eight years later, in 1438, he lost his second wife, whom he dearly loved, and from this blow he never recovered. He retired to Loreto, perhaps with the same malady at his heart as that which had sent Guido, his ancestor, to Assisi. Loreto was considered one of the holiest places in Italy, as possessing the Santa Casa. It was there later that Domenico Veneziano and Piero della Francesca were to paint their frescoes, so soon to be destroyed. It was during his retirement at Loreto, while Federigo, his natural son, ruled as viceregent in Urbino, that Guidantonio founded the Duomo and the Church of San Donato (1439). In 1442 he died, and was buried in the church he had so lately founded and dedicated to San Donato. His son Oddantonio, born in 1427, succeeded him at fifteen years of age. The terrible story of this prince reads like some dreadful fiction. His reign began well, for Pope Eugenius IV gave him the title of Duke ; he was the first of his race to bear it. But he would seem to have been of a weak and vacillating nature, suffering any and every sort of influence to master him. Coming under the spell of that strange and fascinating personality, Sigismondo Malatesta, Lord of Rimini, he was little better than wax in his hands.

It was this man who, according to the folk of Urbino,

brought about the fall of their weak and foolish Duke of
Urbino, Oddantonio, whose city he desired. He sent two
young men of vicious habits, Manfredo de' Pii da Carpi and
Tomaso Agnello da Rimini, to Urbino, who succeeded easily
in debasing his mind and morals, making of the prince who
promised so well a mere devil. At last, at the instigation
of Serafius, a physician, whose beautiful wife had been
seduced by Manfredo, the revolution that Sigismondo so
desired was awakened, and Oddantonio, together with
Manfredo and Tomaso, was murdered. Dennistoun quotes
from an old chronicle in the Oliveriana library an account
of what followed : ' On 22nd July 1444 at lauds (about
3 a.m.) Oddantonio was slain in his own hall, and his
familiar servants Manfredo de' Pii and Tomaso da Rimini
along with him ; and forthwith the people of Urbino in one
voice called for Signor Federigo, who at once took possession
of the state."

Federigo was the natural son of Guidantonio " by a
maiden of Urbino." The Pope, on 22nd December 1424,
formally made him legitimate when he was yet but two
years old. While he was still young, Federigo, who was
destined to attain to so much splendour, was sent as a
kind of hostage to Venice. It was while in that city
that he came under the influence of Vittorino de' Ram-
boldoni da Feltre, the learned professor of Mantua. This
great man was a Greek scholar of no mean attainment,
and his ideal of education soon took possession of the
greatest princes in Italy. He taught Greek, Latin,
Grammar, Philosophy, Mathematics, Logic, Music, and
Dancing at the Casa Goija, the " House of Joy," where
he had settled in 1425 at the invitation of Gianfrancesco II
of Mantua. Nor did he neglect athletics ; in the meadows
of the Mincio shooting and fencing matches were arranged
together with the game of *palla*. Such scholars as could
not afford to pay him he taught for the " love of God."
His pupils included the noblest names in Italy ; all the
children of the Gonzaga house were educated at Casa

Goija, and no doubt met the Duke Federigo in the lecture-room and the meadows. Later, Duke Federigo placed the great scholar's portrait in his palace at Urbino with this inscription : " In honour of his saintly master Vittorino da Feltre, who by word and example instructed him in all human excellence, Federigo has set this here." It was to this man that he owed the fact that his court was famous throughout Italy, as was also that of his son, for culture and refinement and learning. During a hundred and ninety years from Federigo's accession Urbino, unlike any other city in Italy, was free from oppression and disorder, and was governed by the princes of two dynasties, beloved and respected, who followed the tradition Federigo had from Vittorino da Feltre.

Much of Federigo's reign was occupied in fighting. A great general, he seems to have humbled most of his enemies, including Sigismondo Malatesta. Before he had reached his eighth year he had been married to Gentile Brancaleone, and this marriage proving barren, he had in 1454 obtained the Pope's brief of legitimation for his sons Bonconte and Antonio. In 1460, however, he married Battista Sforza, daughter of the Lord of Pesaro. Piero della Francesca, in his pictures on the back of the portraits of Federigo and Battista in the Uffizi, has painted a kind of allegory in memory of the marriage. During the next few years he was still engaged in war, during which time the state was managed to a large extent by his wife, who appears to have been popular. It was after he had been married about four years that he seems to have won the leisure to attend to government at home, and to devote himself to those things which Vittorino had taught him to love.

It seems to have been in 1454 that Federigo began to build the beautiful palace which to-day crowns the hill on which Urbino stands. Perhaps the finest palace in all Italy, it was the work of Luciano Laurana, helped, it may be, by Baccio Pontelli. Castiglione, in his *Cortegiano*, writes of the place as follows : " Among other laudable actions,

Federigo erected on the rugged heights of Urbino a residence by many regarded as the most beautiful in all Italy ; and so amply did he provide it with every convenience that it appeared rather a palatial city than a palace. He furnished it not only with the usual plenishings of rich brocades in silk and gold, silver plate, and such like, but ornamented it with a vast quantity of ancient marble and bronze sculptures, of rare pictures, and musical instruments in every variety, excluding all but the choicest objects."

But it was as a book-collector that Federigo excelled. " To the right and left of the carriage entrance into the great courtyard are two handsome saloons, each about forty-five feet by twenty-two, and twenty-three in height. That on the left contained the famous library of manuscripts collected by Count Federigo ; the corresponding one received the printed books, which, gradually purchased by successive dukes, became under the last sovereign a copious collection."

It was on the 20th August 1474, towards the end of his life, that, with an escort of two thousand horse, he entered Rome, the Pope meeting him in the great doorway of S. Peter's to give him the dignity of duke. This honour, which was his due, conferred with splendid ritual and ceremonies, was not the only dignity which fell to him. On the 18th August 1474, Edward IV of England gave him the Garter, even at that time one of the most splendid honours in Europe.

This truly great man died on the 10th September 1482, leaving a son aged ten years to succeed him. Prudent and wise, he was as good a soldier as he was a prince, and as generous a patron of learning as might be found in Italy.

" In person," says Muzio, " Federigo was of the common height, well made and proportioned, active and stout, enduring of cold and heat, apparently affected neither by hunger nor thirst, by sleeplessness nor fatigue. His expression was cheerful and frank ; he was not carried away by passion, nor showed anger, unless designedly. . . . If his kindness was notable in camp, it was much more so among his people. While at Urbino he daily repaired to the market-place, whither the citizens resorted for gossip and games as well as for business, mixing freely with them and joining in discourse, or looking on at their sports, like one of themselves, sitting among them or leaning on some one by the hand or arm. If in passing through the town he noticed any one building a house, he would stop to inquire how the work went on, encouraging him to beautify it, and offering him aid if required, which he gave as well as promised. . . . Once meeting a citizen who had daughters to marry, he said : ' How are your family ? Have you got any of your girls disposed of ? ' And being answered that he was ill able to endow them, he helped him with money or an appointment, or set him in some way of bettering himself." Hundreds of anecdotes and stories are told of him by the chroniclers and historians, all going to show how much he was beloved, and with reason ; nor is there any that I can find which is to his discredit.

His young son, Guidobaldo I, succeeded him. You may see his portrait to-day in the Colonna Palace in Rome, painted by Santi, as you may see those of his father and mother, painted by Piero della Francesca, in the Uffizi. At the age of seventeen he married Elisabetta Gonzaga, the youngest daughter of Francesco, Marquis of Mantua, but by her he had no children. His household, if we may judge from the precise rules we possess which governed it, was as orderly as his father's. In his peaceful reign he was able to devote himself almost entirely to study and to the chase. His only trouble seems to have been that he was childless. He had adopted his nephew, Francesco Maria della Rovere, as his heir, and kept him near him at Urbino. Suddenly into the quiet serenity of those days in the woods and the gardens, or the great beautiful palace itself, a kind of tiger leapt, Cesare Borgia, that brutal genius, fell upon Urbino suddenly. Without a thought of defence Guidobaldo, together with his nephew, fled to Mantua. Cesare Borgia ransacked the palace, and carried his priceless booty to the Vatican, where the devil himself, masquerading as Pope Alexander VI, waited to receive it. Let it be said in extenuation of Guidobaldo that he was physically a weakling. Once or twice he managed to make headway against the Pope and the Pope's son, but never for long. He retired to Venice really a beggar. Suddenly, almost as suddenly as Cesare Borgia had leapt on Urbino, Alexander VI died. In a moment Cesare's magical empire departed from him, and he himself was a fugitive. Guidobaldo returned to Urbino, and, though much of the booty was never restored to him by the Church, passed the rest of his life among his treasures in the retirement of his court. It was then that the Golden Age began for Italy which in its expression and production has never since been equalled. Every sort of scholar came to Urbino ; great poets, painters, sculptors, architects, engineers, doctors, priests, quacks of every kind, fools and nobles, dancing-masters and beautiful women, musicians, and preachers flocked to the court of one of the most humane princes Italy had ever seen. It was then that Castiglione wrote his *Cortegiano* and his life of Guidobaldo ; it was then that Santi entertained Piero della Francesca, that Melozzo da Forlì came to court, and Luca Signorelli painted his work in San Spirito. In 1505 Pietro Bembo, that fine scholar and stylist, came to Urbino. Born in Venice in 1470, he was in 1505 already famous. A *protégé* of the d'Este princes, he had seen Lucrezia Borgia enter that quiet household. This wanton and beautiful princess, whose acquaintance with every sort of vice was surely unique, seems to have become almost a child again in the serene life of the court of Ferrara. All her hateful childhood and youth seem to have fallen away from her and left her almost a girl again. A great friendship sprang up between her and Pietro

Bembo. Their correspondence, which lasted from 1503 to 1516, is in great part published. And it is there, as I think, in those rhetorical letters in praise of the virtue rather than the beauty of so famous a princess, that we find the best refutation of the inevitable slander as to the purity of their affection. Coming to Urbino in 1505, Bembo stayed there during six years; it was there he met Giuliano de Medici, to whom he owed so much. Going to Rome in 1512 in the company of Giuliano, Leo X, who was made Pope in the following year, appointed him his secretary. How often in his later life he regretted the unfettered existence of those days at Urbino appears from his correspondence again and again.

The duke, who presided over this court of learning and art, was never in good health. A weakling from his birth, it was necessary for him to take his pleasure rather in the somewhat colourless delights of the library, and the salon than in the field. " His passage," says Dennistoun, " from mortality was peaceful; and death, which he considered desirable, spread like a gentle slumber over his stiffening limbs and composed features. At midnight of the 11th of April 1508 his spirit was released from its shattered tenement." Thus died the last of the House of Monte-feltro.

He was succeeded by the first duke of the House of Rovere Francesco Maria. This passionate man was a soldier rather than a scholar. His adventurous reign is full of murder and war. " He was a prince of very violent temper," says Symonds; " of its extravagance history has recorded three remarkable examples. He murdered the Cardinal of Pavia with his own hand in the streets of Ravenna; stabbed a lover of his sister to death at Urbino; and in a council of war knocked Francesco Guicciardini down with a blow of his fist. When the history of Italy came to be written, Guicciardini was probably mindful of that insult, for he painted Francesco Maria's character

and conduct in dark colours.   At the same time this Duke
of Urbino passed for one of the first generals of the age.
The greatest stain upon his memory is his behaviour in the
year 1527, when, by dilatory conduct of the campaign in
Lombardy, he suffered the passage of Frundesberg's army
unopposed, and afterwards hesitated to relieve Rome from
the horrors of the sack.   He was the last Italian condottiere
of the antique type. . . . During his lifetime the con-
ditions of Italy were so changed by Charles v's imperial
settlement in 1530 that the occupation of condottiere
ceased to have any meaning."   Driven from Urbino by the
Pope Leo x, who conferred his dukedom upon Lorenzo de
Medici, he would by no means submit, but was not strong
or rich enough to beat the Pope.   In 1522, however,
Francesco Maria returned to Urbino.   Leo x was dead,
Lorenzo de Medici was dead, and Catherine his heir, soon
to be Queen of France, did not press her claims.

Francesco Maria's son Guidobaldo, by Leonora Gonzaga,
whom he had married in 1509, succeeded him.   Of Guidobaldo II, surnamed Guidobaldaccio, there is little to say.
He quarrelled with his subjects and retired to Pesaro,
where he built the great palace, now the Prefettura, opposite
the church of S. Domenico.   In the autumn of 1574 he
appears to have gone to Ferrara to visit Henry III of
France.   On his way back to Pesaro, " during the great
heats," he fell ill and died on the 28th September.   On
the 30th January 1548 Guidobaldo had married Vittoria
Farnese, by whom he had a son and two daughters.   It
was this son, Francesco Maria II, who succeeded him, the
last Duke of Urbino.   He was born on the 20th February
1549.   His autobiography, extending from his birth to
the marriage of his son, is an extraordinary work, full of
curious information.   It is this sad and mystical duke
whom Mr. Shorthouse has drawn so vividly for us in *John
Inglesant*.   He seems to have felt something of the same
irresistible desire for solitude that forced Guido il Vecchio,
his predecessor, into a Franciscan cell at Assisi.   Married

first to Lucrezia d'Este of Ferrara, whom he did not love, he permitted her to return to Ferrara, and later married Livia della Rovere. It seems to have been in his loneliness, deserted by his wife, that he became occupied with those haunting thoughts about religion which were so eagerly fostered by the Papacy that in 1631 they resulted in his bequeathing his Duchy to the Church. In youth we read that he used a flame vanishing into air as his device, with the motto, *Quies in Sublime*—" There is rest on high " ; later he took a terrestrial globe with the legend, *Ponderibus librata suis*—" Self-poised." He grew more and more into a kind of uninstructed and ungoverned monk. His son by his second marriage, Prince Federigo-Ubaldo, was ruined in his youth. Spoiled by his father, " taught to regard his subjects as dependants on a despot will," he died in 1623 a victim to his own lusts and debaucheries. From this blow Francesco Maria never recovered. We see him, a kind of querulous shadow, pass across that fantastic stage at Urbino, ready to listen to the ranting of madmen and fantastic Lutherans and mad monks. Meantime he was in reality the plaything of the Pope. As the cat deals with the mouse, so the Papacy dealt with this poor, half-witted creature. In 1624 the last Duke of Urbino died, and his lordship became the absolute property of the Holy See.

In spite of all the patronage and splendour of the Counts and Dukes of Urbino, there is little enough left to-day in their city to remind us of the hosts of artists they entertained at their court and employed in decorating the magnificent palace where they lived, and the churches they endowed or protected. The palace is, indeed, spoiled and changed, though it be still the finest monument in Urbino. Built by Luciano Laurana, the Illyrian (1468–1482), the master of Bramante, for the great Federigo, " the Great Christian," as Mahomet II called him, it was the greatest and the most splendid of all these palaces of the Signori which were built

in the early Renaissance, and even to-day it is unique in
Italy.   It is not certainly in its size or even in its proportions
that its beauty lies, but in its fitness and in its harmony of
splendour and strength.   It does not impose itself upon us
as so many of the fortress palaces of Italy, built both before
and after, do, but is content to please us with a certain
quiet and homely beauty that, as it seems to me, is just the
quality one looked for in a palace that was not only a place
of refuge or offence, but a home, a home where life came little
by little to have an exquisite but simple ritual, and where
one might happily entertain one's friends.   As you wander
to-day through those corridors, out of which the beautiful
rooms open, so bare now, or turned to the meaner uses of
our time, through the doorways and past the mantelpieces
with their friezes of dancing angels or vines carved by
Domenico Rosselli, you come at last to the little study of
Duke Federigo, where the walls, all of *intarsia*, once shut
out for him the noisy world of battle and intrigue, so that in
complete silence he might meditate, as he was used to do,
on the divine life of the soul, while he looked, as we may
do, out across the city to the indestructible Apennine, or,
climbing up to the platform of the great north tower,
gazed really across his Dukedom.

In Duke Federigo's day and for long after, until indeed
Urbino came again into the hands of the Pope, the Palace
was celebrated throughout Italy for its great library and
its gallery of pictures.   The library is gone, having been
taken to Rome in 1667, but some of the pictures remain,
though a great part of these too are scattered, many of
them hanging in the Uffizi and Pitti Galleries in Florence.

The Palazzo Ducale is itself, of course, one of the most
interesting buildings of the kind in Italy and in many of
its details one of the most beautiful.   Built under the great
Federigo of Montefeltro, possibly after his own plan and
design, it is undoubtedly the most complete and sumptuous
Ducal Palace of the time of the early Renaissance.

Within, the more noble apartments are now a vast

museum sparely furnished with precious furniture and sculpture, and the remains of the ducal collection of pictures, added to which is the spoil of many a church in the Urbino territory.

One comes first into the noble great court and then, entering a door on the right, climbs a fine staircase upon which is a statue of Count Federigo, and over which hangs a curious great lamp. From the window at the top of this staircase one can best see the fine terracotta—a Madonna and Child with four saints—over the door of the church of S. Domenico opposite; a work in white and blue, dated 1449.

One then enters the first of the great apartments, the Sala del Trono, with a noble ceiling decorated with the monogram F.C. (Federigo Conte), and furnished with a fine mantelpiece by Rosselli, transported hither from another apartment. There, too, hangs a great Giottesque crucifix, and under it a marble relief of the school of Donatello of the Madonna and Child with angels. Close by are two terra-cottas from Castel Durante (Urbania), and another marble relief of the Madonna and Child by Desiderio da Settignano.

From this room one passes into the Sala degli Angeli, furnished with splendid doors of intarsia work by Pondelli Fiorentino, and a most lovely mantelpiece carved with dancing nymphs by Rosselli. Thence one comes into the Sala Ariosto, furnished with similar doors of intarsia work by the same master. Out of this room is a balcony looking over the Mercatello to the mountains.

From the Sala Ariosto one passes into the Studio del Duca, the walls of which are covered with intarsias by Giovanni Castellano. Here are several secret recesses. In one of the intarsias is a portrait of Federigo, and in others Faith, Hope and Charity. The ceiling is beautiful and the room is partially hung with bright Flemish tapestries. This room also opens on to the balcony of the Sala Ariosto. Close by is the little Chapel of the Duke, with a splendid stucco roof by Federigo Brandani.

One is now led back through the Sala degli Angeli and the Sala del Trono to the Salone del Magnifico, which contains the Picture Gallery.

Here first we come to a S. Sebastian by Timoteo Viti, above which is a charming portrait of Duke Guidobaldo as a boy ; this is a copy, but the original is lost. Another picture by Viti follows, the Madonna and Child. Close by is a very charming tondo of the Madonna and Child with angels of the school of Filippino Lippi. One then comes to a polyptych by Antonio da Ferrara, of the Madonna and Child and twelve saints, the panels being now separated from the great picture. Above is the Redeemer in Benediction. The work is signed : " ANTONIUS DE FERARIA, 1439."

Above this work hang two pictures by Titian. These two works, which represent the Resurrection and the Last Supper, originally formed the two sides of the processional banner of the Confraternità di Corpus Domini of Urbino. In 1544 this banner was surrounded by ornament by Pietro Viti, but a little later the banner was taken to pieces and the pictures framed as we see them. Neither picture is among the more important of Titian's work.

To the left of Antonio da Ferrara's polyptych hangs a not very charming work by Giovanni Santi of S. John preaching. Close by is a triptych by Giovanni da Rimini, of the Madonna and Child enthroned with four saints ; at the sides the Adoration of the Magi, the Presentation in the Temple, the Last Supper and the Betrayal ; and above the Crucifixion with three (originally four) half figures of saints and the Annunciation.

We then come to a panel of S. Chiara painted on a gold ground by some Umbrian master, and then to a fine little work by Giovanni Santi, a Pietà, of which we only see the half figures. An architectural piece by Laurana follows, and above it is the finest work by Giovanni Santi in Urbino. This is an altarpiece of the Madonna and Child with S. John, S. Francis, S. Jerome and S. Sebastian with the two donors and their little daughter, Biffi of Urbino.

Above, in a ring of Cherubim, God the Father appears in benediction with two angels. Close by is another Pietà, perhaps by Santi, with S. Mary Magdalen, S. Joseph of Arimathea and S. John Evangelist.

From the window in this room we see the Cortile Pensile. Of old, where the little roof runs over the empty windows in the wall opposite, a balcony passed from the Duke's studio to the Duchess's apartments.

Beyond the window hangs a picture of the Deposition by Zuccari and two panels on gold of S. John Baptist and S. George. Above is a splendid Giottesque Crucifix.

One now passes from this great Salone into the ante-camera of the Duchess's apartments, where are some works by Baroccio. Thence one comes into the Sala degli Aranzi, hung with splendid tapestries from Flanders. Here, too, is another S. Sebastian by Santi. The saint stands, his hands joined, bound to a tree in a glorious landscape of hill and valley. On the left three soldiers, directed by the Emperor from a lofty balcony, pierce the saint with their arrows, while on the right kneels a company of religious. Above them an angel appears bearing the martyr's crown.

Close by is a wonderful picture of Justin of Ghent of the Last Supper, in which we see the Duke Federigo and his court. Two pictures by Timoteo Viti follow of S. Roch and Tobit and the angel. Under these is a most curious work by Paulo Uccello. It represents the Profanation of the Host. A woman, it seems, sells the Host to a Jew. The Jew puts it in a frying-pan on the fire and it immediately covers the floor with blood. The people break into the house, and the Host is carried away in procession by the Bishop. The woman is hanged and the Jew burned and the devil goes off with his soul.

Over the mantelpiece is a fine triptych of the Madonna and Child with saints and the story of the Passion, painted on a gold ground by some follower of Gentile da Fabriano. Close by is another work by Timoteo Viti, a rather charming

Nativity, and some more works by Baroccio. Other pictures by this master fill the last room also, the Sala del Baroccio.

From the Ducal Palace one passes to the Duomo, an uninteresting modern building. In the Sacristy, however, in a closed panel in the wall, is a most glorious work by Piero della Francesca, a picture of the Flagellation. This is perhaps the most interesting picture in Urbino, and faded and damaged though it be, it remains a most lovely thing. It is divided into two subjects. On one side Pilate sits under an open portico. Before him, bound to a pillar upon which is a statue of some god, Christ is scourged. On the other side of the picture in a street before noble houses three figures stand more than three times the size of those in the Flagellation scene. They are richly dressed, but whom they are meant to be has never been decided. They are obviously portraits, and Dr. Witting suggests that the figure on the right is Duke Federigo and that on the left the Venetian Caterino Zeno, who was in Urbino in 1474 as ambassador for the king of Persia. Who the figure in the midst may be is not, however, made clear. We shall probably never solve the mystery.

Another interesting picture hangs here in the sacristy of the Duomo beside the Piero della Francesca. It is a large altarpiece by Timoteo Viti representing S. Thomas of Canterbury and S. Martin, the former holding a crystal staff at the top of which is a crucifix. The two saints are enthroned under an arch through which appears a lovely landscape. Before them kneel, so it is said, the Bishop Arrivabeni and Guidobaldo, the Duke of Urbino. But I strongly doubt that this picture has anything whatever to do with Urbino. It comes, I think, from the church of S. Salvatore of Bologna, and was perhaps painted for the chapel of the English there, dedicated in honour of S. Thomas of Canterbury.

Close by this work is a dismembered altarpiece of the Adoration of the Holy Child, perhaps by Santi, and a very lovely fourteenth-century Madonna and Child with eight angels, perhaps by Lorenzo Salimbeni. In the crypt of the church is a Pietà in marble by Giovanni da Bologna.

From the Cathedral one returns to the market-place, between the two hills on which Urbino stands. Climbing the Contrada Raffaelle, one presently comes to the house (No. 278 on the left) in which Raphael was born, where there is still a much damaged fresco by his father, Giovanni Santi, said to represent his mother, Magia Ciarla, as the Madonna and Raphael himself as the Bambino. At the top of the steep Contrada is the Pian del Monte, whence we may get a good view of Urbino, and, to the north, of S. Marino with a glimpse of the sea. Beyond, under an archway, one comes upon all that is left of the old Fortezza.

After returning to the market-place, past the Loggia of the fourteenth-century church of S. Francesco with its noble tower, one turns to the left down the Via Bramante as far as the church of Santo Spirito, which possesses two fine, but small, pictures, parts of an old standard by Luca Signorelli. They are very hard to see well, for they are set high over two small galleries on either side the altar.

Again, one returns to the market-place and follows the way downhill towards the Mercatello by the Via Mazzini, so far as the Via della Posta Vecchia, down which one passes into the Via Barocci. At the end of this street is the small Oratorio di S. Giovanni, which is entirely painted within in fresco by Lorenzo Salimbeni and his brother Jacopo. This little church with its frescoes is undoubtedly the most beautiful and interesting of all the churches of Urbino. Over the altar is a vast fresco of the Crucifixion, a marvellously lovely thing painted on a black background ; indeed, Salimbeni's use of black in all these frescoes is very notable. The group here about the fallen Virgin is fine, and it is curious to note that the rider on the bucking horse on the left turns back his hand in warning, just as one does to-day in the hunting field. From this great scene the frescoes proceed from left to right to tell the

story in double scenes of S. John Baptist, as follows :—
(1) The Annunciation to Zacharias, who writes the name
John on a tablet.   (2) The Visitation of Mary to Elizabeth,
and of both to Zacharias, a most lovely scene full of decorative beauty; note the black robe of the Virgin, twice
repeated in this splendid composition.   (3) The Birth of
S. John—the Blessed Virgin holds him in her arms—and his
circumcision.   (4) The Blessed Virgin departs to her own
house, and the song of Zacharias, a most lovely thing;
and again note the use of black.   The second part of
this fresco represents the flight into Egypt.   The Holy
Family meet S. John on the way.

The second line of frescoes begins again at the altar.
Here, in the first scene (5), S. John preaches in the desert ;
this is partly spoilt.   Then comes (6) the preaching of
Repentance on the banks of the Jordan, and (7) the Baptism of Our Lord, a beautiful scene, and (8) the preaching of S. John to Herod.   There is nothing in all the
Marches comparable with this wonderfully lovely series
of frescoes.

On the left of the altar are frescoes of the Blessed Virgin
and Child enthroned between S. Sebastian and S. John
Baptist, and of the Madonna kneeling on a rock holding
her Divine Son in her arms between two saints.   By this
last is a fresco of the Blessed Pietro Spagnuoli d'Urbino,
who is buried here (1415).   The fine roof should not be
missed.

One other picture at least remains to be seen in Urbino.
This is a fresco of the Madonna of Mercy in S. Maria dell'
Olmo.   But who could hope to sum up the riches of this
stormy, wind-battered, rain-sodden, sun-baked acropolis ?
This at least, however, should not be forgotten, I mean
the church of S. Bernardino.   This is a little convent of
the Zoccolanti which stands at the end of a dusty road on
a hill-top opposite Urbino, from which there is a notable
view of the city, but not of the palace.   S. Bernardino
stands under the cypress-ringed Campo Santo of the

THE VISITATION. BY LORENZO SALIMBENI

S. Giovanni, Urbino

Urbinati. It has itself always been a graveyard, and here, in the little cruciform church under its blind, round lantern, a truly Bramantesque dream of a church all in rosy brick, the Dukes Federigo and Guidobaldo lie. Before the church stretches a little green, where in the early October days crocuses of pale purple blossom just out of the shadow of the mulberry trees which line the hill where it breaks suddenly away in vineyards, purple now with grapes, towards the pale rosy city that crowns the great rock like a diadem.

It was there I took farewell of Urbino, before I set out down the long road for Pesaro, the railway, and home. All that way was presently filled, as I came into the valleys, with great bullock-waggons piled up with vast barrels or boxes with the family sitting on the top, for it was the time of vintage. The happiness of all that !

At evening, my head full of songs, I came into Pesaro by the Rimini gate, thronged to-day with bullock-waggons loaded with grapes. Every forge and carpenter's shop by the wayside was busy mending or renewing the old vats or making new ones, and when a few days later I set out for home, it was in the new bubbling wine my health was pledged, and in the new pressed grapes I, too, drank to all my friends.

INDEX

Printed by
MORRISON & GIBB LIMITED
Edinburgh